T3-BOB-300

SHEMARYAHU TALMON

KING, CULT AND CALENDAR IN ANCIENT ISRAEL

To the memory of Yonina

KING, CULT AND CALENDAR IN ANCIENT ISRAEL

Collected Studies

SHEMARYAHU TALMON

JERUSALEM

THE MAGNES PRESS, THE HEBREW UNIVERSITY

Distributed by the Magnes Press,
The Hebrew University, Jerusalem, Israel

Jerusalem 1986
ISBN 965–223–651–9
Printed in Israel
at Shasag Press, Jerusalem

CONTENTS

PREFACE

The studies collected in this volume have appeared previously in various journals, Festschriften and co-authored volumes. Their republication in this collection is meant to make them more readily accessible to the interested reader.

While the individual essays each concern a specific topic, they all pertain to social issues and problems which confront the student of ancient Israel. Viewed together they reflect my endeavor to achieve a comprehensive understanding of biblical man and his society *from within*, by extracting pertinent evidence first and foremost from the Hebrew Scriptures themselves. With this aim in mind, the texts are investigated by a variety of techniques and methods which inform biblical scholarship. They range from the textual analysis of passages which come under scrutiny, the discernment of literary patterns or motifs and contextual structures, to the elucidation of societal mechanisms and their ideonic underpinnings. Whenever appropriate, the field of investigation is widened, so as to bring into play congruous extra-biblical information derived from ancient Near Eastern sources, and post-biblical writings, such as the Qumran finds and rabbinic literature, which shed indirect light on the issues under discussion. However, in attempting to elucidate pivotal aspects of the ancient Israelites' conceptual universe, pride of place is given to the Hebrew Scriptures, in full agreement with Henri Frankfort's dictum: "the borrowed features in Hebrew culture, and those which have foreign analogies, are least significant."

I have applied the very same approach also in the analytical study of biblical literary concepts, motifs and structuring techniques in another series of essays to be published shortly in a forthcoming volume.

The selected studies included in the present collection were written over a period of some three decades. Accordingly, they bear the imprint of the state of research at the time when each one was put to paper. Viewed in conjunction, they reflect my own thoughts on characteristics of the biblical society as they developed over the years.

No attempt was made to bring the studies up-to-date, but rather they were republished in their original form. Obvious mistakes and typographical errors were emended to the limited degree to which such emendations can be accomodated in a photographic reproduction. However, I have utilized the wider latitude for adaptations and rephrasing in the here-presented English version of studies which were translated from a Hebrew or German original.

Because of these circumstances, and since the essays were first published in conformity with varying editorial requirements, no unity could be achieved in the present edition with respect to the system of quotations, references, sigla, etc.

The preparation of this collection of studies for republication was in part carried out while I was a Fellow in the Institute for Advanced Studies at the Hebrew University of Jerusalem. I am indebted to the Director of the Institute and the entire staff for providing excellent research facilities in a congenial athmosphere.

Several of my students assisted me at various stages in the preparatory work and in proofreading. My thanks are due to Mr. E. Arad, Dr. P. Cowe, Dr. W. Fields, and especially to Miss D. Josef who also took care of the indexes.

I wish to thank the Academic Committee of The Magnes Press and its chairman, Prof. H. Beinart, for their resolution to publish this volume of my selected essays, and three more which are in various stages of being processed for publication. The staff of the Magnes Press and foremost its director, Mr. B.Z. Yehoshua, supervised with great care the somewhat complicated production of this volume.

My thanks are due to all of them, and to the editors and publishers of the original versions of these studies who willingly granted permission to have them republished in this collection.

I dedicate this volume to the memory of my late wife, Yonina Talmon-Garber, Professor of Sociology at the Hebrew University, whose scholarly acumen and sociological perception were a source of unfailing support and left and imprint on my work beyond her untimely death.

KINGSHIP AND THE IDEOLOGY OF THE STATE

The Sources

As WITH most matters of belief and social thought, the Bible deals with monarchy not systematically but primarily by observing actual events. Exceptions to this rule are the "Law of the King" (*miṣvat ha-meleḵ*; Deut. 17:14–20),[1] the "Statute of the King" (*mišpaṭ ha-meleḵ*; I Sam. 8:10–17), Nathan's prophecy (II Sam. 7:4–17),[2] Gideon's declaration (Judg. 8:22–23), and perhaps Jotham's fable (*ibid.* 9:7–20). The biblical concept of monarchy must therefore be dealt with as an idea and as a social organization, by framing fragmentary information which the scholar extracts from the text, explains, and tries to synthesize into one system of thought. It is by no means to be expected that by connecting one clue or one fragment to another it will be possible to present a comprehensive view of monarchy in the biblical period or of the political ideology from which it sprang. The discussion must perforce remain fragmentary.[3]

Moreover, the bits of information to be gleaned from the biblical texts do not always tally. Sources might even contradict one another, and this is not at all surprising. The biblical literature developed over the course of centuries. It therefore reflects concepts of the monarchy at various stages of its development, the diverse reactions and changing attitudes toward it of generations of scribes, and echoes of contrasting opinions about it which were entertained in Israel at any one point in time as well as at various periods.

The problem presented by the heterogeneity of sources concerning the concept of monarchy is compounded by the difficulty of dating them. Most biblical statements, whether pro- or anti-monarchy, bear no signs which would enable them to be dated, especially when they are contained in literary anthologies such as the book of Psalms, which crystallized progressively over a lengthy period. The same holds true for the historiographical and prophetic literature, our principal source for understanding the concept and nature of monarchy in the

[1] I have used here the traditional term *miṣvat ha-meleḵ* even though it would be more appropriate to call the chapter *mišpaṭ ha-meleḵ*, since it is linked with *mišpaṭ ha-kohănīm* (Deut. 18:3) in the framework of the law code which pertains to conditions in the land of Canaan.

[2] Topically this matter is related to Solomon's dream (I Kings 3:5–14; II Chron. 1:7–12) and Solomon's prayer (I Kings 8:12–26; II Chron. 6:3–17).

[3] Cf. Jacobsen's treatment of what is known about the political-ideological development of Mesopotamian society, "Early Political Development in Mesopotamia." *ZA*, 52 (1957), 91–140 (= *Toward the Image of Tammuz and other Essays*, ed. by W. L. Moran [Cambridge, Mass., 1970], pp. 132 ff.).

biblical period. Even where a superscription specifies the date of writing a book, there is no way of telling when specific individual passages concerning the monarchy were composed or committed to writing. A precise presentation of the development of political thought or of the view of the monarchy in the Bible is therefore impossible. This is especially difficult in surveying the time when the monarchy actually sprang into being between the period of the Judges and the days of Samuel.

Despite these limitations, the biblical sources still remain the major basis for every study of the concept of monarchy. We have no extra-biblical evidence which directly illuminates the ideological foundations of the monarchy in Israel or informs us of the ways in which royal power was exercised. Extra-biblical sources, by way of comparison, can serve to fill out the picture which emerges from the biblical account by pointing out similar or identical characteristics in the Israelite kingdom and ancient Near Eastern kingdoms, and by highlighting what was peculiar to Israel in contrast to the monarchical regimes of surrounding nations. With regard to the early monarchical period, we depend especially on the relatively meager information concerning the ethno-political entities in Transjordania whose social structure at that time was similar to that of Israel: Edom, Moab, and Ammon. For the period of the United Kingdom—when the Israelite monarchy was at the height of its development—we have at our disposal the more numerous references to the monarchical regimes in the Cisjordanian Canaanite city states of Syria, Tyre, Sidon, and Ugarit, as well as sources from the Mesopotamian empires. It should be remembered, however, as Frankfort said, that the elements of Israelite culture which supposedly were drawn from neighboring civilizations, or whose like can be found there as well, are less important threads in the fabric.[4] Similar or even identical terms and phrases in the literatures of different peoples can express differing conceptual loads. The exact meaning of biblical phrases and terms dealing with monarchy should therefore be derived from their own linguistic context and the immediate contextual matter and are not to be defined on the basis of the socio-political vocabulary of other ancient Near-Eastern peoples.[5]

The Idea of the State in the Biblical Period

The concept of the state results from Israel's viewing its own place in history and the place of the surrounding peoples as a reflection of the principles upon

[4] H. Frankfort, *Kingship and the Gods*, Chicago, 1948, p. 339.

[5] As is done, e.g., by the "Myth and Ritual" school, upon the conjecture that the peoples of the ancient Near East, including Israel, had a common ideological-religious substratum. A survey and criticism of this approach can be found in M. Noth, "Gott, König, Volk im Alten Testament," *ZThK*, 47 (1950), 157 ff. = *Gesammelte Studien zum Alten Testament*, München (1966), pp. 188 ff.; F. I. Rosenthal, "Some Aspects of the Hebrew Monarchy," *JSS*, 9 (1958), 17.

which the world was created—a set of concentric circles. The political system is considered the historical embodiment of the complex of relationships between men, established by God at the creation of the world: on the international plane in defining the relations between Israel and her neighbors, and on the intra-national in delineating the functions and stipulating the rights which govern the relations between the deliverer-ruler (*mōšīaʿ-nāgīd*) and the community he leads. Ideally, the laws of creation permeated the foundations of the Israelite historical-national existence which, for the biblical writers, reached its fullest expression in the United Monarchy. There is practically no definition of the political sphere which is not conceived of and couched in terms of monarchy, because only under the monarchy did Israel crystallize as a people with a common faith and consciousness of a common origin and establish a national territorial framework on a basis of political sovereignty. The idea of state[6] and the concept of monarchy are one.

In identifying the concept of state with that of monarchy, Israel was no diferent from most ancient Near-Eastern peoples. The biblical traditions concerning these peoples also speak of them in terms and imagery of monarchy.[7] Similarly, both Israel and her neighbors conceived of divine rule as monarchical.[8] Such epithets and definitions applied to mortal kings as *nāgīd*, *mōšīaʿ*, *sār*, *šōfēṭ*, etc. also apply to the heavenly kingdom, especially with respect to two types of imagery drawn from the life of society: military leadership[9] and legislation.[10]

It does not concern us here whether the terminology of political monarchy was derived from the image of the god-king or whether notions of government on the terrestrial plane were transferred to the celestial sphere. A single world of concepts permeated Israel's historical existence, from its beginning after the Exodus unto the "later days:" when it was a self-contained political entity, and when it was integrated into the general political structure of the ancient Near-

6 Apart from I Kings 20:14–19, the term *mᵉdīnāh* appears only in the later biblical books—Ezek., Eccl., Lam., Esther, Dan., Neh. By and large it is used for secondary administrative units within the kingdom—provinces of a sort—either inside or outside Israel. Sometimes it is parallel to *mamlāḵāh*, e.g. Ezek. 19:8; Eccl. 2:8; Lam. 1:1.

7 The political organization of the Gibeonites, who apparently were not indigenous to Canaan, was a confederacy of cities, ruled over by elders (gerontocracy). Even though the Bible likened Gibeon to a metropolis, a seat of royalty (Josh. 10:2, cf. II Sam. 12:26), a king of Gibeon is never mentioned (cf. Josh. 9–11;II Sam. 21). Among the Philistines, who originated in the Aegean, monarchical government apparently developed after contact with the inhabitants of Canaan. Perhaps one of the five Philistine governors (*sᵉrānīm*) who ruled the cities of the Pentapolis at times took over command of the joint army and while he held office would be called "king" (I Sam. 21:11–16; I Kings 2:39–40). Cf. B. Mazar, "The Philistines", *Proceedings of the Israel Academy of Sciences and Humanities* I, no. 7, Jerusalem (1964).

8 Cf. Ex. 15:18; Isa. 24:23; 52:7; Jer. 10:10 Micah 4:7; Zech. 14:9, 16; Ps. 47:9; 96:10; 99:1; 146:10, etc.

9 See, e.g.: Ex. 15:2 ff.; Isa. 34:1 ff.; Hab. 3:8, 13; Ps. 68, 1–3,etc.

10 See especially Isa. 33:22.

Eastern nations; in terrestrial reality and in relation to the celestial realm. The parallelism of terms of government common to all aspects of Israel's existence, actual-political and ideal-religious alike, correctly reflects a basic conceptual principle of socio-political leadership which remained constant. In the biblical period Israel viewed monarchy as the quintessence of social life.

Biblical Israel viewed the socio-political order not as static but as a developing, changing mechanism. This is also true of the monarchy, which by a historical process gradually grew out of the confluence of internal social factors and external political pressures, and was influenced in its variations by the types of monarchical government prevalent among the nations with which Israel maintained mutual relations from the time of the conquest of Canaan until the ultimate loss of political sovereignty. In other words, the monarchical regime was not perpetuated in the form in which it emerged in the time of Saul. From the very beginning, elements and principles inherent in it found expression in historical reality in executive agencies which constantly changed form. This dynamism which marks the history of Israelite government from the outset should guide any discussion of the idea of state and the concept of the monarchy in the biblical period.

A Kingdom of Priests and a Holy Nation[11]

The essence of Israel's special status is defined in a programmatic divine statement in the book of Exodus: "Now then, if you will obey Me faithfully and keep My covenant, you shall be My treasured (or special) possession[12] among all the peoples. Indeed, all the earth is Mine, but you shall be to Me a priestly kingdom and a holy nation"[13] (Ex. 19:5–6; cf. Deut. 7:6, 14:2, 26:18). Israel's social existence was founded on the premise of being distinct from all peoples by virtue of divine election. The election is meant to be realized in historical actuality in the political framework of the kingdom to be founded after the Conquest of Canaan, when the geo-political conditions are conducive to its realization. The biblical writer viewed the independent national kingdom in the Promised Land as the embodiment of an ancient vision. The definition of

[11] A survey of the scholarly discussion of this subject with extensive bibliography is given by W. Moran, "A Kingdom of Priests," *Gruenthaner Memorial Volume, The Bible in Current Catholic Thought*, ed by J. L. McKenzie, New York (1962), pp. 7–20; G. Fohrer, "Priestliches Königtum (Ex. 19:6)," *ThZ*, 19 (1963), 359–362 = *Studien zur Alttestamentlichen Theologie und Geschichte* (1949–1966), *BZAW*, 115, Berlin (1969), 149–153.

[12] The etymology of the noun *s^egullāh* is uncertain. In Ugaritic (*UT* 2060:16, 7, 12) and in Akkadian documents from Boghazköi (*KUB* III, 57:4, 5, 6) it appears to have the connotation of "pledge," "covenant." It has a similar meaning in biblical Hebrew, as can be learned from its recurring formulaic employment (Deut. 7:6; 14:2; 26:18; Mal. 3:17; Ps. 135:4; Eccl. 2:8; I Chron. 29:3).

[13] In this connection, *goy* is synonymous with *'ām* (cf. Deut. 7:6; 14:2; 26:18). The qualitative differentiation made by E.A. Speiser does not apply here. See his: "'People' and 'Nation' of Israel," *Oriental and Biblical Studies*, ed. by J. J. Finkelstein and M. Greenberg, Philadelphia, 1967, pp. 160–170.

Israel as a priestly kingdom and a holy nation therefore reflects the ideological principles which are the foundation of monarchy.[14] Israel's covenant with God elevates the political national existence to the rank of a social-religious experience based on the mutually complementary cooperation of people and king under divine supervision.[15] The territorial and political sovereignty and the idea of religious submission are the warp and woof of the Israelite monarchy.

The Covenant of Sinai bridges the divine promise of royalty to Abraham—the father of the Hebrews—and the future covenant with King David and his descendants. The blessing of Abraham uses phrases and historical-conceptual motifs which parallel the statement in Ex. 19:5–6, and which refer to Israel as God's chosen people, marked by the political-territorial quality of a monarchy in the land of Canaan: "... and I will make nations out of you, and kings shall come forth from you. And I will establish My covenant between Me and you and your descendants after you throughout the generations for an everlasting covenant, to be God unto you and to your descendants after you. I will give to you, and to your descendants after you, the land of your sojournings, all the land of Canaan, as an everlasting possession; and I will be their God"[16] (Gen. 17:6–8; *ibid.* 16 and 35:11). Similar language and imagery appear in Nathan's

14 Biblical and extra-biblical parallels show that the word *mamlākāh* in this and some other passages has the same meaning as *melek*—"king," e.g. Deut. 3:21; I Kings 10:20; Ps. 68:33; Amos 7:13—where *beit mamlākāh* is parallel to *miqdaš melek;* I Kings 5:1: *mamlākōt* = II Chron. 9:26: *m*ᵉ*lākīm;* I Sam. 10:18 MT: *mamlākōt*, V: *regum*. Similarly in Phoenician inscriptions, *mmlkt* = *mlk*. Cf. H. L. Ginsberg, *Studies in the Book of Daniel*, New York (1948), index s.v. *mmlkt; idem*, *BASOR*, 111 (1948), 25. Additional examples are adduced by Moran, *op. cit.*, pp. 11–13. *Gōy-mamlākāh* should be considered a hendiadys, a composite designation of Israel's national essence (cf. I Kings 18:10; Isa. 60:12; Jer. 18:7–9; II Chron. 32:15, etc. See Moran, *ibid*). In like manner, *kohănīm* should be understood as complementing *qdš*, being synonymous in meaning. For the purpose of parallelism the two bilateral expressions were broken up and the two halves rejoined cross-wide. On this matter, cf. E. Z. Melamed, "Break-up Pattern of Stereotype Phrases, etc.," *Scripta Hierosolymitana*, 8, Jerusalem (1961), 115–153; S. Talmon, "Synonymous Readings in the Textual Traditions of the Old Testament," *ibid.*, p. 335 ff.; Y. Avishur, "Pairs of Synonymous Words in the Construct State (and in Appositional Hendiadys) in Biblical Hebrew," *Semitics*, 2 (1971–72) 17–80. In the adjectival construct *mamleket kohānīm*, the *nomen rectum kohānīm* defines the *nomen regens mamleket* = *melek*, just as in the parallel phrase *qdš* defines *gōy*. The statement purports to define Israel's peculiarity as a treasured people: priestly sanctity will distinguish the kingdom, i.e., the people and its ruler.

15 This idea is reflected in the words of the Psalmist (114:1–2), who states that when Israel went out of Egypt, the people was God's holy dominion: *hāitāh Y*ᵉ*hūdāh l*ᵉ*qod*ᵉ*šō, Yisrā'ēl mamš*ᵉ*lōtāw*. Cf. further II Chron. 29:21, where the triad, *Y*ᵉ*hūdāh, miqdaš, mamlākāh*, serves to define the national entity of the Judean kingdom. On the interchange of *mamlākāh-memšālāh* in Ps. 114:2, see below, note 21.

16 *V*ᵉ*hāyītī lāhem le'lohim-vihyitem lī s*ᵉ*gullāh* (Ex. 19:5) are mutually complementary. Cf. further Ezek. 37:23; Hos. 2:25, and contrast *ibid.* 1:9 and perhaps also 3:3–4.

prophecy (II Sam. 7), and in a more concise form in the Royal Psalm 110:3–4: "Your people offer themselves willingly in the day of thy warfare; in adornments of holiness . . . The Lord hath sworn and will not change his purpose: You are a priest for ever after the manner of Melchizedek." Notwithstanding the uncertain meaning of the passage, the four words *'amḵā, qōdēš, kohēn, malkī (ṣedeq)* evidently paraphrase Ex. 19:6 with the intent of applying the formula of the covenant between God and His people to this covenant with the Davidic dynasty which, for the poet, represented the essence of Israel's nationhood.

The similarity in language and motif which, on the one hand, apply to the ethnic and national entity, and on the other to the monarchy, indicates the centrality of kingship in biblical political thought. Israel from its very beginning was destined to become a kingdom, just as monarchy was destined for Israel. All pre-monarchical social institutions were considered merely introduction to and preparation for the sublime gift of royal splendor. Israel's history throughout the biblical period unfolds under the banner of kingship.

The Savior

Socio-political leadership, in any form, is viewed in the Bible as a function of God's divine Covenant with Israel. In the period of Israel's political self-crystallization—between the Conquest of Canaan and the Settlement to the beginning of the Monarchy—the Covenant centered around the military and political experience and was concretized in the "savior," the divinely appointed emissary who brought his people deliverance from their enemies.

At first the savior is appointed *ad hoc*. The term of his appointment is commensurate with the duration of the danger. His mission consists of fulfilling a specific task. The delineation of his mission accords with the nature of the peril and guarantees that the power given him will remain temporary. Since the appointment answers a specific need, it ends when that need is satisfied. In theory, therefore, Israel required no formal limitations of the rights and obligations inherent in the mission because they were determined by the task itself. In practice, however, the divine spirit was never removed from a leader, from Moses to Samuel. All biblical traditions concerning saviors report the leader's death (Judg. 3:11), usually at a ripe age (*ibid.* 8:32).[17] Even when no mention is made of his death, it is understood from the text that he died while still "in power" (*ibid.* 3:30, 5:31). This clearly indicates that when divine inspiration alighted upon a chosen person, it stayed with him all his life (*ibid.* 16:31; I Sam. 7:15).

His mission to save Israel from its enemies determined the savior's position among his compatriots. Along with the spirit of God came some of the divine

[17] Cf. further Deut. 34:5–7; Josh. 24:29–30 = Judg. 2:8–9; *ibid.* 12:7, 10, 12, 15.

authority and the people obeyed him in socio-political matters because his power derived from God's sovereignty.[18] Being delivered by the savior obliges the people to bear his yoke as well. As the one who crystallizes the covenantal promise in the historical realm, he has the right to limit the freedom of his people, just as has the Covenant.

The establishment of the Covenant is subject to Israel's agreement to enter into it (Ex. 24:7; Deut. 5:24). Similarly, for the concept to be translated into action, the savior's mission must be sanctioned by the people. Just as there can be various forms of divinely appointed leadership, so there can be various forms of the people's acceptance: by acclamation after the fact—as with Moses, Gideon, or David—or by *a priori* agreement—as with Jephthah and Saul;[19] by all the people (*'īš Yisrā'ēl, bᵉnei Yisrā'ēl*) or by the people's representatives (*ha-zᵉqēnīm, ziqnei Yisrā'ēl*)—as with Moses, Joshua, and Gideon—or by part of the people—as with Deborah, Jephthah, David, Rehoboam, and Jehu. Just as the bestowal of the divine spirit upon a person is understood to be *ad hoc*, so is Israel's readiness to accept the authority of such a person, for the immediate purpose of helping him carry out his specific mission. The people, however, generally gave the savior consent for life. There is not a single example of a pre-monarchical savior being ousted by the people or its representatives.

Because the savior's course of action and the relationship between him and the people were pragmatically determined *ad hoc* and were not governed by any institutionalized patterns, some scholars have defined the Israelite type of government as "primitive democracy."[20] This definition, however, does not satisfactorily express the essence of political leadership in Israel from the days of Joshua, and perhaps even of Moses, to the days of Solomon. The Bible describes the patriarchal age as essentially peaceful and tranquil, but after the Exodus and especially after the invasion into Transjordania, the situation changed drastically. The biblical traditions realistically depict the internal-social and the external-political conditions which determined the concept of leadership and the image of

18 This is emphasized in the traditions about Moses, the prototypical divine emissary (see, e.g., Ex. 4:1–17; 19:9), and is echoed in God's words to Samuel: "for they have not rejected you, but they have rejected me from being king over them" (I Sam. 8:7).

19 The tradition of Saul's coronation after defeating the Ammonites puts the agreement *post factum* (I Sam. 11; 12:12).

20 The term was introduced by Th. Jacobsen to define the ancient Mesopotamian form of government. (See: Th. Jacobsen, "Primitive Democracy in Ancient Mesopotamia," *The Image of Tammuz, etc.*, pp. 157–162.) It was subsequently applied to the Israelite society in the biblical period. See, for instance: C. U. Wolf, "Traces of Primitive Democracy in Israel," *JNES*, 6 (1947), 98–108; R. Gordis, "Primitive Democracy in Ancient Israel—The Biblical Edah," *Alexander Marx Jubilee Volume* (New York, 1950), pp. 369–388. Cf. S. Talmon, "The Judean 'Am-Ha-aretz in Historical Perspective," *Papers of the Fourth World Congress of Jewish Studies* I, Jerusalem, 1967, pp. 71–76. P. A. H. de Boer totally rejected the claim that there was any democratic element in the Israelite form of government in the biblical period: "Israel n'a jamais été une démocratie" ("Vive le Roi," *VT*, 5 [1955], 227).

the savior in this crucial period. Historical vicissitudes confined him to the military sphere. His holy enthusiasm, stemming from divine inspiration, propelled him to only one goal: the holy war to save Israel from its enemies. The historiographical books again and again reiterate the same motif: Israel's cries which induced the Lord to send a savior to rescue His people from its plight. Joshua and the Judges, Saul and David attained power because of their military prowess. Their achievements in battle gave legitimacy to their divine mission.

The savior's success in accomplishing his mission depended on the cooperation of the people's army. As long as there were no mercenaries in Israel until David introduced them, the hero-savior's power of action derived directly from Israel's military might. This made him dependent on popular sanction, and enabled the people to control his activities. The democratic elements in the pre-monarchical Israelite society resulted from the prevailing give-and-take relationship between leader and led in the military sphere which was then the focus of sociol-political life. This reciprocity, though lacking constitutional definition, marked the social system of Israel from Joshua to David as a *de facto* "military democracy."

The Founding of the Monarchy

A dominant element in Israel's socio-political thought prior to the reign of David is the principle that appointment to leadership by divine inspiration and popular consent is always *ad personam* and non-transferable, either by inheritance or, after the days of Moses and Joshua, even by designation. The outgoing ruler never appointed his successor. This principle of discontinuity in the chain of leadership resulted in interregnal gaps between saviors. These were periods of decline in Israel's political ascendancy. The shortcomings inherent in the non-continuous rule of divine emissaries were felt in the fate of the people in the Conquest period, when Israel was forced to battle with the autochthonous population of Canaan for possession of agricultural (Jos. 17:14–18; Judg. 1:19, 34–35; 18:1–31) and pasture lands (I Chron. 4:39–43; 5:9–10; 7:21, 8:13), and for political supremacy in the area. The ups and downs of the prolonged military struggle led to the recognition that, for the people to exist as an independent political entity, a centralized government and predetermined procedures of succession were essential prerequisites. This was not recognized at once, but only after an extended, multiphased historical process. Its effects were first felt in Israel's offer to Gideon, which contains a capsule definition of the change needed in the governmental institutions: "Rule[21] over us, both

[21] The verb *mšl*, used there, and *mlk* which is widely employed in biblical Hebrew, are synonymous. Cf., e.g., Zech. 6:13: "... and he (Zerubbabel) shall bear royal honor, and shall sit and rule (*umāšal*) upon his throne," with I Kings 1:35: "... and he (Solomon) shall come and sit upon my throne; for he shall rule (*yimlok̲*) in my stead ..." (similarly, vv. 17, 24, 30). See also H. T. Boecker, "Die Beurteilung der Anfänge des Königtums

you and your son, and your son's son also" (Judg. 8:22). However, the implementation of the demand to replace the sporadic rule of the judge-savior by instituting a monarchy was delayed until the middle of the eleventh century B.C.E. when ecological-economic and socio-organizational factors combined with external political circumstances finally tipped the scales in favor of a more centralized and continuous form of government.

Saul's rise to power was not different from that of the Judges. As the *šōfēṭ* (judge) in his time, Saul was inspired by the strength of the fervor which seized him. He drew his authority from the inspiration that qualified him to stand at the head of the community. Like the saviors who preceded him, Saul received popular sanction to act. Thus the monarchy was not created *ex nihilo* as a revolutionary eruption of a new form of government without roots in the preceding social system. On the contrary, the nascent monarchy was imbued with the same values which had been basic to the social leadership in Israel from its very beginning: a charismatic, authoritative mission based on a pragmatic military democracy.

The founding of the monarchy was accompanied by criticism and attempts to block its emergence. It is widely held that traces of the struggle against it are reflected primarily in Gideon's refusal to accept hereditary rule (Judg. 8:23), Jotham's fable (Judg 9:8–15),[22] Samuel's address which precedes the Statute of the King (I Sam. 8:4–22), and his speech after Saul's coronation (*ibid.* 12 :16-24).

The opposition was many-faceted. Jotham's oration was directed specifically against Abimelech's kingship, and cannot be deemed a statement of principle.[23] It therefore recommends no alternative form of government. Gideon, however, posited the prophetic ideal "the Lord will rule over you" (Judg. 8:23)[24] as a principle opposed to any form of human overlordship perpetuated by dynastic succession.[25] Similarly, Samuel was concerned lest the concept of divine rule

in den deuteronomistischen Abschnitten des I Samuelbuches," *Wissenschaftliche Monographien zum Alten und Neuen Testament*, 31 (Neukirchen, 1969), 20. The synonymity of the terms undermines M. Buber's contention that משל here implies a formal government which is conceived as essentially different from monarchy (*Königtum Gottes*, Berlin, 1932, pp. 3 ff.).

[22] M. Buber discerned two strata in the book of Judges, one anti-monarchical and the other pro-monarchical (*op. cit.*, pp. 57 ff.). However, this conjecture is open to criticism and must be re-examined. See Talmon, "In those Days there was no King (*meleḵ*) in Israel," *Proceedings of the Fifth World Congress of Jewish Studies* I, Jerusalem, 1969, pp. 135–144 (Hebrew) = in this vol. 39–52.

[23] The issue was discussed by E. H. Maly, "The Jotham Fable—Anti-Monarchical?" *CBQ*, 22 (1960), 299–305. See also U. Simon, "Jotham's Fable—The Fable and its Interpretation and Literary Framework," *Tarbiz*, 34 (1964), 1–34 (Hebrew).

[24] Y. Kaufmann correctly demonstrated that Gideon's declaration has absolutely nothing to do with a theocratic priestly government but is advocating a prophetic-emissary form of government. (See *Tolᵉdot*, I-III, pp. 694 ff.).

[25] It is often held that Gideon only refused in theory, but in actual fact accepted the monarchy. See G. Henton Davies, "Judges VIII," *VT*, 13 (1963), 151–157.

be at stake when the people demanded that he appoint a king (I Sam. 8:7, 10:19), and therefore proclaimed "the Lord is your King" (I Sam. 12:12, cf. *ibid.* 19–20 and Obad. 21). In the long run, however, the attempts to prevent the implementation of the monarchy were abortive. Once the idea of terrestrial kingship had taken root it grew and gathered strength, and Israel was never to abandon it. From the time of its inception, the monarchy withstood every internal crisis, until it was abolished by external adversaries. If there remained any opposition to the monarchy during its historical existence, as is claimed, this resulted not from negative experiences with monarchical government, but rather had its roots in the pre-monarchical period. From the days of David, the anti-monarchical sentiment that existed, was merely the echo of historic memory and had no real influence on the life of society. No proof to the contrary can be derived from the solitary statement in Hosea (13:10–11): "Where now is your king to save you from all your enemies,[26] and your saviors of whom you said—'Give me a king and prince.' I have given you kings in my anger and I have taken them away in my wrath," which some wish to interpret as a relatively late negation of monarchy as such. If these verses indeed refer to the earthly king, and not to foreign cults of the Moloch type (cf. *ibid.* 7 ff.), they are but a reflex of the polemic from the days of Saul and Samuel, as can be gathered from the literary and topical similarity with I Sam. 8, 10, 11, 12.[27]

The traditions about the emergence of the monarchy in the days of Samuel[28] contain an element which has no traces in the preceding polemic nor in the later prophetic rebuke of the kings: "Give us a king *like all the nations* . . . and we too will be *like all the nations* . . ." (*ibid.* 8:5, 20). Similar language is found in the Law of the King in Deut. 17:4: "I will put a king over me *like all the nations around me.*" It appears that Samuel took absolutely no exception to the people's wish to be like the other nations in the matter of monarchy,[29] implying tacit acceptance like that of the author of the Law of the King (Deut. 17:1). It is reasonable to assume that in this matter the Bible accurately reflects Israel's history. At the time of the founding of the Israelite monarchy, Israel was socially and politically

[26] Reading with J. Kennedy, *An Aid to the Textual Amendment of the Old Testament*, Edinburgh, 1928, pp. 28, 104, *mikol ṣārēikā* instead of MT: *b^e kol 'āreikā*, which is mostly emended to *v^e kol sārēikā uš^e fāṭūkā*. See, among others, J. Wellhausen, *Die Kleinen Propheten*, 3, Berlin (1898), p. 19; W. R. Harper, *Hosea*, Edinburg, ICC, 1910, p. 400; M. J. Buss, The Prophetic Words of Hosea, Berlin, *BZAW*, 111 (1969), p. 74; BH, etc. NEB presupposes: *v^e šoftēikā b^e kol 'ārēikā*.

[27] See Y. Kaufmann, *ibid.* pp. 697 ff. Hosea's criticism of government and of rulers in his day is found in such other passages as 7:3–7; 8:4, 10, etc., most of which show opposition to an independent Ephraimite monarchy (*ibid.* 1:4–5).

[28] These traditions are not of one cloth, and all or part of them are probably not contemporaneous with the events. However, the basic realistic non-mythical quality of the Israelite monarchy is discernible in the matter-of-fact presentation of Samuel's negotiations with the elders of Israel.

[29] The expression usually has negative connotations. See, e.g., II Kings 17:15; Ezek. 5:6–14; etc.

similar to the nations of Canaan, especially the Transjordanian nations, and above all Edom.[30] Because of this affinity, the Bible pays special attention to Edomite history. Genesis 36 (cf. I Chron. 1:35–54) contains a capsule account of the history of Esau-Edom which parallels in its scope the more expanded presentation of the history of Jacob-Israel covered in Gen. 29—I Sam. 12. Genesis 36 gives a concise survey of the story of the eponym-hero Esau and his descendants who became tribes, their settlement in the Seir region, and the founding of their national state, ending with a list of "kings who ruled in the land of Edom before a king reigned in Israel" (Gen. 36:31 ff., cf. I Chron. 1:43 ff.).[31]

The Edomite chronicle does not reflect a dynastic system but, rather, records the names of eight rulers, no two of whom are father and son, and not one of whom ruled in the city of his predecessor. It reflects, therefore, a socio-political situation similar to that mirrored in the book of Judges. The biblical writer was obviously aware of parallels between the forms of government which obtained in Israel and Edom in the period between Moses and the establishment of monarchy: a national leadership of kings-judges with no permanent seat of centralized administration and no institutionalized transfer of power.

The same parallelism can be discerned in the later phases of the history of government in the two states. The first possible reference to dynastic rule in Edom comes in a fragmentary retrospective note from the days of Solomon which speakes about Hadad the Edomite of royal descent who fled to Egypt when David and Joab made war against Edom, and who returned to his land in the time of Solomon. It can be surmised that he is Hadar—the last in the Edomite King-List—or his son or grandson, if that Hadad actually lived in the days of Saul. In any case, by combining all these bits of information, one reaches the conclusion that at approximately the same time—in the second half of the tenth century B.C.E.—the Edomite and Israelite systems of government underwent a period of crisis, and in both states dynastic monarchies began to emerge.

30 The distinct affinity with Edom is reflected in the patriarchal and the Conquest traditions (Num. 20:14 ff.; Deut. 2:3 ff.), and also in prophetic literature (Amos 1:11; Obad. 10–12; Mal. 1:2).

31 Nöldeke's suggestion to identify the first name in the roster—*Bela‘ ben B*^{e}*‘ōr*—with *Bil*^{e}*‘ām ben B*^{e}*‘ōr* who was Moses's contemporary (Num. 22–24), is reasonable. He may be the unnamed king of Edom, referred to in Num. 20:14. *Hădād ben B*^{e}*dād*, who smote Midian in the plains of Moab (Gen. 36:35), could have been Gideon's contemporary, who also vanquished the Midianites in that area. It is therefore possible that the last one mentioned in the list—Hadar (in I Chron. 1:51, Hadad)—ruled in Edom in the days of Saul (I Sam. 14:47). See: Th. Nöldeke, *Untersuchungen zur Kritik des Alten Testaments*, Halle, 1869, p. 87; Ed. Meyer, *Die Israeliten und ihre Nachbarstämme*, Halle, 1906, pp. 376–377; J. R. Bartlett, "The Edomite King-List of Gen. XXXVI, 31–39 and I Chron. 1, 43–50," *JThS N.S.*, 16 (1965), 301–314; *idem*, "The Land of Seir and the Brotherhood of Edom," *ibid.* 20 (1969), 1–20; Y. Kaufmann, *op. cit.*, p. 781.

Neither biblical nor external sources inform us as to the type of government in Moab and Ammon before the period of Saul. An anonymous king of Ammon is mentioned in the Jephthah episode (Judg. 11:12 ff.). The traditions about Saul and David mention Nahash king of Ammon (I Sam. 11:1–2; 12:12). Only from the time of David is mention made of a dynastic monarchy in Ammon: Nahash's son Hanun succeeded his father in the capital Rabbath-Ammon (II Sam. 10:1; I Chron. 19:1–2)[32]

A chronistic comment in Numbers 21:26 refers to the first king of Moab without giving his name (cf. *ibid*, 20:14). Shortly after mention is made of Balak son of Zippor, king of Moab,[33] who was allied with Balaam son of Beor. The book of Judges mentions Eglon king of Moab (13:12 ff., cf. 12:9). In I Samuel 22:4 a Moabite king, a contemporary of Saul and David, is mentioned. However, the first reference to dynastic monarchy in Moab appears in the Mesha inscription[34] (mid-9th century B.C.E.), in which Mesha claims that his father reigned before him in Moab for thirty years.[35]

Although there is no decisive proof, we may perhaps conjecture that the socio-political development of Moab and Ammon was similar to that of Israel and Edom: a non-continuous government from the time of their settlement in Transjordania in the thirteenth century B.C.E. and the establishment of national states. Dynastic monarchy centered in a capital began at the end of the tenth or the beginning of the ninth century.[36] It would follow that at the time of the emergence of monarchy, Israel shared in the socio-political culture of the Transjordanian ethnic groups which, like Israel, were in a stage of transition to permanent settlement based on a mixed economy of cattle-breeding and agriculture and in the process of national and political solidification.

Against this background one must study the biblical documents which were meant to set normative guidelines for the monarchy in Israel: the Law of the King (Deut. 17:14–20) and the Statute of the King (I Sam. 8:11–16).

[32] It cannot be determined whether Shobi son of Nahash from Rabbat Bene Ammon who helped David in his flight before Absalom (II Sam. 17:27) was of the royal line, though this is probable.

[33] The formula *melek̲ leMō'āv* (Num. 22:4) resembles that found in Gen. 36:31 with reference to Israel—"*lifnēi melok̲ melek̲ livnēi Yisrā'ēl.*" In other passages, Balak is called *melek̲ Mō'āv* (Num. 22:10; 23:7; Josh. 24:9; Judg. 11:17, 25; Micah 6:5).

[34] S. Morag identified the Moabite name משע with the Hebrew noun *mōšīa'*, and put forward the hypothesis that the name was given to that king on account of his military victories (*Eretz-Israel*, 5 [1958], 138–144 (Hebrew).

[35] An explicit allusion to primogeniture in Moab or Edom is found in II Kings 3:27, depending on whether one interprets the verse as a reference to Mesha's son or, as seems preferable, to the son of the Edomite king (thus David Kimḥi, quoting his father, and also some modern commentators).

[36] A. Alt, "Die Staatenbildung der Israeliten in Palästina," *Kleine Schriften*, II, pp. 1–65.

Mišpaṭ ha-m^e lūḵāh (THE LAW AND STATUTE OF THE KING)

The Law of the King and the Statute of the King probably preserve parts of a social contract which laid down quasi-constitutionally the rights and duties of the king. This is the *mišpaṭ ha-m^e lūḵāh* (the Law and Statute of the King) which Samuel proclaimed and committed to writing subsequent to Saul's coronation (I Sam. 10:25) as attesting the covenant between the king and the people before God.[37] Of this document only a selection of prescriptive and proscriptive ordinances which apply to the king have been preserved in the Bible. Some of these have been transmitted in a circumstantial formulation in Deuteronomy[38] and some seem to underly the polemic formulation in which Samuel presented the Law and Statute of the King to the people who came to ask for a king to be appointed. These details do not complete the picture. The exact stipulations of the covenant between king and populace remain unknown, as do the punishments to be dealt to a violator, customarily found in similar legal documents both in the Bible and in the ancient Near East. The reason might be sought in the fact that the Bible preserved only a selection of these matters, i.e. those which are directly applicable to the socio-political situation at the time of the birth of Saul's monarchy.[39] It stands to reason that in the course of time there developed further statutes, possibly transmitted orally, which were no less binding than the Law and Statute of the King.[40]

Parallels in content and style as well as similarities between the structure of

[37] The proposed identification of *mišpaṭ ha-meleḵ* (I Sam. 8:9–17) with *mišpaṭ ha-m^e lūḵāh* (*ibid.* 10:25) is debated in scholarly circles. See: M. Segal, *The Books of Samuel²*, Jerusalem, 1956, p. 81 (Hebrew); S. Talmon, *mišpaṭ ha-meleḵ, A. Biram Jubilee Volume*, Jerusalem, 1948, pp. 45–56 (Hebrew); E. E. Halevy, "*mišpaṭ ha-meleḵ*" *Tarbiz*, 38 (1969), 225–230; J. Pedersen, *Israel, its Life and Culture*, London 1946, III–IV, p. 99; M. Noth, *Überlieferungsgeschichtliche Studien*, Königsberg, 1943, p. 58; J. de Fraine, *L'aspect religieux de la royauté israëlite*, Rome, 1954; E. Mendenhall, *BA*, 27 (1954), 71; G. Fohrer, "Der Vertrag zwischen König und Volk in Israel," *Studien zur Alttestamentlichen Theologie und Geschichte*, pp. 330–351; H. Wildberger, "Samuel und die Entstehung des Israelitischen Königtums," *Baumgartner Festgabe*, *ThZ*, 13, (1965), 442–469 = in this vol. 53–67.

[38] F. Horst distinguished two layers here: the basic law and its legal exegesis. See: F. Horst, *Das Privilegrecht Jahwes*, Göttingen, 1930, pp. 87, 99; L. Köhler, *Die hebräische Rechtsgemeinde* (1931), p. 17 ff.; J. Pedersen, *Israel*, III–IV, p. 101; K. Galling, "Die israelitische Staatsverfassung in ihrer vorderorientalischen Umwelt", *AO*, 28, 3/4 (1929), 32; A. Alt, "Die Heimat des Deuteronomiums," *Kleine Schriften*, II, pp. 250–275; G. von Rad, *Studies in Deuteronomy*, London, 1953, pp. 50, 62; Hempel, *Die althebräische Literatur*, Wildpark-Potsdam, 1934, pp. 140 ff.; K. Rabast, *Das apodiktische Recht im Deuteronomium und im Heiligkeitsgesetz*, Berlin, 1948, pp. 10 ff.

[39] See: S. Talmon, *loc. cit*; E. A. Speiser, *Judges*, 280–287; I. Mendelsohn, Samuel's Denunciation of Kingship in the Light of the Akkadian Documents from Ugarit, *BASOR*, 143 (1956), 17–22.

[40] However, such statutes were not recorded in the Bible because all legislation was concentrated in the Pentateuch and attributed to Moses. The Law of the King in Deuteronomy seeks to anchor the laws pertaining to the king in that formative period.

the Law of the King and the order of events connected with the founding of the monarchy in the days of Saul attest to the connection between these two issues. The Law of the King consists of three parts: an introit (Deut. 17:14–15) and an epilogue (vv. 18–20) of a theoretical basic nature which frame a cluster of specific prohibitions and instructions (vv. 16–17). Similarly three parts can be discerned in the account of Saul's coronation: an introduction (I Sam. 8:4–9) and an epilogue (*ibid.* 10:25; 12:13–14, 24–25) dealing with the bases of the monarchy, and between them a series of matters which bear upon the actual arrangements of the monarchical government (*ibid.* 8:11–17).

The conclusion of the Law of the King contains references to the threefold covenant between the king and the people before God: the king is commanded to write for himself "a copy of the [King's] Law", *et mišneh ha-Tōrāh ha-zōt*, the wording of this specific pericope, so that he may learn to fear God, observe and act in accord with the prescribed ordinances (Deut. 17:18–19). Similarly, Saul's coronation concludes with the writing of the Law and Statute of the King—although by Samuel and not by the king (I Sam. 10:25)—and in Samuel's exhortation to the people and its king to obey the Lord and serve Him faithfully (*ibid.* 12:13–25).

On the basis of this comparison it may be conjectured that the Law and Statute of the King which Samuel wrote down and placed before the Lord,[41] i.e., most certainly placed in the hands of the priests of Mizpah (cf. Judg. 20:1, I Sam. 7:5–13), was of the *mišneh ha-Tōrāh* (copy of the [King's] Law) type referred to in the Law of the King pericope (Deut. 17:18).

We should bear in mind that the preserved text of the Statute of the King has been distorted because of the polemical tone in which it was presented. However, we can still reconstruct from it two basic issues without which there would be no continuity in a monarchy or in any type of government that concentrates in its hands the administration of the state. Both of these were considered fundamental to the monarchy in ancient Near-Eastern states such as Ugarit and Alalakh.[42] They are the organization of the army and the administration of the realm, each demanding that taxes be levied.

1. Establishing an army, training soldiers and officers, furnishing arms, and organizing cavalry and chariotry are dealt with in the following passages which, somewhat freely translated, read: "He will take (of) your sons, and appoint them charioteers, and runners before his chariot" (I Sam. 8:11, cf. I Kings 9:22); "(and) he will appoint them captains of thousands, and captains of fifties" (cf. I Sam. 22:7); " . . . and to make weapons and the furnishings of his chariots" (*ibid.* 8:12). In actually granting authority to the king to draft people for the

[41] Similar traditions about reading a document and committing it to writing are recorded about Moses (Deut. 31:14–30) and Joshua (Josh. 8:32–35; 24:19–26). Compare further the acts of Josiah (II Kings 23:1–3 = II Chron. 34:29 ff.) and Nehemiah (Neh. 10).

[42] See Mendelsohn, *op. cit.*

army, there is no difference between the king and the "savior" of old. However, the king's role is not confined to calling up the army in time of emergency as it had been under the Judges. This method was adequate in its own day when Israel's wars were waged against nomadic tribes such as Midian and Amalek, or against the East Jordanian peoples whose military organization and equipment were similar to those of Israel. The descriptions of these wars make no mention of chariots and horsemen.[43] Most "savior" traditions, such as those about Ehud, Gideon, Jephthah, and Samson, speak exclusively about infantry battles. An exception is the war of Deborah and Barak against Sisera (Judg. 4–5), the first to transfer the Israelites' war effort from Transjordania and the mountains of Cisjordania to the coastal plain and the great valleys whose inhabitants threatened Israel "because they had iron chariots" (Josh. 17:16, 18, Judg. 1:19, 4:3, etc.).

The introduction of cavalry and a chariot force is a distinct function of the monarchical regime.[44] The chariot must be operated by a unit and not by an individual and entails training teams and tactically co-ordinating several units. The charioteers and horsemen had to be available for drills and manoeuvers. Chariots and horses meant establishing stables and provision centers. By their very nature, cavalry and chariot corps are professional units which cannot be organized and mobilized by clans and tribes. Because of all this, in Israel and probably elsewhere, a central government, like the monarchy, was indispensable for the introduction of chariots and cavalry. It is for this reason that the matter was taken up in the Law of the King in Deut. 17, and was given even more emphasis in the Law of the King in I Sam. 8. True, in Saul's days, plans for the development of mounted forces were not yet implemented.[45] because he was still struggling with primary problems of organizing and arming the infantry (I Sam. 13:19–22). Nevertheless, the delays in implementation do not contradict the traditions about Saul's election, which stated that military considerations, especially the demand to strengthen the Israelite army by cavalry and chariots, were an important or even decisive factor in the people's demand to establish a monarchy. The ideal king was conceived by the Hebrews in that period as a warrior-king and savior who would effectively lead the Israelite army in battle—"who didst lead out and bring in Israel" (II Sam. 5:2).

2. It was the king's responsibility to provide for the full-time military and administrative personnel who had left their previous occupations and means of livelihood. In a period, like David's, of military victories and conquests,

[43] See Num. 20:14–21; 21:21–35; 31:1–54; Deut. 2–3, etc.

[44] Cf. Y. Yadin, *The Art of Warfare in Biblical Lands in the Light of Archaeological Discovery*, Ramat Gan, 1963, 243 ff.

[45] Even David did away with most of the chariot horses which he captured, leaving only a hundred (II Sam. 8:4, cf. Josh. 11:6, 9). A cavalry and chariotry force was actually introduced in Israel only by Solomon (I Kings 10:26; 5:6–8).

these expenditures would be at least partially covered by booty and tribute collected from vanquished enemies. However, under Saul, at a time of defensive wars, such means were expected to come from the people by tithes imposed on produce and livestock, and by conscription to the royal labor force. The authority invested in the king to levy taxes and to impose corvée duties is reflected in the following verses: "He will take your men-servants and your maid-servants, and your best young men,[46] and your asses and put them to his work" (I Sam. 8:16), "and he will take your daughters to be perfumers, and to be cooks and bakers" (*ibid.* 13), "and you will be for him servants (or slaves)."[47] "He will tithe your flocks (*ibid.* 17), your seeds [probably produce],[48] and your vineyards (and give to his officers and to his servants);"[49] "and he will take your fields, and your vineyards, and your best olive yards, and give them to his servants" (*ibid.* 14–15; cf. *ibid.* 22:7). Taxing the people either for *ad hoc* requirements (II Kings. 15:19–20; 23:35) or permanently (Amos. 7:1) was recognized in the biblical period as a legitimate right of the monarchy.[50] According to biblical tradition, general taxation supervised by a royal officer—*'ăšer 'al ha-mas*—was introduced in Israel only in the days of Solomon within the administrative framework of the realm which he developed (I Kings 4–5, especially 4:6; cf. *ibid.* 12:18 = II Chron. 10:18). The biblical term *mas* is to be understood as an apocopated form of *mas 'ōvēd* i.e., corvée, and usually refers to imposed labor obligations.[51] But it stands to reason that the term also refers to taxes in the form of tithes levied from agricultural produce and from livestock. Probably the foundations of taxation were laid by David, possibly even by Saul. An indirect allusion to taxation may be found in Saul's promise to whomever would vanquish Goliath that "his family will be free (*ḥofšī*) in Israel" (I Sam. 17:25), which presumably means "free from tax." As long as the tax remained within

[46] καὶ τα βουκόλια Septuagint: "and your cattle." The combination "your cattle and your donkeys" reflects a standard element in the agricultural economy of that period (I Sam. 9:1–5 ; 11:5; cf. Job 1:3, 14; 42:12, and Gen. 12:16).

[47] It seems that originally the reference was to *'ăvādīm* in the sense of the king's officers (cf. I Kings 9:22), a title familiar from ancient seals. However, in Samuel's polemic wording of the Statute of the King the honorific term was given a negative slant by placing it next to *'ăvādīm ušᵉfāḥōt*.

[48] Perhaps it should be "your olives" *zēitēikem* as in v. 15.

[49] It is probable that *vᵉnātān lᵉsārīsāv va-'ăvādāv* is a synonymous reading of *vᵉnātan la 'ăvādāv* in v. 14. The term *sārīs* is used mainly in the late books of the Bible (Jer., Isa. 40 ff., Esther, and Daniel), and is not found at all in Joshua, Judges, and Samuel. In the Pentateuch it is used only with reference to Pharaoh's court. The term is first applied to an Israelite royal officer in I Kings 22:9.

[50] Taxation may have indirectly spurred the national economy because it forced the farmer to increase production so as not to have to lower his standard of living as a result of the king's levy on his produce.

[51] See: A. F. Rainey, "Compulsory Labour Gangs in Israel," *IEJ*, 20 (1970), 191–202; S. Talmon, "The New Hebrew Letter from the Seventh Century B.C. in Historical Perspective," *BASOR*, 176 (1964), 29–38, and bibliography there = in this vol. 79–88.

reasonable limits and was spent on recognized public requirements, it was accepted by the people as a necessary evil. No protest was raised until the burden of taxation became too heavy, as was the case under Solomon (I Kings 12:3–16).

The preceding analysis shows that the Statute of the King reflects the technical military and socio-economic situation of the Israelites from the days of the Judges to the time of David and Solomon. It bears the imprint of generations not yet actually experienced in institutionalized government. Historically and logically this "Law" finds its place in the dynamic development of the biblical society from the discontinuous leadership of the "saviors," who had no national machinery or organization, to the structured multi-faceted network of royal administration.

There is no reason to doubt the essential historicity of the biblical account of the founding of the monarchy in Samuel's time. Saul, Israel's first king, was elected in the wake of negotiations between the elders representing the people and the charismatic, divinely-appointed Samuel, who were partners in the national leadership of that time. The pragmatic formulation of the people's demands as expressed by the elders—"give us a king to save [rather than 'to judge'] us"—and their insistence even in the face of Samuel's objections indicate that the negotiations were conducted on the basis of clear knowledge of the obligations and privileges that went with the monarchy. The people were willing to limit individual as well as tribal-local freedom in order to enjoy the military and political benefits expected from a continuous rule of kings. At the time of its foundation Israel did not look upon the monarchy as a social ideal but saw it rather as a pragmatic solution to the problems of the day.[52] This attitude is clearly reflected in the words of the elders at the conclusion of their negotiations with Saul: "There shall be a king over us; that we also may be like all the nations; and that our king may rule us, and lead us, and fight our battles" (I Sam. 8:19–20). Because of its inherent military character, the monarchy preserved the democratic characteristics of the regime of the savior-judges. Without the cooperation of the people, the king was incapable of carrying out his principal task—to save Israel from its enemies. The monarchy came into being on the basis of a freely contracted covenant—the Law and Statute of the King—which was intended to preserve the balance between the ruler's power of action and the people's right to consent or refuse. By virtue of these criteria, the rule of the kings in biblical Israel may be defined as "participatory monarchy,"[53] a monarchy based on the participation of the people and their representatives in executing the political and administrative activities directed by the king.

[52] H. Frankfort, *Kingship and the Gods*, Chicago, 1948, p. 339: "The Hebrews knew that they had introduced it [i.e., the kingship] on their own initiative, in imitation of others and under the strain of emergency."

[53] For an analysis and a definition of the term used here, see C. Pateman, *Participation and Democratic Theory*, Cambridge, 1970.

The Institutionalized Monarchy

Saul's kingdom marks the watershed between the period of the Judges and the institutionalized monarchy. Through it, certain principles which characterized the leadership of savior-emissaries were fused into the monarchical model which developed under David and Solomon and even in the times of the divided monarchy. This is shown in the terminology, imagery, and motifs pertaining to the monarchical government,[54] which are but variations of terms and concepts marking the premonarchical government. Titles such as *šōfēṭ*,[55] *mōšēl*, *nāsī'*,[56] and *mōšīa'*[57] apply to the king just as they applied to pre-monarchical rulers. To these were added new designations such as *nāgīd*.[58] Despite etymological differences, the use of these terms in *parallelismus membrorum* and their interchangeability in parallel passages indicates that they were considered synonymous during, as well as preceding, the monarchy. At the same time, however, the social life of Israel changed. Internal factors which affected social development clothed themselves in new ideologies and terminologies, and crystallized in forms of political organization resembling those of neighboring peoples.

The transition from the rule of the saviors, whom the people obeyed because they were divine emissaries who proved their claims to leadership by successful action, to the rule of kings with power inherited (but still rooted in the idea of a personal mission) led to an ideological crisis which permeated the biblical traditions concerning the beginnings of the institutionalized monarchy. By its very nature, the institutionalized monarchy is dynastic. In contrast to previous forms of social leadership which stood on the principle of discontinuity and appointment *ad personam*, the transfer of office from father to son was accepted as basic to monarchical government. Indeed, from the days of Saul the right of succession within the royal family was considered the norm (I Sam. 13:13–14).

[54] See: J. A. Soggin, "Zur Entstehung des alttestamentlichen Königtums," *ThZ*, 15 (1959), 401–418; *idem*, "Charisma und Institution im Königtum Sauls," *ZAW*, 75 (1963), 54–65. M. Buber, "Die Erzählung von Sauls Königswahl," *VT*, 6 (1956), 113–173.

[55] For the synonymity of *šōfēṭ* and *meleḵ* see, e.g., Hos. 7:7; 13:10; Ps. 2:10, etc. Further, Micah 4:14, where *šōfēṭ Yisrā'ēl* refers to the king of Judah. Cf. S. Feldman, "Biblical Motives and Sources," *JNES*, 22 (1963), 102; W. Richter, *Die Bearbeitungen des Richterbuches in der deuteronomischen Epoche*, Bonn (1964), p. 130.

[56] Although etymologically different, the terms *nāsī'* and *meleḵ* are often used as synonyms in biblical literature. This fact should be the starting point for any attempt to explain Exekiel's preference for *nāsī'* in his vision of the future Israelite kingdom, without discarding altogether the traditional title *meleḵ*. Cf. Ezek. 37:24: *vᵉ'avdī Dāvīd meleḵ 'ălēihem* with v. 25: *vᵉ'avdī Dāvīd nāsī' lāhem*.

[57] Cf. e.g., I Sam. 9:16 with Isa. 19:20 in reference to Ex. 3:7, 9; 6:2–8, and with the formula of salvation repeatedly employed in the book of Judges, and see Boecker, *op. cit.*, pp. 20–22.

[58] I Sam. 9:16–17; 10;1; 13:14; 25:30; II Sam. 6:21; 7:8, etc. and also Ezek. 28:2.

Saul certainly intended to pass on his power to his son Jonathan and considered David a threat to the establishment of his dynasty: "Then Saul's anger was kindled against Jonathan and he said unto him . . . 'as long as the son of Jesse liveth upon the earth, thou shalt not be established, nor thy kingdom'" (I Sam. 20:30–31). After the death in battle of Saul and Jonathan, Abner unhesitatingly made Saul's son Ishbaal king over Israel (II Sam.2:8–9), as a matter of course. The dynastic principle received its full ideological, systematic expression in Nathan's prophecy bringing God's promise to David: "Thy house and thy kingdom shall be made sure forever before thee [read: 'before me']; thy throne shall be established forever" (*ibid.* 7:16; cf. 13, 25–26, 29; I Kings 3:6; 5:19; Ezek. 37:24–28; II Chron. 13:5–7). Whenever this prophecy was composed, a matter widely discussed in scholarly circles,[59] there can be little doubt that it contains thoughts and sentiments from the period of David. This is confirmed by the fact that David's sons Absalom, Adonijah, and Solomon saw themselves as prospective successors to the throne, and that this was undisputed by the king's entourage and all Israel alike. However, at that time, no definite system of succession had been agreed upon. This caused the wars of succession among David's sons, each of whom attempted to capture the monarchy, backed by courtiers and faithful supporters from among the populace. The issue was decided by David, who designated Solomon heir and successor over his older brother Adonijah (I Kings 1:32–35; cf. II Sam. 3:4; 5:14). Similarly, Rehoboam appointed Abijah in preference to his older brothers (II Chron. 11:18-22). With Solomon's enthronement the dynastic principle was established. After Solomon's death, no one contested Rehoboam's right to succeed his father (I Kings 11:43—12:1), even though the people demanded that Solomon's taxes be alleviated (*ibid.* 12:4–17).

The same principle applied not only in Judah but also in Ephraim. Ahijah the Shilonite who appointed Jeroboam king over the northern tribes promised him everlasting kingship, just as Nathan had promised David: "And I will take thee,[60] and thou shalt reign over all that thy soul desireth, and shalt be king over Israel. (And it shall be) if thou wilt hearken unto all that I command thee, and wilt walk in My ways, and do that which is right in Mine eyes, to keep My statutes and My commandments, as David My servant did, then I will be with thee and will build thee a sure house, as I built for David, and will give Israel unto thee" (I Kings 11:37–38; cf. I Sam. 13:13). However, since Jeroboam

[59] See Y. Kaufmann's treatment of the subject "Nathan the Prophet at the King's Court," *Collected Essays*, Tel Aviv, 1966, pp. 180–184 (Hebrew); M. Noth, *Gesammelte Studien zum Alten Testament*, München, 1966, pp. 334–35; G. W. Ahlström, "Der Prophet Nathan und der Tempelbau," *VT*, 11 (1961), 113–127.

[60] The phrase is redundant and is employed here for the sole purpose of evoking an association with Nathan's prophecy: II Sam. 6:8. There it is material, since it harks back to I Sam. 16:11.

did not live up to the conditions of his covenant with God, the promise of a dynasty for all generations as given by Ahijah (I Kings 14:7–14; cf. II Kings 9:9) was revoked, just as Saul's kingdom was taken from him by Samuel who had appointed him in the first place (I Sam. 13:14; 15:10–28), and just as the rule over the ten northern tribes was denied to the Davidic house (I Kings 11:7–13, 29–36). Similarly, the often repeated reference to "Baasha and his house" (I Kings 16:3, 7, 11, 12) implies that Baasha's rule had been intended to be dynastic. And indeed, he was succeeded by his son Elah, but, Zimri's conspiracy put an end to Baasha's line (*ibid.* 16:9 ff.). Also, the chronistic summary of Jehu's reign indicates that initially he had been promised an enduring dynasty by the prophet who appointed him, though this is not expressly mentioned (II Kings 9:1–10), but forfeited the pledge because of subsequent wrongdoings and was granted a line of four generations only: "And the Lord said unto Jehu, 'Because thou hast done well in executing that which is right in Mine eyes, and has done unto the house of Ahab according to all that was in My heart, thy sons to the fourth generation shall sit on the throne of Israel'" (*ibid.* 10:30–31). There is therefore no basis to A. Alt's contention that the court revolutions, more frequent in Ephraim than in Judah, constitute evidence that the ideology of a disjunctive rule by saviors from the period of the Judges was prepetuated in the North also after the establishment of the monarchy.[61] It follows that even though for the larger part of its history, Ephraim's royal rule was non-dynastic, kings often being dethroned and replaced, this should not be taken as evidence that a different concept of monarchy prevailed in the North, but rather as a sign of the internal weakness of the monarchy, the causes of which should be sought in the social structure or in external political circumstances. Conceptually, the dynastic monarchy was as firmly rooted in Ephraim as it was in Judah.

The paucity of our sources does not permit any final decision regarding the laws of succession. The Bible usually uses the neutral statement "and his son ruled after him." It is reasonable to assume that in the course of time primogeniture was accepted in Israel as, presumably, it was among the neighboring nations. Primogeniture is expressly mentioned in the tradition about Jehoshaphat: "And their father gave them great gifts, of silver, gold and precious things, with fortified cities in Judah; but the kingdom gave he to Jehoram, because he was the first born" (II Chron. 21:3). Nevertheless, we encounter in Israel, as in other nations,[62] younger sons who were preferred over the elder, either because a king loved the mother of the son designated as his successor, or because of a court cabal (II Kings 23:30; cf. *ibid.* v. 36), because of foreign intervention.

[61] A. Alt, "Das Königtum in den Reichen Israels und Judas," *VT*, 1 (1951), 2–22 = *Kleine Schriften*, II, pp. 116–134.

[62] The Assyrian kings Esarhaddon and Ashurbanipal were not first-born and were appointed rulers already in their fathers' lifetimes.

The internal consolidation of the dynastic concept was strengthened by the increasing contact between Israel and her neighbors. As stated, there is reason to believe that dynastic monarchy, which was customary in the Canaanite city-states, took root among the Transjordanian peoples at the same time that it was adopted in Israel, i.e. in the period of David and Solomon. At that juncture, we observe a clearly discernible trend towards centralization in that area of the ancient Near East. Capital cities became focal points of the royal administrative network spanning the country. Next to the royal palace, central temples sprang up, symbolizing the stability of the monarchy.[63] The king, who often served as a priest or assumed the title of priest, took overall charge of the cult.[64] The peoples in the area maintained close political and economic contact. They were all subject to Mesopotamian culture influence[65] which by its very nature was open to the absorption of foreign elements. The situation was conducive to the integration of the kingdom of Israel in the political and cultural fabric of the Syro-Palestinian sphere. The belligerent expansion under David and Solomon's economic enterprises opened a window for Israel to the world of ideas of the neighboring peoples and their socio-political ideologies.[66] The parallel social development, language affinities with the immediate neighbors, and the existence of a *lingua franca*—Akkadian or Aramaic—facilitated assimilation. From the days of the United Monarchy, an unprecedentedly distinct trend towards Canaanite-Mesopotamian acculturation characterized biblical Israel. The literature of the monarchical period—the Former and Latter Prophets, and especially the book of Psalms—contains a plethora of images and motifs familiar to us from Ugaritic literature and from North-West Semitic inscriptions. They testify to the continually increasing participation of Israel in the surrounding world of beliefs and ideas.

Under the influence of the court style which typifies the literature of neighboring monarchies, the idea of the savior-king, God's elect, evoked imagery and phraseology which brought the king and his office within the heavenly sphere. The king was cloaked in a sanctity never bestowed upon the savior-

[63] Cf. A. L. Oppenheim, *Ancient Mesopotamia*, Chicago, 1964, pp. 124–126.

[64] For biblical references to priest-kings, see Gen. 14:18 and Ps. 110:4; II Sam. 8:18 (cf. I Chron. 18:17). The combination is also found in Phoenician inscriptions, e.g., *tbnt khn 'štrt mlk ṣdnm*. Cf. H. Donner–W. Röllig, *KAI* I, 2–3 (Text 11, 1; 13, 1; 14, 5); M. Noth, *op. cit.*, n. 5, p. 194.

[65] See E. A. Speiser, "The Idea of History in Ancient Mesopotamia," *Oriental and Biblical Studies*, Chicago, pp. 270–312; *idem*, "Authority and Law in Ancient Mesopotamia," *ibid.*, pp. 313–324.

[66] See B. Mazar, "The Aramean Empire and its Relations with Israel," *BAr*, 25 (1962), 98–120 = *BAr Reader*, II, New York, 1964, pp. 127–151; *idem*, "The Philistines and the Founding of the Kingdoms of Israel and Tyre," *Proceedings of the Israel Academy of Sciences*, I, 7, Jerusalem, 1966, 356–377; A. Malamat, "The Kingdom of David and Solomon in its Contact with Egypt and Aram Naharaim," *BAr*, 21 (1958), 96–102 = *BAR* II (1964), 84–98.

judges: whosoever harms the king will not go unpunished (I Sam.26:9,23; II Sam. 1:14—15); to curse the king was considered a capital offense (*ibid.* 19:22), like cursing God (I Kings 21:10 cf. Ex. 22:27); one would call upon the king to witness, as one called upon God (I Sam. 12:3), and people would take an oath by his name (II Sam. 15:21). The king sheltered his people (*ibid.* 21:17; Lam. 4:20) just as God gave protection to Israel. The identity of metaphors applied to the king and to the Diety eventually led to the depiction of the king as the first-born son of God (Ps. 2:7–9; 89:27–28),[67] probably borrowed from Near-Eastern mythic-religious terminology. The image obviously does not imply an actual biological father-son relationship, as is sometimes maintained,[68] but rather an adoption formula to provide the king with a special place among those enjoying God's protection.

At first sight, the cultural affinities of Israel with her neighbors, appear to have resulted from the intercourse of an élite stratum with their peers in other nations. However, a closer look reveals a somewhat more purposeful and structured relationship. We seem not to be dealing solely with processes of unplanned acculturation but with intentional assimilation on the part of the Israelite kings and royalist courtiers. For them, the cultures of Canaan and Mesopotamia provided welcome models of government and socio-political ideologies which focused on the image of the king.[69]

In contradistinction to the historical conception of monarchy lacking any ideological dimension, which was the original Israelite view,[70] other Near-Eastern peoples considered the monarchy a basic element of creation.[71] Kings had ruled the world from the beginning of time. The sanctity of primordiality permeated the institution of monarchy and the person of the king. From this world of ideas, Israel derived concepts and motifs out of which it wove an ideology of monarchy principally based on the Davidic house, but also leaving its impressions on Ephraimite concepts. The monarchistic ideology set out to make the Davidic dynasty transcend the realm of historic singularity and implant it in primeval antiquity: "Thou Bethlehem Ephrathah, which art smallest

[67] Most of these terms are derived from Nathan's prophecy (II Sam. 7:12–14), which is the most concentrated expression of biblical Israel's monarchistic ideology. Cf. further the metaphorical reference to the king in court-etiquette fashion as "angel of God" (I Sam. 29:9; II Sam. 14:17; 19:28; Zech. 12:8).

[68] G. Widengren, *Sakrales Königtum im Alten Testament und im Judentum*, Münster, 1955, pp. 62 ff.; A. R. Johnson, *Sacral Kingship in Ancient Israel*, Cardiff, 1955; M. Noth, *op. eit.*, (n. 5), 157–191.

[69] See K. H. Bernhardt, "Das Problem der altorientalischen Königsideologie im Alten Testament," *VTS*, 8 (1961) pp. 67–90.

[70] See *Enc. Miqr.*, IV (1962),. s.v. *meleḵ, mᵉlūḵāh*, esp. cols. 1085, 1088; G. H. Fohrer, *Israels Staatsordnung in Rahmen des Alten Orients, op. cit.*, pp. 309–329; Soggin, *op. cit.*, p. 5.

[71] The Sumerian King List opens with the words, "When kingship came down from heaven." See: S. N. Kramer, *The Sumerians*, Chicago, 1963, pp. 328–331; Th. Jacobsen, *The Sumerian King List*, Chicago, 1939; A. J. Sachs–D. J. Wiseman, "A Babylonian King List of the Hellenistic Period," *Iraq*, 16 (1954), 202–211; A. L. Oppenheim, *op. cit.*, p. 145.

(youngest) among the clans of Judah, out of thee shall one come forth a ruler of Israel whose roots are in the distant past, in days gone by (or possibly: in the days of creation)" (Micah 5:1). The Davidic line is like the people of Israel whose political and territorial existence is also rooted in the dawn of history: "When the Most High gave to the nations their inheritance, when He separated men, He set the borders of the peoples according to the number of the children of Israel" (Deut. 32:8). The survival of the Davidic kingdom and that of the people of Israel are both compared to the eternality of the laws of creation: just as these laws will never be annulled, so God will never cast away His chosen people nor the seed of His servant David (Jer. 33:25–26; cf. *ibid.* 31:35–36; Ezek. 37:23–28; Ps. 89:3–5, 29–30; 110:3–4, etc.).

The monarchical ideology sought to free the government of kings from the polemics in which it had been embroiled at its inception and to invest it with ideological justification. The elevation of the monarchy beyond mundane history upset the balance between the power of action granted to the king and the controlling power of consent invested in the people on which the smooth working of the participatory monarchy was based. There was a definite danger that kings might develop a tendency towards an autocracy deriving its power from its own unlimited and unconditional sanctity, as was true of ancient Near-Eastern monarchies. In opposition to such trends, tempering lines of thought emerged and crystallized; in them can be discerned variations on concepts which had determined the political structure of Israel at the time of the savior. The two forces which had interacted in the founding of the monarchy—the prophet, representing the divine, and the people—now forged new principles and institutions which would contend with the monarchy over the definition of its place in the socio-political fabric, within the framework of the Covenant between Israel and God and between the king and the people.

Changes in the Relations of King and People

The boundaries of Saul's kingdom were identical with the area settled by the Israelites. Saul's wars were primarily defensive and preventive and were not aimed at territorial expansion and annexation. Conquered territories were not incorporated into the Israelite political system (I Sam. 14:47–48). Foreign populations, such as the inhabitants of the Canaanite cities, remained outside the political framework of the national state, or else were assimilated into the Israelite ethnic fabric, like the Kenites and Gibeonites, thus completely losing their national identity.[72]

This situation changed radically in David's time. Conquered states were absorbed into the political framework of the empire at different levels of incorporation, without losing their national and ethnic identity. In Solomon's day

[72] Individuals of foreign extraction were completely assimilated into the Israelite society and could even be found in the king's entourage; cf. Doeg the Edomite (I Sam. 22:9).

there even developed a rather liberal socio-religious outlook (not to be mistaken for syncretism)[73] which provided an ideological basis for the ethnic and religious pluralism of the citizenry.[74] Concurrently the diverse components of the realm evinced a variety of attitudes towards the king of Israel, the "king of kings." The concept of Israel as a "priestly kingdom and a holy nation" (i.e., a holy state) was lost on the non-Israelite ethnic elements. Similarly meaningless for them was the concept of the king's mission as savior of Israel, which was a function of God's covenant with His people. A rationalist political conception of kingship replaced the image of the king as God's emissary.

The politicization of the image of the king, which probably emanated from ethnically foreign elements in the population, brought with it significant changes in the relationship of the Israelite citizens to their monarch. The growth of the one-nation state of Saul's time to the multi-national empire under David was accompanied by a process of socio-economic and cultural-religious differentiation in the Israelite stratum of the population. Signs of this transformation can be discerned in the changing character of the army, which had been the backbone of the pragmatic democracy of the period of the saviors. David conscripted an army of mercenaries partly from the foreign conquered populations, such as the Cherethites and Pelethites (II Sam. 8:18; 20:23). As a result, the importance of the people's army dwindled and its influence in matters of state waned. At the same time, the king's status and tasks changed and his role in the body politic was redefined. Toward the end of David's reign, the image of the king as Israel's military leader which had brought the people to choose him as their ruler (*ibid.* 5:1–3) began to fade. His participation in military matters became symbolic, as is evidenced by his merely ceremonial conquest of Rabbath-ammon (*ibid.* 12:27–31; cf. *ibid.* 21:15–17).[75] Professional officers like Joab, Abner, and Benaiah replaced the savior-king at the head of Israel's army. The gap between the king and the people in one of the vital areas of political life could not be bridged even by the increasing royal participation in other areas such as the judicial (*ibid.* 14:1–11; 15:2–6), in which the saviors of old had not been involved.

Solomon's reign, which was entirely peaceful, was marked by a total loss of the close relationship between people and king which had characterized the period of the great war-leaders. Nothing remained of the former image of the savior-king envisioned by the people in Samuel's day: "And he shall go out before us and fight our wars" (I Sam. 8:20). In contrast, Solomon is depicted as inexperienced in military matters, a mere youngster who could not lead an army

[73] See: J. A. Soggin, "Der offiziell geförderte Synkretismus in Israel während des 10. Jahrhunderts," *ZAW*, 78 (1966), 179–204.

[74] See: S. Talmon, "The Biblical Concept of Jerusalem," *Journal of Ecumenical Studies*, 8 (1971), 300–316.

[75] Similarly, Assyrian kings credited themselves with military ventures which never took place or in which they did not take part.

into battle (I Kings 3:7). The military expansion of David's days gave way to Solomon's tendency to stabilize existing borders and develop a system of static defense which demanded massive building projects (*ibid.* 5:1–8; 9:15–19; 11:26–28). The means were provided by taxing the population (*ibid.* 4:7 ff.; 5:2–3, 7–8, 27–32), collecting duties from transit trade passing through Israelite territory (*ibid.* 10:14–15), and developing independent economic enterprises as a monopoly of the crown (*ibid.* 9:26–28; 10:22). These projects necessitated creating a ramified administration (*ibid.* 4:2–19; 9:23) and establishing channels of communication between the king and his subjects. There emerged a stratum of royal officers and courtiers between the king and the people (*ibid.* 12:6–7), who represented the king vis-à-vis the populace. This development reached a peak in the days of Rehoboam, the first generation when the idea of a hereditary monarchy was properly realized. The negotiations between Rehoboam and the people who were to confirm his kingship, if Solomon's corvée were alleviated, reveal first signs of formal implementation of participatory government. In order to reach a decision, Rehoboam consulted with a "royal council" which, according to the biblical sources, was first established under Solomon (*ibid.* 12:1–15). Scripture does not enlighten us about the nature of this council[76] nor indicate the composition of the group negotiating on behalf of the people. The results, however, prove its real power: for the first time in its history, the socio-political leadership in Israel deposed its ruler. It is of interest to note that, despite his increased power, the king was more vulnerable than any previous type of leader. Not one of the pre-monarchical saviors had been removed from office by the people, even though some encountered antagonism and even open opposition (Num. 16; Judg. 8:1–3; 12:1–6 and perhaps 15:9–13, etc.). On the other hand, with the institutionalization of the monarchy, the political system was recurrently rocked by internal rebellion and political upheaval (II Sam. 15–18; I Kings 11:26 ff.). Assassination of kings by rebels was common not only in Ephraim (*ibid.* 15:27–28; 16:8–12; II Kings 9–10; 15:10, 14, 25) where hereditary monarchy did not take firm root, but even in Judah where the Davidic dynasty became well-established (*ibid.* 11:1, 16; 12:21; 14:19; 21:23). Even though it cannot be proved, in most cases the rebels probably came from the

[76] A. Malamat compared these groups with similar bodies in Sumer, emphasizing their institutional character: "Organs of Statecraft in the Israelite Monarchy," *BAr*, 28 (1965), 34–65. This view is opposed by G. Evans, "Rehoboam's Advisers at Shechem," and "Political Institutions in Israel and Sumer," *JNES*, 25 (1966), 273–279, but note Malamat's reaction answer in *BAr Reader*, III (1970), n. 9. See also H. Tadmor, "'The People' and the Kingship in Ancient Israel: The Role of Political Institutions in the Biblical Period," *Journal of World History*, XI, 1–2 (1968), 1–23. For a different interpretation of such phenomena, see S. Talmon, "The Judean 'Am Ha'aretz," *Papers of the Fourth World Congress of Jewish Studies*, I, Jerusalem, 1967, pp. 71–76. = in this vol. 68–78.

army hierarchy or from the royal retinue who opposed the king because he failed in his task as military leader.[77]

These developments disclose the diminishing immunity of political leadership in Israel which was intended to, and in actual fact did, counterbalance the increased power which the kings derived from dynastic continuity. It seems that there developed intuitively non-institutionalized means of socio-political checks and balances which succeeded in renewing the balance of power between the king and the people, and helped to perpetuate even in the institutionalized monarchy certain principles from the time of the saviors.

I. The Political Function of Divine Inspiration

In the pre-monarchical age, the divine Spirit was exclusively revealed in Israel in the person of the savior. The savior's unique charisma afforded him a special position in his society. Because Covenantal promises were embodied in him alone, no one could criticize him on behalf of the Covenant and in the name of its giver. From the beginning of the monarchical period there was a bifurcation of the divine Spirit in Israel. The Spirit revealed itself in two types of social functionaries: the king-savior and the messenger-prophet, each of whom claimed precedence over the other. Appointment as a ruler (*nāgīd*) no longer came directly to the man selected, as with Moses and the Judges, but was transmitted by a man of God (*'īš 'ĕlōhīm*).[78] The anointing of Saul and David by the prophet Samuel became the prototype for future generations.

The bifurcation of the divine Spirit is discernible in the appreciation given to the kings in biblical literature. The deeds of the savior-judges were evaluated by only one criterion: their success in accomplishing their military mission. Saul was initially measured by the same yardstick. After he had defeated Ammon in a holy war, no one dared any longer to oppose his leadership (I Sam. 11:12–15; cf. 10:26–27). However, his later achievements in the political arena, the victory over Amalek and over all his enemies, were judged by religious-ideological standards, unrelated to historical reality. Prophetic inspiration appointed itself judge over the king and his actions. Starting out by hailing Saul's political achievements, that he "fought against all his enemies everywhere, against Moab, Ammon, Edom, the kings of Zobah and the Philistines," the report then

[77] In the chronistic summaries of assassinated kings there is not one occurrence of the term *ugᵉvūrātō* which is commonly found concerning kings who died while still in power: *vᵉyeter divrĕi . . . ugᵉvūrātō* is found in connection with David (I Chron. 29:30), Asa (I Kings 15:23), Jehoshaphat (*ibid.* 22:46), Hezekiah (II Kings 20:20) in Judah, and with Baasha (I Kings 16:5), Omri (*ibid.* 16:27), Jehu (II Kings 10:34), Jehoahaz (*ibid.* 13:8), Joash (*ibid.* 14:15), and Jeroboam (*ibid.* 14:28) in Ephraim.

[78] This is emphasized in the book of Samuel before and after Saul's election (I Sam. 15:1, 17–19; 13:13–14; 15).

incongruously continues: "and wherever he turned he failed" (*ibid.* 14:47; cf. 15:10–28). Similarly, Scripture reports negatively about Jeroboam that "he did that which was evil in the sight of the Lord," and then continues by praising him: "He restored the border of Israel from Lebo-hamath unto the sea of the Arabah, and (God) saved them (Israel) by the hand of Jeroboam the son of Joash . . . The rest of the acts of Jeroboam, and all that he did, and his might, how he warred and how he recovered Damascus and Hamath, . . . they are written in the book of chronicles of the kings of Israel" (II Kings 14:24–28).

Prior to the monarchy, divine inspiration was never removed from a man who had been revealed a savior, even if he went wrong. Samson's marriage to a Philistine woman indeed angered his parents (Judg. 14:3; cf. Gen. 26:34–35; 27:46), but the Bible justified his action "for he looked for a pretext [to fight] against the Philistines" (Judg. 14:4), and the Spirit remained upon him (*ibid.* 14:6). Gideon, by erecting the Ephod in his city Ophrah, sinned, and caused others to do so: "And all Israel went astray after it . . . and it became a snare unto Gideon and to his house" (*ibid.* 8:27). Even so, his mission was not terminated.

In the monarchical period, however, the very mission of the savior-king could be voided because of his failings. The first king was also the first leader to be deposed. Samuel who crowned Saul also dethroned him (I Sam. 13:13–14; 15:26–28). Because of Solomon's sin in marrying foreign wives (as Samson had done) and building high places (like Gideon's at Ephod), the rule over ten tribes was divested from his son Rehoboam (I Kings 11:1–13) and assigned to Jeroboam (*ibid.* 29–39). Ahab's transgression led to his son's being deprived of the throne and Jehu was anointed king over Israel by the emissary of Elisha the prophet (II Kings 9).

The very possibility that the rule of a king could be terminated *de jure* for religious and doctrinal considerations, and not only *de facto* after revolts, differentiated the Israelite monarchy from that of neighboring nations, and curbed the development of absolutism characteristic of monarchical governments at all times. The threat that the king's mission could be revoked should he not comply with the statutes of the divine Covenant and the social contract with the people, as interpreted by the prophet, meant that even the institutionalized dynastic monarchy in Israel retained the principle that continuity of leadership was not automatic, neither in the lifetime of a king, nor from generation to generation.

Against the background of these changes in political ideas and practice, the significance of anointing with oil must be examined. The practice was obviously an innovation of the monarchical regime, and unheard of in the era of the saviors. Anointing, though, is known from biblical sources in such contexts, as reference to the High Priest (Ex. 28:41; 29:7, 36; 40:13–15; Lev. 8:10–12; Num. 3:3; 35:25, etc.), who was called the "anointed priest" (Lev. 4:3, 5, 16; 6:15), to a prophet (I Kings 19:16; cf. Ps. 105:15), or to cultic implements (Gen. 31:13;

Ex. 30:26; 40:9–11; Num. 7:10, 84, 88, etc.). Extra-biblical sources show that the practise of anointing kings was common to many ancient Near-Eastern monarchies including the Canaanite city-states. However, *māšiaḥ* (= "the anointed one"), the title applied to the king, has thus far been attested only in the Bible, where it always occurs in either the construct form—*m^ešiaḥ YHWH* (I Sam. 24:7, 11; 26:9, 11, 16, 23, etc.), *m^ešiaḥ 'ĕlohēi Ya'aqōv* (II Sam. 23:1), or with a possessive suffix—*m^ešīḥī* (I Sam. 2:35; Ps. 132:17), *m^ešīḥekā* (Hab. 3:13; Ps. 84:10; 132:10 etc.), *m^ešīḥō* (I Sam. 2:10; 12:3, 5; Isa. 45:1, etc.), *m^ešīḥāi* (Ps. 105:15). The Bible mentions explicitly anointing only certain kings:* David (I Sam. 2:4; 5:3; Ps. 89:21), Solomon (I Kings 1:39), Jehu (II Kings 9:1 ff.), Joash (*ibid.* 11:12) and Jehoahaz (*ibid.* 23:30). The Jewish sages deduced from this that a king was anointed only if he had founded a new line. A king coming to the throne in dynastic succession was anointed only if his rights had been contested (Yer. Sheqalim 49, 3; Horayot 47, 3). However, the recurring use of the term "anoint as king" (*māšaḥ l^emelek*: Judg. 9:8, 15, etc.; II Sam. 2:4; I Kings 19:15, etc), to mean "enthrone," and the often employed term *m^ešiaḥ YHWH* indicate that anointing was fairly widespread, and that possibly every king in Judah and Ephraim was anointed, although our sources are silent about the fact.

The anointing was done by the High Priest (I Kings 1:39; II Chron. 23:11), apparently with the "holy oil" kept in the Tabernacle and later in the Temple (Ex. 25:6; 37:29; Lev. 8:2; I Kings 1:39), or by a prophet (II Kings 9:6 ff; cf. I Kings 19:15–16) on divine command. The Bible also mentions anointing by the people. Such was the case with Solomon. According to I Chron. 29:22, the people acclaimed him king by anointing him at the customary coronation banquet.[79] Similarly with Joash: "and they made him king, and anointed him; and they clapped their hands, and said 'Long live the King'" (II Kings 11:12),[80] and with Jehoahaz: "And the *'am ha-'āreṣ* took Jehoahaz the son of Josiah, and they anointed him (the last phrase is missing in II Chron. 36:1) and made him king in his father's stead" (II Kings 23:30).[81]

The above analysis suggests that in Israel anointing was not a purely sacred act but also a socio-political one.[82] It gave formal expression of approval of the king by the representatives of the people or by the prophet or priest as representatives of the religio-cultic dimension, or by both. Even though conceptually the act of anointing lent the king immunity through sanctity (I Sam. 24:7, 11;

* Saul (I Sam. 10:1),

[79] The reference is missing in the parallel account in I Kings 1:38–48, where only an anointing by Zadok and Nathan is recorded (v. 45).

[80] The parallel in II Chron. 23:11 reads: "Jehoiada [the priest] and his sons anointed him."

[81] Cf. II Sam. 19:11: "And Absalom whom we anointed over us died in war," as a parallel to the term *melek* used in *ibid.* 15:10.

[82] See: E. Kutsch, "Salbung als Rechtsakt im A. T. und im Alten Orient," *BZAW*, 87 (1963).

26:9, 11, 16, 23; II Sam. 1:14–16; Ps. 105:15 = I Chron. 16:22), factually it gave expression to the king's dependency on his constituents, symbolizing the people's control over the monarch. In historical reality, the act of anointing was a ceremonial manifestation of the checks and balances inherent in the basic conditions of the covenant of monarchy which the participatory monarchy imposed upon the king.

The image of the anointed king, scion of a dynastic line, as realized in the Davidic house, contained two essentially contradictory principles: the concept of inspired leadership deriving its power from personal charisma, which by definition is non-consecutive, coalesced with the idea of an automatically continuous government drawing its strength from an institutionalized charisma of office.[83] The principle of election by the divine spirit was grafted on to the system of dynastic government, which in essence is void of any religious and ideological dimension. This unexpected amalgam of seemingly contradictory concepts raised the dynastic monarchy to the level of a basic principle of biblical ideology. Nathan's prophecy and related traditions (II Sam. 7; I Kings 8:22–26; I Chron. 28:4–7; II Chron. 6:16–17; 13:5, etc.), in which the House of David was assured of God's everlasting benevolence and support, produced in biblical literature the image of an ideal king who became a sign and symbol for all generations: a king blessed with understanding and wisdom, on whom the spirit of the Lord rests; a righteous king and savior under whose leadership Judah and Ephraim would be reunited to overcome their enemies: "Behold the days are coming, says the Lord, when I will raise up for David a righteous shoot, and he shall reign as king and deal wisely, and shall execute justice and righteousness in the land. In his days Judah will be saved, and Israel will dwell safely. And this is his name by which he will be called, 'The Lord is our righteousness'"[84] (Jer. 23:5–6; cf. Isa. 11:1–10; Jer. 22:1–4; Hos. 3:4–5; Amos 9:11–15; Micah 5:1–8; Hag. 2:20–23, etc.).

The biblical writers conceived of the monarchy as the pillar of national existence and the pivot of Israel's historical experience. A deep-seated pious hope for Redemption was implanted in the monarchy and in the anointed king of the Davidic line. Generation after generation lived with the expectation that in their day the ideal anointed king would reveal himself and would realize the divine promise affirmed and reaffirmed in God's Covenant with the patriarchs, with Israel at Sinai, and with David. The hope did not focus on the image of a unique Messiah but was kept alive by the vision of a dynasty of anointed kings. The belief received its fullest expression in the prophetic vision of "the latter

[83] This distinction is based on the terminology introduced by M. Weber in *Gesammelte Aufsätze zur Religionssoziologie*, III, Das *antike Judentum*, Tübingen, 1921 = *Ancient Judaism*, transl. H. H. Gerth and D. Martindale, Glencoe, Illinois (1952); J. A. Soggin, "Charisma und Institution im Königtum Sauls," *ZAW*, 75 (1963), 54–65.

[84] Or possibly: by this name the Lord will call him: "our righteous [one]."

days" (*'aḥărīt ha-yāmīm*), which draws most of its ideas and images from the historical experience of national life, from the splendor of the Davidic and Solomonic realm. In the period of the United Kingdom, Israel had realized its desire to live as a nation in its own land, secure and thriving, its social fabric firmly established to a degree never experienced, in any period of Israelite history.

Israel's political ideology in the biblical period, to all intents and purposes, must be identified with the idea of monarchy. The Books of Samuel and Kings, and the passages in the Pentateuch, the Latter Prophets, and the Psalms, which reflect the institution of the monarchy and its ideological foundations, essentially constitute the *politeia* of Israel in the biblical period.[85]

[85] To distinguish from M. Buber's attempt in his *Königtum Gottes*, Berlin, 1932 (= *Kingship of God*³, transl. R. Scheimann, London, 1967), to discern in the book of Judges the religio-political credo of biblical Israel.

“IN THOSE DAYS THERE WAS NO מלך IN ISRAEL”

Judges 18–21

A. The formula “in those days there was no מלך in Israel” recurs, as is well-known, four times in the Book of Judges: twice in each of two tradition clusters considered to be additions to the book: the tale of Micah’s temple and the Danite migration (Judg 17:1–18:31), and the story of the concubine at Gibeah (Judg 19:1–21:25). The phrase appears twice in its short form as a statement: “in those days there was no מלך in Israel” (*ib.* 18:1; 19:1), and twice in expanded form with the appended phrase: "איש הישר בעיניו יעשה" (*ib.* 17:6; 21:25). This latter expression has been taken as indicating the shortcomings and faults which its author thought to be characteristic of the period in which the events described in these two tales occurred.

Most interpreters maintain that the formula is an editorial addition rather than an integral component of the book.[1] Many are of the opinion that it was not even penned by the authors of the appendixes to the book, *viz.* the tales of Micah’s idol, the Danite migration and the concubine at Gibeah, but is to be considered an addition to the appendixes.[2]

The appendixes themselves are not judged to be of one cloth but rather to comprise several sub-traditions. Since the formula under consideration appears in two distinct forms, one short and one expanded, it has been contended – by Eissfeldt, for example – that the constituent sources of these tales can be discerned in the formula.[3] Other scholars distinguish the work of arrangers and redactors in the composition of the book. The last of these presumably integrated the formula into the tales, thus putting the final touch to the editorial work on the Book of Judges.

Modern interpreters concur in the opinion that the formula postdates the period of the Judges and the Book of Judges. They disagree, however, as to how much later it is, and for what purpose it was appended. Scholars who

1. M.Z. Segal ascribes the formula to the second of the authors of the book, whom he designated “B” (“Studies in the Book of Judges,” *Tarbiz* 1 (1930) 17 (Hebrew).
2. See, *e.g.*, A.B., Ehrlich, *Randglossen zur Hebräischen Bibel*, vol. 3 (Leipzig, 1909) 145.
3. O. Eissfeldt, *Einleitung in das Alte Testament*[3] (Tübingen, 1964) 348.

prefer an early date place it in the time of David[4] or the Divided Kingdom.[5] Gray tends to the opinion that in all likelihood it reflects a priestly tradition of the royal sanctuaries in Beth-el and Dan.[6] Those who tend to date the formula rather late ascribe it to the redactor of the Priestly Code (R^P), who lived after the Babylonian Exile.[7] One view assumes that the author of the formula wanted to advertise the deuteronomistic ideology of a unified and centralized cult in opposition to the plurality of sanctuaries reflected in the above tales – Mount Ephraim, Dan, Bethel, Mizpah and Shiloh. Another opinion holds that since the author of the formula obviously takes a dim view of periods in which there was no king, his negative attitude implies that he held in high esteem the monarchial period which, as it were, was not affected by such anarchistic trends.[8]

The formula presents several other problems of a literary-structural character, but we shall not deal with them here since our concern is to examine the socio-historical ideology which, according to interpreters, is encapsulated in the formula.

The opinion in which modern interpreters concur is that the formula "in those days there was no מלך in Israel" evidences a monarchistic tendency. This in fact is already apparent from the ancient translation which render the Hebrew noun מלך as מלכא (T, Syr), βασιλεύς (G), *rex* (V), *e.e.*, king, monarch. All these are based on the premise that the noun מלך in the formula carries the same semantic value as it does in the majority of its occurrences in the Bible.

The word occurs predominantly in the biblical literature of the monarchical period. In this literature, which reflects the institution of monarchic government, the noun מלך pertains always to the person of a ruler and to the type of monarchic rule which developed in Israel after David. Thus it came to be used with a specific technical connotation. This uniform employment resulted in every verse in which the noun מלך appears being dated after the emergence of the monarchy. It is therefore almost *a priori* determined that in

4. B.Z. Luria, "The Incident of the Concubine of Gibeah," in *Studies in the Book of Judges*. Israel Society of Bible Studies (Jerusalem, 1967) 477 ff.; 489–490 (Hebrew).
5. Kuenen, Driver, Budde, Cornill, Moore and others ascribe the formula to R^{EJ} who, they believe, lived in the days of Manasseh, King of Judah. See G.F. Moore, *Judges, ICC* (Edinburgh, 1895) 369; S.R. Driver, *Introduction to the Literature of the Old Testament* (Edinburgh, 1913) 170.
6. J. Gray, *Joshua, Judges, Ruth* (London, 1967) 239.
7. C.F. Burney, *The Book of Judges* (London, 1920) 410–411.
8. R.H. Pfeiffer, *Introduction to the Old Testament*[2] (New York, 1948) 321; Moore, *op. cit.* 382; Burney, *ib.*

our formula as well מלך refers to a monarchic ruler and to monarchic government, which are presented as superior to and more desirable than the leadership of the Judges from which the book derived its name. Because the formula appears only at the end of the Book of Judg 17–21, both ancient and modern interpreters were of the opinion that whoever interpolated it into those traditions had meant to present it as an introduction to the monarchical period which followed the comparatively less-laudable period of the Judges.[9] Rabbi Isaiah of Trani said (*ad* Judg 21:25): "He [the writer] wishes to begin the next book [*i.e.*, the Book of Samuel] with the kingdom of Saul. Therefore he states that until then no king had yet [עדיין] arisen in Israel." Eissfeldt likewise inserts the German counterpart of Rabbi Isaiah's עדיין in his translation: "In jenen Tagen gab es *noch* keinen König."[10] This understanding of the text had to deduce that the appendixes to the book, and especially the formula under consideration, present a viewpoint favorable to the institution of kingship. This is in contrast to the anti-monarchical attitude which characterizes most of the Book of Judges, *viz.* the cluster of traditions pertaining to the period of the Conquest (Judg 1:1–36), the historiosophical introduction (*ib.* 2:1–3:1) and the body of the book which consists of the individual Savior-Judges episodes. The praise of kingship which many scholars discern in the formula "in those days there was no מלך in Israel" stands in contradiction to the tone of ridicule which pervades the portrayal of kings and their officers in the Book of Judges, and which reflects on the appreciation of monarchical government as such. This trend is evident, for example, in the description of Adoni-bezek and the seventy kings whose thumbs and big toes he had cut off and who gathered food under his table (*ib.* 1:6–7); Ehud's killing of Eglon, king of Moab (*ib.* 3:20–22); the death of Sisera at the hands of Jael, the wife of Heber the Kenite (*ib.* 5:24–27), and the killing of Abimelech the son of Jerubbaal by means of a millstone thrown by a woman from the tower roof in Thebez (*ib.* 9:51–54). To these one must add the deprecatory tone evident in Gideon's command to Jether his first-born to slay Zebaḥ and Ṣalmunna, the kings of Midian: ולא שלף הנער חרבו כי ירא כי עודנו נער (*ib.* 8:20). All this is epitomized in the open rejection of Abimelech's kingship and of monarchic rule in general which, according to some, is the main tendency of Jotham's parable (*ib.* 9:7–20). This piece may echo his father Gideon's refusal to establish in Israel a government which is transferable from father to son (*ib.* 8:22–23), which by definition would be monarchic or would tend to develop into a monarchy.

9. O. Eissfeldt, *op. cit.* 179.
10. *Op. cit.* 348.

In contrast to the ridiculed, scorned figures of kings, the courage and success of the Judges is extolled. Men such as Ehud the son of Gera, Barak, Gideon, Jephtah, and Samson vanquish their royal enemies and subdue kingdoms and their rulers. The dualism reflected in the evaluation of monarchy in the diverse components of the book gave birth to a theory, developed especially by Martin Buber, that the Book of Judges is comprised of two conjoined sources, one anti-monarchistic and one pro-monarchistic.[11] The latter is encapsulated in the extended formula "in those days there was no מלך in Israel and every man did that which was right in his own eyes." This literary-historical source attempts to present the period of the Judges as one of both ritual-religious and socio-political anarchy. For Buber, the conjunction of the two ideological strands in the Book of Judges evidences the controversy between those loyal to a "primitive theocracy" led by a "charismatic leader," in the phraseology of Max Weber, upon whom the spirit had descended, and a "monarchistic-calculating" faction supporting dynastic monarchistic-centralistic government, which stands in complete opposition to non-mediated, direct theocracy.

B. We can see that discussion of the formula which recurs in the appendixes to the Book of Judges transcends the limits of linguistic-literary research, and touches upon societal issues and problems of socio-political thought in Israel pertaining to the transition period from the rule of Judges to monarchical government. Thus it is only logical that we turn our attention to the meaning of the pivotal term מלך in that formula. We must determine whether its connotation here is indeed necessarily identical with its connotation in those books of the Bible which date from the period of the Kingdom, as maintained – almost axiomatically – by commentators. Concurrently, we should consider another possibility: that the noun מלך carried several denotations distinct from one another to a greater or lesser degree, either synchronically or as the result of a diachronic semantic development. The examination of this second possibility is especially significant in view of the fact that we are discussing a formula which epitomizes, as it were, a critical juncture in the history of Israel – the transition from the rule of Judges to monarchy. Its interpretation therefore may be derived either from subsequent semantic developments, as in fact is posited by most interpreters, or from an earlier usage as will be postulated here.

Before entering into a discussion of this matter, we must take issue with the presentation of the formula "in those days there was no מלך in Israel and every

11. M. Buber, *Königtum Gottes* (Berlin, 1932), esp. chap. 2; W. Richter, *Traditionsgeschichtliche Untersuchungen zum Richterbuch* (Bonn, 1963) 338–339.

man did that which was right in his own eyes" as not only indirectly laudatory of the monarchy but also clearly critical of the institution of rule by a Judge. According to this interpretation the author of the phrase disapproved of the religio-social anarchy apparent in the tales of Micah's idol, the Danite migration and the Gibeah affair. If indeed this was the author's appreciation of the period, how could he have blamed the institution of the Judges for the failings of Israel in the above incidents? It can hardly go unnoticed that no Judge is mentioned in the appendixes which recount those acts and events. Neither the abominable behavior, the "Schandtat" of the men of Gibeah, nor the inter-tribal schism that precipitated the fratricidal war in which the Benjaminite city of Gibeah and practically the whole tribe of Benjamin were wiped out, occurred at a time when a Judge ruled in Israel. Thus the circumstances as related in the appendixes force us to conclude that the crucial formula is not at all concerned to contrasting rule by a Judge with that by a monarch, or with giving preference to the latter over the former. It rather gives expression to the desirability of an orderly government, albeit temporary, as was operative in the period of the Judges, as opposed to the anarchy that pervailed in a leaderless Israel.

The absence of an authoritative leader is indicative of the episodes recorded in the two appendixes to the Book of Judges in which the formula "in those days there was no מלך in Israel" is exclusively used; it also characterizes the cluster of conquest traditions in Judg 1:1–2:5 and distinguishes it from the Savior-Judges traditions which form the bulk of the book. Precisely in that first chapter the anti-monarchic trend reverberates at its strongest, *viz.* in the report in which Adoni-bezek the conqueror of kings is held up to mockery and scorn. Concurrently, that same cluster illustrates the disintegration of the unity of Israel which, according to tradition, had been forged by Moses and continued into the time of Joshua. Now the tribes, we read, fight individualy and among themselves, with only Judah and Simeon cooperating in the common war against the Canaanite inhabitants of the land (Judg 1:3). The salient theme of these traditions is the history of non-success, the description of the failure of the tribes to conquer the Promised Land. That period too could be characterized by the caption "in those days there was no מלך in Israel and every man did that which was right in his own eyes."

Who then is the מלך of which the texts speak? In view of the foregoing remarks, we have to conclude that in the formula under discussion it should not be translated *rex*, monarch or king but rather that the term מלך is here fully synonymous with שופט, the common denotation of the leader in the Book of Judges. The criticism expressed in the formula בימים ההם אין מלך בישראל refers to those periods in the history of Israel "in which there was no judge, overseer or ruler" – שלא היה שופט, שוטר ומושל – in the words of the mediaeval commentator Abarbanel.[12]

E.A. Speiser says of the Judge that he was "originally someone with authority to decide what administrative action was needed and, when necessary, to issue warnings and mete out punishment. He was arbiter or punitive officer, as the case might be . . .".[13] This implies that in that period the judge performed functions which in the future the king was to perform. In effect there is no great difference between the two words in terms of this significance; the distinction is more one of degree than of essence. Thus only at a time when there was no king/ruler or judge/leader in Israel could deeds be perpetrated such as those described in the appendixes to the Book of Judges. Again we can only concur with the understanding of the crucial formula by a mediaeval interpreter, David Kimḥi (*ad* Judg 18:1): "In all the days of the Judges no man would do what was right in his own eyes; only of these three episodes – of Micah, the tribe of Dan and the concubine of Gibeah – it is said that there was no מלך in Israel. These events occurred between [the days of] Samson [who was a Judge of Israel] and [those of] Eli; the time between them was as it was, when there was no Judge in Israel and each man did as was right in his own eyes."[14] Abarbanel presents a similar interpretation which identifies מלך with שופט (*ad* Judg 18:1): "There were many days [*viz.* in the pre-monarchic period] when they had no מלך; what they were missing and lacking now were the *Judges*. Therefore Scripture should have said, 'when there was no שופט in Israel.'"

In contrast to the opinion of Kimḥi and Abarbanel – that the events dated to the early period of the Judges. Rashi concurs with the interpreteation of Eli, when "Samson the judge was [bound] in fetters of wretchedness and iron" (Abarbanel) – other traditional interpreters hold that the episodes should be dated to the early period of the judges. Rashi concurs with the interpretation of the Sages: "From here [*i.e.*, from the formula 'in those days there was no מלך in Israel'] we can deduce that this event happened at the very beginning [of the period] of the Judges." Likewise Gersonides (Ralbag): "This incident occurred after the death of Joshua and before the rule of Othniel (the first Judge – Judg 3:7–11), the son of Kenaz. The Danite tribe sought a territory to settle after the death of Joshua because at that time the tribes fought each individually for

12. Commentary to the Former Prophets, *ad* Judg 17:1.

13. E.A. Speiser, "The Manner of the King," in *The World History of the Jewish People – Volume 3: The Period of the Judges*, ed. B. Mazar (Tel Aviv, 1971) 281.

14. Cp. also *b. Tal. Hul.* 57b.

their lots." This dating has been accepted by some modern scholars as well.[15]

This view is utterly convincing. As noted, the absence of a Judge is common both to the cluster of traditions in chapter one — which is not part of the main body of the Book of Judges[16] — and to the appendixes at the end of the Book. According to biblical historiography as expressed at the end of the Book of Joshua and the beginning of the Book of Judges, during that period Israel found itself under the unstable leadership of the "Elders" who came after (literally, "outlived") Joshua (Josh 24:31; Judg 2:7). Only in the period of time between Joshua and Eli, described in the first chapter of the Book of Judges, and in the appendixes, when there was no Judge, did priests officiate in Israel. No mention whatsoever of a priest is made in the body of the Book, *i.e.*, not in the introduction nor in the traditions of the Savior-Judges (Judg 2:1–17:31). In the appendixes priests are expressly mentioned (*ib.* 17:5; 18:4), and even by name: Phinehas the son of Eleazar the son of Aaron (*ib.* 20:26–28) and Jonathan the son of Gershom the son of Menasseh/Moses — מ׳נשה (*ib.* 18:30). Likewise, mention is made of holy places and of holy objects (*ib.* 17:4–5; 18:17–20, 24, 27, 30; 20:26–27, *etc.*). Only in the appendixes and in chapter one do we find reports of oracular inquiries in matters of public interest, concerning the tribe of Dan (*ib.* 18:5–6) or all the tribes of Israel (*ib.* 20:27). In the instances set in Beth-el where "the ark of the covenant of God [was housed] in those days, and Phinehas, the son of Eleazar, the son of Aaron, stood before it . . .", the opening phrase of the request for divine advice is: "And the children of Israel asked of the Lord" — exactly as in Judg 1:1, where Israel inquires of the Lord which tribe should lead the onslaught on the Canaanites. It is logical to assume that there too it was addressed to a priest, and perhaps that same Phinehas, son of Eleazar, in the same sanctuary at Beth-el. Moreover, the phrasing of the request and of the divine oracle recurs in both instances almost word for word:

Judg 1:1–2 — מי יעלה לנו אל הכנעני בתחלה להלחם בו. ויאמר ה׳ יהודה יעלה
"Who shall go up first for us against the Canaanites, to fight against them?" and the Lord said, "Judah shall go up . . ."

Judg 20:18 — מי יעלה לנו בתחלה למלחמה עם בני בנימן. ויאמר ה׳ יהודה בתחלה
"Who shall go up first to battle against the Benjaminites?" And the Lord said, "Judah shall go up first."

The socio-religious similarity and the literary parallelism between chapter one and the appendixes to the "Book of the Saviors" leads us to the conclusion

15. See A. Aharoni, *Israel in the Biblical Period* (Jerusalem, 1962) 207 ff.

16. See S. Talmon, "Judges, Chapter One," in *Studies in the Book of Judges* (Jerusalem, 1967) 15 ff. (Hebrew).

that the story of the Danite migration, and by analogy also that of Micah's sanctuary, as well as the tale of the concubine of Gibeah and the report of the tribal war against Benjamin, were originally placed together with chapter one at the beginning of the Book of Judges.[17] A hint to this effect is still evident in the present text of the book: Judg 1:34 tells us that the tribe of Dan was forced to migrate to the north of the country because of Amorite pressure: וילחצו האמרי את בני דן ההרה כי לא נתנו לרדת לעמק – "The Amorites pressed the Danites back into the hill country, for they did not allow them to come down to the plain..." Since Dan is mentioned in the list of tribal wars after the northern tribes of Zebulon (*ib.* 1:30), Asher (*ib.* 1:31–32) and Naphtali (*ib.* 1:33), it stands to reason that the author of the first chapter of the Book of Judges refers to that self-same migration described in the appendix. It may be surmised that because of the comparative length of this narrative unit, which expanded into what amounts to a novella (Judg chs. 17–18), quite disproportionately to the relatively short notes on the other tribes (chap. 1), the arranger (מסדר) of the Book of Judges transferred the novella to the end, in the form of an appendix, and retained only a brief reference to it – a sort of *custos* – in its previous location at 1:34.

The same can be said for the story of the war of Benjamin and the tale of the concubine at Gibeah. In content and character – an inter-tribal war during a period in which there was no leader – the proper place for these items is within the framework of the tradition cluster pertaining to the early days of conquest and settlement. And indeed it would seem that in a preceding redactional stage the present appendix also belonged to the cluster. Again, the editor of the Book of Judges has left an indication to this effect in the mention of הבכים, apparently an epithet of Beth-el, in Judg 2:1 as another *custos.*[18] The name was probably given to the city after the Gibeah war, playing on the incidents related in Judg 20:26 – "Then all the children of Israel, and all the people, went up, and came unto Beth-el, and *wept* (ויבכו) and sat there before the Lord..." (cp. also v. 23) – and again in 21:2 – "And the people came to Beth-el and sat

17. See Talmon, *op. cit.* 27 ff. Malamat has also discussed these similarities recently, but he explains them exclusively in terms of style and motif, and does not interpret the recurring mention of priests of the third generation after the Exodus, historically and chronologically. See: A. Malamat, "The Danite Migration and the Pan-Israel Exodus-Conquest: A Biblical Narrative Pattern," *Bib* 51 (1970) 1–16.

18. This may explain the break in the middle of the verse – *pisqāh be-ʾemṣaʿ pāsūq* – in Judg 2:1 after the word הבכים. I have attempted to explain it as alluding to an extra-textual homiletic or liturgical interpolation, based upon the Gibeah tale in Judg 19–21. See S. Talmon, "*Pisqāh Be-ʾemṣaʿ Pāsūq* and 11QPs^{a}," *Textus*, vol. 5 (1966) 11–21.

there till evening before God, and lifted up their voices and cried loudly and wept (ויבכו בכי גדול)."[19]

Thus the Danite migration which is associated with the episode of the theft of Micah's idol, and the Gibeah war occurred, respectively, in the days of Phinehas son of Eleazar, son of Aaron, and Jonathan son of Gershom, son of Menasseh/Moses, both being of the third generation after the Exodus from Egypt. The proper literary context of these tales is the cluster of traditions which constitutes the first chapter of the Book of Judges. Incidents are related there which predate the early days of the "Saviors," that is, they are set in the *interregnum* after Joshua, in a period in which there indeed was not *yet* a *king–judge* שופט–מלך in Israel – at least in the view of the editors of the Books of Joshua and Judges, and also of the compiler of the Former Prophets.

We conclude therefore that the formula "in those days there was no מלך in Israel and every man did that which was right in his own eyes" actually praises the rule of Israel by the Judges. We can notice here an internal relation between the two appendixes to the Book of Judges, on the one hand, and the Book of Ruth, on the other hand, which reflects the situation of juridical, political and religious order as it obtained "in the days when the Judges judged" (Ruth 1:1).[20] Rashi remarks there, very much to the point, that those were the days "before there ruled King Saul when those generations were led by Judges. [The story of Ruth] occurred in the days of Ibzan [who is mentioned after Jephthah – Judg 12:8–10] whom the Sages identified with Boaz."

19. The LXX also reflects this interpretation, presenting, as it were, a triple translation: ἐπὶ τὸν κλαυθμ̃να κὰι ἐπὶ Βαιθηλ καὶ ἐπὶ τὸν οἶκον Ισραηλ. Interestingly enough, this association of בכים in Judg 2:1 with Bethel, is also reflected in a midrash which identifies the "angel" – מלאך of the episode related in Judg 2:1–5 as Aaron's grandson Phinechas who reportedly officiated at Bethel at the time of the Gibeah incident (Judg 20:28): ויצא מלאך ה׳ מן הגלגל אל הבכים. וכי מלאך היה, והלא פינחס היה . . . (see: *Lev. Rab.* 1, 1, ed. Margaliot, 2, line 4 ff.) – A parallel tradition, which associates "weeping" – בכה – with Bethel can be found in Gen 35:8 – "And Deborah, Rebeccah's nurse died, and she was buried below *Bethel* under the oak; and the name of it was אלון בכות". A further echo may be discerned in Hos 12:5: וישר אל מלאך ויכל ב כ ה ויתחנן לו ב י ת . א ל ימצאנו ושם ידבר עמו.

20. One can find vestiges of a similar appreciation in the almost triumphal description of the Passover celebrated in the days of King Josiah: "For there was not kept such a passover from the days of the Judges that judged Israel, nor in all the days of the kings of Israel, nor of the kings of Judah" (2 Kgs 23:22). The author of Chronicles interpreted the verse as indicating that Israel *did* keep the Passover in the period of the Judges, as implied in the reading: "And there was no passover like to that kept in Israel from the days of Samuel the prophet; neither did any of the kings of Israel keep such a passover as Josiah kept . . ." (2 Chr 35:18). See further, S. Talmon, "Jeroboam's Cult- and Calendar Reform", = in this volume, 127–128.

To sum up: the formula "בימים ההם אין מלך בישראל איש הישר בעיניו יעשה" epitomizes the transition from the period of the *Elders* who followed after Joshua, when Israel was without an individual leader, to the new era of successive "charismatic" leaders who saved Israel through the spirit of God which descended upon them. A last echo of this positive approach to the institution of the Judge-King can be discerned in the words of the representatives of the people to Samuel when his own sons were recognized to be unsuited to assume the leadership over Israel (1 Sam 8:5–6): "שימה לנו מלך לשפטנו ככל הגוים".[21] These words herald a new era in the socio-political history of the Israelite society and its government. Even in his abdication speech Samuel makes positive mention of some of the Judges, the pre-monarchic leaders of Israel: "And then the Lord sent Jerubbaal, and Bedan, and Jephthah, and Samuel, and delivered you out of the hands of your enemies round about, and you dwelt in safety" (1 Sam 12:11). His words comprise an interesting juxtaposition of a salient term from the Book of Judges – which amounts almost to a quotation from Judg 8:34: "And the children of Israel remembered not the Lord their God, *who had delivered them out of the hand of all their enemies round about*" – with a formula characteristic of the literature of the monarchical period: "And Judah and Israel *dwelt safely*, every man under his vine and under his fig tree, from Dan even to Beer-sheba, all the days of Solomon" (1 Kgs 5:5; cp. Mic 4:4; Jer 32:37; Ezek 28:26; 38:14; Zech 14:11, *et al.*).[22] This juxtaposition may be taken as another linguistic indicator of the transition from the period of the Judges to the period of the monarchy.

C. We now wish to adduce some corroborative evidence to strengthen our hypothesis that in the formula with which we are concerned the denotation of the term מלך differs from that which developed in Israel after the time of David, and that it denotes here a form of government which preceded classical monarchy. We submit that the non-dynastic, non-monarchistic meaning of מלך can still be discerned in other early biblical texts which, because of the current interpretation, have been classified as anachronisms or later additions, for example, the difficult verse which introduces the Blessing of Moses: "There was a מלך in Jeshurun. When the heads of the people were gathered, all the tribes of Israel together" (Deut 33:5). Wellhausen,[23] Graetz, Cornill, Stade and many

21. Cp. 1 Sam 8:19–20.
22. The phrase also appears in literature which is not necessarily monarchic in outlook, *e.g.*, Lev 25:18–19; 26:5; Isa 47:8.
23. J. Wellhausen, *Prolegomena zur Geschichte Israels* (Berlin, 1895) 256, n. 1.

others surmised that the text refers to Saul, the first king of Israel, and that the word was out of place in the pre-monarchic context.[24] Rashi, Abarbanel, Maimonides and several modern interpreters see in the word מלך a reference to the God of Israel.[25] Ibn Ezra, however, presents an interpretation which seems more likely to be correct: "It is Moses from whose mouth the heads of the people heard the Torah interpreted, and who was like a king."[26] This interpretation establishes a proper connection between verse five and the one preceding it – "Moses commanded us a law, an inheritance of the congregation of Jacob." Thus, in opposition to the hypothesis set forth by many scholars, we should not consider Deut 33:5 a secondary interpolation which should be deleted from the context.[27]

The term מלך in the sense of a non-dynastic ruler appears in the Bible not only in reference to Israel but also to other nations. It is employed in Gen 36 in the context of an Edomite tradition which can be defined as a condensed version of the history of Edom, which parallels the much more expanded and detailed account of the history of Israel as unfolded in the Pentateuch and in the Former Prophets: the development from the nuclear family of Esau (Gen 36:1–4) to the league of the Edomite tribes (*ib.* 15–19) and their settling in the mountains of Seir (*ib.* 8–9, 20–21). As is known, this chronicle concludes with the roster of "המלכים that ruled in the land of Edom before there reigned a מלך over the children of Israel" (*ib.* 36:31–39; cp. 1 Chr 1:43–53).[28] The list is not the record of a royal dynasty but rather a schematic enumeration of the names of eight rulers – none of whom is the son of his predecessor nor the father of his successor, and none of whom reigns in the city in which his predecessor reigned.[29] The socio-historical picture that emerges is very similar to that

24. The antiquity of the Blessing of Moses has been stressed by I.L. Seeligmann, "A Psalm from Pre-Regal Times," *VT*, 14 (1964) 75–92 (this study also includes a bibliographic survey of scholarly discussion of this issue).
25. See *e.g.*, C. Steuernagel, *Das Deuteronomium* (Göttingen, 1923) 175; Driver, *op. cit.* 394; Ehrlich, *op. cit.*, vol. 2 347; E. Rosenthal, "Some Aspects of the Hebrew Monarchy," *JJS*, 9, 1–2 (1958) 112.
26. For Moses as a royal figure, see J.R. Porter, *Moses and Monarchy: A Study in the Biblical Tradition of Moses* (Oxford, 1963); Joh. Pedersen: *Israel*, vol. 3–4 (Copenhagen, 1940) 662–666; G. Widengren, "King and Covenant," *JJS*, 81 (1957) 18.
27. See Seeligmann, *op. cit.* 78–79. It is methodologically unsound to solve an exegetical crux by textual emendation.
28. The linguistic similarity between לפני מלך מלך and בימי שפוט השופטים (Ruth 1:1) was discerned already by Rashi in his comment on Gen 36:31. For מלך לבני ישראל . . . cp. 1 Kgs 22:17 לא אדנים לאלה.
29. The historical impact of Esau's genealogy has been discussed in detail by Ed. Meyer, *Die Israeliten und ihre Nachbarstämme* (Halle, 1906) 328 ff. esp. 370 ff. The first part of the list

revealed in the Book of Judges: a discontinuity from judge to judge, respective of family, tribal relations or the seat of government.[30] Moreover, in parallelism with the schematic expressions through which the author of Judges attempts to establish a semblance of continuity between the *Saviors* such as "and *after him* was" (ואחריו היה, Judg 3:31) or "and *after him* judged" (וישפט אחריו, *ib.* 12:13),[31] the author of Gen 36 employs the formula "and he reigned *in his stead*" (וימלך תחתיו, *ib.* 36:33–39).[32]

There is much to recommend Noeldeke's suggestion that the first king, Bela the son of Beor (*ib.* 36:32–33), should be identified with Balaam the son of Beor[33] who lived in the days of Moses (Num 24 *passim*),[34] and that the first Hadad on the list, the son of Bedad, who was the fourth Edomite king and who

is found also in the Greek addition to Job 42:17(d) where Job is identified with Jobab (Gen 36:33), an identification which is rabbinic in origin: Ιωβαβ ὦ καλόυμενος Ιωβ. See H.M. Orlinsky, "The Tribal System of Israel and Related Groups in the Period of the Judges," *OA*, 1 (1962) 17.

30. This is also the opinion of Speiser, who nevertheless subscribes to the usual definition of מלך. He concludes that "the institution of kingship presupposes a more developed system of government in ancient Edom", E.A. Speiser, *Genesis, AB* (New York, 1964) 282.
31. In the roster of David's heroes (2 Sam 23:9, 11; 1 Chr 11:12) אחריו does not indicate chronological succession. The term serves there as an element of enumeration, or even simpler, of association. – Similarly, Persian *pasāva* has been explained as a word "das nicht konsequent auf einen späteren Zeitpunkt hinweist, sondern oft einfach als überflüssiges Wort erscheint", so much so that "viele . . . Gelehrte ignorieren stillschweigend dieses Wort". Quoted from M.A. Dandamaiev, *Persien unter den ersten Achämeniden* (*6. Jhrhdt. v. Chr.*), übersetzt von H.D. Pohl, (Wiesbaden, 1976) 128. Disagreeing with this view, Dandamaiev himself takes *pasāva* to mean "danach, nachdem".
32. Kaufmann makes an essential distinction between these terms: "The minor judges do not come one *in place of* the other [as in the biblical terminology referring to kings – S.T.] but rather one *after* the other. This means that they did not officiate in orderly succession, but rather arose sporadically, as the other [major] judges of the same period," (Y. Kaufmann, *The Book of Judges*, (Jerusalem, 1964) 47; likewise, W. Richter, *ZAW*, 77 (1965) 40–72. This distinction is unwarranted. "One *after* – אחר – the other" is used in reference to dynastic succession (*e.g.*, 1 Kgs 1:20, 27; 15:4) and in reference to priests (Exod 29:29–30). Conversely, the phrase "one *in the stead of* – תחת – the other" can be found to refer to sporadic leadership (2 Sam 17:25; 1 Kgs 2:35; and especially Gen 36:33–39).
33. Speiser, *op. cit.* 280, maintains that the similarity between the names Belaᶜ and Balaᶜam is coincidental.
34. Thus, we should perhaps turn to the list for the name of the king of Edom who lived in the time of Moses and whose name is not specified in Num 20:14–21. According to the list he would be Belaᶜ the son of Beᶜor, or Jobab the son of Zeraḥ. As already noted, the Sages and LXX identify Job with Jobab. This would explain the statement "Moses wrote his book and the sections of Balaᶜam and Job" in *b.* Bab. Bath. 14 b.

smote Midian in the field of Moab (Gen 36:35–36), was a contemporary of Gideon, who also vanquished the Midianites (Judg 6–8).[35] One may further presume that the second Hadad, the last to appear on the list (Gen 36:39), immediately antedated or was a contemporary of Saul, of whom it is written: "and [he] fought against all his enemies round about, against Moab, and against the children of Ammon, and against Edom, and against the kings of Zobah, and against the Philistines; and whithersoever he turned himself he put them to the worse [ירשיע, which probably should be emended to יושע].[36] And he did valiantly and smote the Amalekites and delivered Israel out of the hands of them that spoiled them." (1 Sam 14:47–48).[37] It follows that, according to biblical chronology, the period during which the eight kings of Edom reigned coincided with the period of wars in eastern Transjordan in the days of Moses and with the period of settlement when the Judges ruled until the early days of the monarchy. Thus, in context and meaning the term מלך employed in the roster of Edomite kings is synonymous with the term שופט as used in the Book of Judges, and is equally identical in denotation with מלך in the formula under consideration.

The semantic similarity – even interchangeability – of שופט–מלך is evident also in their occasional use as synonyms in biblical parallelisms, *e.g.*, in Hos 7:7; 13:10; Ps 2:10 (cp. Dan 9:8, 12). Similarly, the two terms appear as synonyms of שר (Exod 2:14; Hos 13:10; Amos 2:3; Mic 7:3; Zeph 3:3; Ps 148:11; Prov 8:16;[38] cp. Amos 1:15; Jer 49:3, *et al.*). This stylistic-pragmatic

35. See Meyer, *op. cit.* 381.
36. In accordance with the LXX reading οὗ ἂν ἐστράφη ἐδῴξετο. This reading is similar to a characteristic formula of the Book of Judges found, *e.g.*, in 2:16: "And the Lord raised up judges who saved them out of the hand of those that spoiled them" (cp. also *ib.* 2:18; 3:9, 15, 31; 6:14; 10:1, *et al.*). The author of the Book of Samuel employed this formula in reference to David, but with an interesting change: "And the Lord gave victory to David wherever he went" (2 Sam 8:14).
37. In this we differ from Ed. Meyer who denies any historical validity to the tradition which ascribes to Saul a victory over Edom (1 Sam 14:47), and takes it to be a mere imitative duplication of a Davidic tradition (*op. cit.* 355, n. 2; but cp. 381). That historiographical note in 1 Sam 14:47–48 is possibly reflected in a poetic version in Balaam's final oration (Num 24:15–22). Ed. Meyer claims that David was the first to subject Edom to Israelite suzerainty (*op. cit.* 355). If his view is accepted, the second Hadad of the Edomite king list could be identified with "Hadad the Edomite of royal descent" whom 1 Kgs 11:14 mentions as one of Solomon's adversaries.
38. Cp. Isa 40:23. The couple שר–מלך is also found in the *'ztwd* inscription, text a–b 12, 3 (H. Donner, and W. Röllig, *Kanaanäische und Aramäische Inschriften*, Bd. II (Wiesbaden, 1964) 37.

rather than etymological synonymity appears primarily in the non-historiographic literature.[39]

In summarizing our discussion, we can say that:

(a) The noun מלך in the formula "in those days there was no מלך in Israel" in the appendixes to the Book of Judges, does not require that the formula be dated later than the the early days of the monarchy, because the term מלך does not necessarily and exclusively refer to monarchic-dynastic rulers. Its denotative equivalent approaches that of שופט.

(b) The above formula therefore refers to a period in the history of Israel during which there was no ruler at all. It is reasonable to assume that the notation refers to the time between the leadership of Joshua and the beginning of the period of the Judges. Thus we can conclude that the author of the formula was of the opinion that the events described in the appendixes occurred not long after the death of Joshua. This assumption is reinforced by the fact that the passages mention priests of the house of Aaron and Moses who are of the third generation after the Exodus from Egypt.

(c) Because the author of the formula lays the blame for the political and religio-cultic anarchy which marked those times on the absence of a מלך-Judge, we can infer an implied measure of indirect praise accorded by him to the rule of Israel by Judges.

39. This synonymity can be substantiated from Ugaritic, Akkadian and Phoenician literature; however, this issue will be dealt with separately. For the present, see the Ugaritic texts: 51 IV:43–44 (*CTA* 4 IV:43–44); 'nt V:40–41 (*CTA* 3 V:40–41); further *RSP* I, II 365, 267 and bibliography registered there.

"THE RULE OF THE KING"
1 Samuel 8:4–22

Critical Bible scholarship has accepted as an established fact that Israelite society during the Biblical period, developed along lines conforming to the principles of the theory of evolution; *i.e.* that earlier and simpler states gradually led up to a complex and variegated society. That these earlier stages are not represented in Biblical literature is due to this literature having been compiled or edited during the Second Temple period. Later authors were responsible for writings which reflected their own conceptions. At times their ingrained habits or oversights allowed anachronisms to appear in the text, and at others they deliberately sought to anchor the values and laws of a later society in the initial period of Israel's emergence as a people. This literary tampering needs to be corrected. Once as detailed and exact an analytical study as possible has been made, the authentic, though incomplete, picture will come to light of the history of Israel and the gradual emergence of its social institutions. Each section of the Biblical narratives will have to be retested by this criterion, and so assigned its proper place in the progressive development of material and conceptual patterns.[1]

Obviously, it is impossible to reconcile this historical-evolutionary approach with the account of the history of Israel and the emergence of its social institutions recorded in the Bible. Hence a rearrangement of Biblical literature must be undertaken. Indeed, the Biblical account always lies open to the suspicion of having been tampered with by a later, editorial hand. Hence wherever there is an attempt to fit factual, historical situations into systematic, ideonic settings, the tendency of the critics is, generally, to remove such chapters from the location assigned to them by the Bible and to relocate them in later times. The scholars subscribing to this view are firmly convinced that, at the inception of their history, the people of Israel were incapable of the abstract, spiritual exercise necessary for extracting common denominators from isolated events and, by generalization, to fit them into patterns of principles which would make it possible to predict the future. All Biblical laws are, from the start, explained as *ad hoc*, as having emerged from

1. See Alt, A., "Die Urgestalt des Reiches Israel", *Kleine Schriften* 2 (1953) 15–17.

past historical experiences, and not as *a priori* laws which were to prepare for a specific situation and lead along channels marked out in advance.

In addition to what has been stated above, we must further draw attention, in dealing with the foundations of the Israelite kingdom, to a guiding principle accepted as axiomatic by scholars Bible. They have decided, once and for all, that ancient Israel was, by its very nature, a theocracy,[2] that it recoiled from any type of control resulting from any manifestation of power which was not limited by subservience to the pure monotheistic faith as reflected in the Pentateuchal legislation and the pleadings of the prophets. Hence, during all the long period of its existence, the monarchy, as such, was never accorded a defined, legal status,[3] but was merely tolerated instead as a "necessary evil". While in Judah, David's reign and the election of his house brought about a change in this view, the theocratic opposition continued, actively and passively, in Ephraim down to the very destruction of the political independence of the state.[4]

The prophet Samuel was designated as the outstanding exponent of theocratic opposition during the period preceding the destruction of the First Temple. He stood at the cross-roads – at the point where occasional (charismatic) leadership gave way to the establishment of a secular monarchy. At first Samuel fought resolutely against the new order then gaining ascendancy. Finally, however, the force of historical events – the Philistine assaults – compelled him to yield. The establishment of a

2. This popular view was examined and rejected by Kaufmann, Y., *History of the Religion of Israel* (Hebrew) (1938) III 686–706.
3. Alt, A., "Das Königtum in den Reichen Israel und Juda," *VT* I (1951) 1 ff.
4. *Ib.* 12 ff., 19–22.

   This is not the place to study the basis of the view and examine its details. Suffice it to note that the view is open to criticism because of its faulty logic, which makes the whole thesis disputable. The most ardent supporters of theocracy were, obviously, the personalities of the Second Temple period: Ezra, Nehemiah and their disciples. The Israelite kingdom came to an end with the destruction of Jerusalem. For those who returned from Babylon, the monarchical system was no longer a vital necessity, nor even a realistic possibility. Judea was a Persian satrapy, enjoying limited social and religious autonomy. Under such circumstances, the idea of "a kingdom of priests and holy nation" flourished. And it was indeed these personalities who, apparently, instituted the pattern of social and political laws enshrined in the Bible, which was marked by a complete detachment from the patterns of their own lives. Yet for some reason or other, these persons are not suspected of having been the ones to infuse the historical writings of the divine rule of Israel through the medium of emissaries. Here the approach should be reversed. Ancient historical fact is reflected precisely in those chapters and events which portray secular government, its development and power, government which reflects the real reaction of the people to the problems besetting them during the period of conquest and settlement.

permanent, central authority capable of providing the means of repelling the enemy incursions, which imperilled the existence of the state, had become a necessity.

Before entrusting the reins of office to Saul, Samuel made a final effort to deter the people from their objective. He failed. In his famous address (1 Sam 8) warning the people of the yoke monarchical rule would impose upon them, scholars seek to find the impressions of later historical experiences. They contend that this address characterises the absolute tyranny that became manifest in the later reigns of despotic Israelite kings and which first began to emerge, at the very earliest, in the days of Solomon. Clearly, then, this address could not have been the invention of Samuel. Antagonists of the royal house, living much later, at a date which scholars cannot determine with any precision, or even agree upon, put the words into his mouth and thereby described as an inherent feature of monarchy the tyrannical and degenerate rule of the generations preceding theirs.[5]

(1) Does this address, at base, really give an unfavourable picture of kingship, and does it therefore express the antagonism of the people to the tyranny, exploitation and despair engendered by a form of government which had proved a failure?

(2) Are the situations portrayed in that address really different from the actual life-patterns prevalent in the period of Samuel and Saul? Do they, accordingly, lack that grasp of historical reality necessary for assigning them their location, as a Biblical passage, in the chain of history?

We shall demonstrate convincingly that Samuel's speech cannot be excised from the period of the beginning of the kingdom, and that it is precisely this period which furnishes the background of reality that constitutes the *Sitz im Leben* for this speech.

Two contradictory views of Samuel's speech have already been given expression in rabbinic literature: the one regarding the address as a warning calculated to deter the populace from establishing a monarchy, the other regarding it as specifying the basic elements of any monarchy. We quote (*b. Sanh.* 20b): "R. Judah said in the name of Samuel: Whatever is stated in the passage referring to the king is permitted to him. Rav said: This portion was only stated as a warning to them, for it is said (Deut 17:16) 'You shall surely place a king over you' – that his awe be upon you." While Maimonides inclined to Samuel's view,[6] the ancient Targumim and medieval commentators[7]

5. Lods, A, *Histoire de la Litterature Hébraïque et Juive* (1950) 313–323.
6. Laws of Kings 2:3.

followed the view of Rav. And this latter trend is also evident among modern scholars.[8]

Rav links "the rule of the king" set forth in the Book of Samuel with the "commandment pertaining to the king" appearing in Deuteronomy (17:14–20). Nor has the connection between the two been overlooked by modern scholars. It is almost certain that the distinctly negative tone partially submerged in the "commandment pertaining to the king" (*ib.* vv. 16–17) influenced the commentators in their exposition of "the rule of the king."[9] Therefore it must be stressed that R. Judah, who cited the Amora Samuel, does not make any such connection. He bases his legalistic interpretation of the prophet's remarks upon an examination of that address itself. These polarized views of Samuel's address stem, in the main, from the contradictory interpretations of the divine authorization to Samuel to accede to the demands of the populace (1 Sam. 8:9): "Now therefore hearken to their voice, albeit thou shalt earnestly warn them, and thou shalt declare unto them the rule of the king that shall reign over them."[10]

In the Bible, the expressions: עוד־העיד "forewarn"; נגד־הגיד "declare"; and משפט "rule" carry various connotations. It would therefore be appropriate to examine them one by one and so determine the extent of their possible signification in the passage referred to above.

The hif'il of the verb עוד is used in the Bible to signify:

(l) The giving of testimony;

(2) The adducing of witnesses (Deut 4:26; 30:19; Jer 32:10);

(3) The establishing of a law ("statute and ordinance") (2 Kgs 17:15; Neh 9:34). It is almost certain that this last meaning stems from the custom of designating witnesses at such assemblies;

(4) An admonition directed towards the person entrusted with the responsibility of carrying out the law;

(5) And from here there derives the meaning of "warning" alone (Gen 43:3; Jer 42:19), the sense in which the word is used most frequently. It is

7. Rashi, R. Levi b. Gershom.
8. Leimbach, K.A., *Die Bücher Samuel* (1936) 43 ff.; Segal, M.Z., *The Book of Samuel* (Hebrew) ed. Kahana (19ll) 16 ff.; Smith (*ICC*, 57) does not adopt a definite position: "... this is his customary behaviour, Yhwh will allow him, perhaps authorize him, so to act."
9. Leimbach *op. cit., ib.*: "The arbitrary practice of the absolute potentate, of the oriental despot; and it is self-understood that this practice did not meet with the Lord's approval."
10. Schultz, A., *Das erste Buch Samuel* (KHAT) (1919) 124, interprets this passage as an expression of the despair of God who yields to the demands of the continually wicked people. But this is not correct.

impossible to deduce the intention of the author here with any precision from the linguistic form alone.[11] The proper connotation can only be discovered by reference to the context.

The hif'il of נגד־הגיד is synonymous with "say-tell-notify" and sometimes also conveys the proximate meaning of "predict", "announce (good tidings)."[12] It is not synonymous with עוד־העד in the sense of "warning."[13] The Septuagint reflects the most frequent general denotation of the word ἀγγαλεῖς αὐτοῖς[14] while the Vulgate gives the meaning as "predict", *et praedic eis*.

The real intent of the word is not, then, self-evident. This can only be deduced from its predicate; and so the phrase "the rule (*mišpāt*) of the king" should then give the key to the meaning of the verse as a whole.

Mišpāt in the Bible is used to designate:

(1) the exercise of the function of judging;

(2) the location of the judging, the court of justice;

(3) the object, or content of the litigation;

(4) the result of the judging, *i.e.*, the verdict, from where

(5) there derives the sense of the rules governing the rendering of judgment, accordingly a synonym for "law", "commandment", *etc.* In a less exact signification, *mišpāt* signifies an action customarily, repeatedly performed, a type of "law" or "rule", as it were, which lacks juridical authority (1 Sam 2:13).

Even in respect of this idiom, apparently, it is impossible to make any decision about the meaning of the term, since this will depend upon the viewpoint of the reader and cannot be determined from the text alone. And the same consideration gives rise to the conflicting Tannaitic viewpoints quoted in the continuing discussion in the Talmudic passage cited above. "There is a corresponding difference of opinion among Tannaim: R. Judah declares: The passage was given in order to warn them, as it is said: 'Thou shalt appoint a king over you' – that his awe be upon you." Yet this selfsame Tanna, R. Judah, the exponent of the unfavorable view of the king, regards the establishment of the monarchy as one of the three commandments

11. The ancient versions use verbs corresponding to the various connotations of עוד listed above. T.J.: אסהדא תסהיד בהון, LXX: διαμαρτυρόμενος διαμαρτύρηΔ αὐτοῖς, Vulgate: *verumtatem contestare eos*.

12. See Gesenius, W. *Wörterbuch*; Koehler-Baumgartner, *Lexicon in Veteris Testamenti Libros*.

13. For this reason the expressions העד תעיד and והגדת להם are not to be carelessly interchanged, as Leimbach did.

14. So T.J.: ותחיו להון

devolving upon the children of Israel immediately upon their entry into the land of Canaan: "to appoint a king over themselves, to exterminate the seed of Amalek, and to build the Temple" (*Sanh. ib.*).

In ancient Jewish tradition the positive attitude toward "the Rule of the King" was predominant. What caused the later, and especially the modern, commentators to reject this view in favor of the negative interpretation of the term? It appears that the prophet Samuel's exposition of the "Rule of the King" made its interpretation as a legal term rationally unacceptable. Surely, the commentators averred, it could not be possible for the king to be permitted to seize the daughters and sons of the people and press them into his service without any protest being raised! Scripture, then, must be recounting the undesirable practices the kings enforced on their subjects.

It follows then that Samuel's words themselves should be subjected to a close scrutiny to determine what they indeed convey and whether the description of kingship they portray really contradicts the principles on which the people – and the Scriptural author – wished to base the rule of the monarch.

At first sight we are astonished by the fact that Samuel's sharply provocative remarks failed to elicit the slightest change in the attitudes of the elders and populace assembled before him. When he finished speaking, they did not argue with him; neither did they seek to mitigate the severity of the future he predicted for them, nor did they attempt to reassert the prestige and usefulness of the kingdom they were to establish. Their retort was final and unequivocal: "Nay; but there shall be a king over us." Only someone who had deliberated over every aspect of a problem, its advantages and drawbacks, and had all along anticipated the reactions of the opposing side, could have answered so forcefully and decided with such finality. Samuel did not tell the elders anything they did not know. His remarks could not then have deflected them from the path they had chosen. Their first demand,[15] "Now give us a king to judge us like all the nations", was not in any way blunted by his speech. And this time, they stated their reasons explicitly: "There shall be a king over us, and go out before us and fight our battles" (*ib.* 8:20). Their reasons were not ideological, but practical.[16] They did not seek a monarchy for its own sake. They were not dazzled by its glamor. They saw in it the one possibility for solving their most urgent problem, one

15. Or their demand at the commencement of the meeting, if we wish to regard all of chapter 8 as a continuous account.
16. Frankfort, H., *Kingship and the Gods* (1948) 339: "The Hebrews knew that they had introduced it (*i.e.* the kingship) on their own initiative and under the strain of emergency."

which the system of Judges was not capable of coping with: the establishment of a standing army capable of repelling the Philistine invader.[17]

We shall now proceed to an analysis of Samuel's speech. At the very first reading, the passage reveals a lack of order which, apparently, is intentional, argumentative, and deliberate. The remarks, in fact, consist of three units or topics:

(1) v. 11: "He will take your sons and appoint them unto him for his chariots, and to be his horsemen; and they shall run before his chariots."

v. 12a,c: "And he will take your sons to appoint them unto him captains of thousands and captains of fifties[18] and to make his instruments of war, and the instruments of his chariots."

v. 13b: "And ye shall be his servants."[19]

(2) v. 17a: "He will take a tenth of your seed and your vineyards, and give them to his officers and his servants."

v. 14: "And he will take your fields and your vineyards and your oliveyards, even the best of them, and give them to his officers and his servants."

(3) v. 13: "And he will take your daughters to be perfumers, and to be cooks, and to be bakers."[20]

v. 16: "And he will take your manservants and your maidservants and you goodliest young men,[21] and your asses and put them to his work."

v. 12b: "And to plow his ground and reap his harvest."

Arranged in this order, Samuel's remarks reveal their main intent. Essentially, we are confronted here with three main principles which underly the establishment of any centralized government and which constituted an unavoidable necessity for the Israelite monarchy as well. The form in which the principles are presented is explained by the political and economic circumstances attending Israelite society prior to David's and Solomon's reigns, in whose times decisive changes occurred in the internal structure of Israelite society as well as its foreign policy.

17. This reasoning is discernible in the remarks of the elders who came to offer the crown to David: "In times past, when Saul was king over us, it was thou that didst lead out and bring in Israel" (1 Sam 5:2).
18. The LXX reads: "Officers of fifty and officers of hundreds"; Pesh.: "Officers of thousands and officers of hundreds and officers of fifty and officers of ten."
19. This phrase may also be included in the third unit – all depends on the meaning of the term "servants".
20. It is possible to add here: "And you will be servants unto him" (v. 17). See below.
21. Perhaps the reading of the LXX is to be preferred: καὶ τὰ βουκόλια ὑμῶν τὰ ἀγαθά.
22. See Caspari, W., *Thronbesteigung und Thronfolge der israelitischen Könige* (1917) 174–175; 249–253.

Being familiar with the structures of the neighboring monarchies, both Samuel and the elders were fully aware of these principles.[22] It is almost certain that Israelite society gave due consideration to these facts, at least in essence, in previous attempts at the establishment of a centralized government. The realization, that their tribal organization and the charismatic, discontinuous leadership of the Judges were insufficient to assure the permanent survival of the people of Israel in strife-torn Canaan, did not dawn on them, after all, with any suddenness. The appeal of the "men of Israel" to Gideon – or their offer "rule over us, both thou, and thy son and thy son's son also, for thou hast saved us out of the hand of Midian" (Judg 8:22) – stemmed from the very same reasons which impelled the elders of the people to turn to Samuel with their demand. Both then and now, a monarchy was sought after as the one efficient means of defence. Even in the days of Gideon, the people recognized the features that distinguished a monarchy from the rule of the Judges – namely, the continuity of the government. Then, however, the idea was still somewhat vague, the institutional terminology had not yet crystallised: "Rule over us, both thou and thy son and thy son's son." Samuel's times followed after the attempts in the days of Gideon and Abimelech, and after the people had examined, and learned from, the world around them. Accordingly the elders now formulated their claim explicitly: "Appoint for us a king to judge us." The meaning and character of this type of government are summed up in the term "king", which carries various institutional implications and denotes certain known powers. The biblical authors succeeded in discerning the gradual, protracted historical process, as they faithfully recorded the dull and hesitant beginnings on the one hand and the crystallisation and emergence of the concept from potentiality to actuality on the other. The awareness of this historical process will make intelligible the elders' adamant stand and Samuel's yielding to their demands. This time the ideas had been fully clarified before they were brought up for discussion.

The Gideon incident was an attempt to obtain the advantages of continuous government and to eliminate the principle of charismatic leadership by according permanence to the ruler's family. Hereditary government was offered to the savior and judge, who was acknowledged as chosen of God. The two types of leadership could not, however, exist together. Gideon realized this; and so did Samuel. And the people had become aware of it too. The two functions were separate and distinct. In the days of Gideon the idea of bestowing separate leadership assignments prevailed over the concept of continuity. In the days of Samuel, priority was accorded to enduring government. In the days of Gideon, the kingship was offered to God's emissary after he had proved himself by his military prowess; in Samuel's time, the rule would be entrusted to a mighty warrior, and ratification of his individual assignments would be sought subsequently.[23] There was nothing really novel in the present situation. It was only that now the scales were tipped in favor of the principle of permanent government. Only the principle of conferring leadership for a specific assignment had lost its priority. In David's time, the two types would reach a balance and the idea would be born of a "king-messiah". It would strike root in Judah but find no place in the northern kingdom.[24] Samuel and Saul, then, stand consciously and intentionally at the cross-roads. The people took sides in the dispute – they decidedly preferred a representative, continuous government.

Viewing the events from this standpoint forces us to conclude that at the time when the Israelite kingdom was founded, the basic principles defining the rights and obligations of the king had already been formulated. The approach of the delegation of elders to the charismatic leader has the ring of historical truth about it. Saul was anointed as the result of a free discussion between the political powers sharing the leadership: the emissary of God and the representatives of the people. Saul did not "seize the kingdom" as one "exalting himself to reign" and by relying on naked force.[25] One must by no means overlook the conspicuously constitutional character marking the episode of Saul's accession.[26]

Now Samuel's speech hinges on the fundamental principle of the "Rule of the King", which sets limits to the royal prerogative and defines the king's obligations. At the same time, however, Samuel's speech was political in tone in the interests of persuasion, his remarks addressed only to controversial issues. Only later, after the anointing ceremony had taken place, was the "Rule of the King" presented in complete form and properly formulated. Then Samuel "told the people of the rule of the kingdom,[27] and wrote it in a book, and laid it up before the Lord" (1 Sam 10:25).[28]

23. So, at least, according to the present sequence of the biblical narrative. There is a common tendency among scholars, however, to place chap. 2, the account of the war against Nachash, before the anointment of Saul, and to regard his victory over the Philistines as the cause for his accession. See Alt, A. *Kleine Schriften* 2 (1953) 15 ff.
24. Alt, *ib.* 19–22.
25. Not so Abimelech whose rule lacked any contractual basis; the consent was based on sheer force and the support of his followers (Judg 9:1–8).
26. See Caspari, *op. cit.* 148–152.
27. There is no distinction between משפט המלך and משפט המלוכה; they are not to be set up as separate concepts.
28. Mendenhall, G.E. *BA* 18, 3 (1954) 71: "The king was made king by covenant. Though we do not have details enough to analyze its form, there can be no reasonable doubt that Israel was bound by an oath to obey the king, with Yhwh acting as witness."

As has been stated, it was quite foreseeable that Samuel's argument would fail, since the very cloak of evil covering his remarks failed to conceal their essentially positive elements.

The king was chosen in order to establish a national, standing army ready to serve the people at all times. The tribal forces had been utterly routed by the Philistines, who excelled in their stable political organization, in their developed arts of warfare and in their superior weapons. The policy of mobilizing a national militia in times of national peril had proved a disappointment in the confrontation with an enemy capable of launching an attack anywhere along an ill-defined boundary and with forces of unpredictable size. Only a regular army, quite large in numbers, concentrated in centers from where they could be speedily dispatched to close up any breach in the front lines, could assure real relief. With such forces, it was also possible to develop uniform tactics and to organize the troops around a permanent officers corps. These could act in times of need, as the nucleus of a national militia, by supplying the military leadership.

The army had, as far as possible, to be armed with the most up-to-date weapons. This was especially important at that time. The Philistines had prohibited the Israelites from forging their own weapons: "Now there was no smith found in all of Israel for the Philistines said: 'Lest the Hebrews make them swords or spears . . .' So it came to pass in the day of battle that there was neither sword nor spear found in the hand of any of the people that were with Saul and Jonathan; but with Saul and Jonathan his son was there found" (1 Sam. 13:19–22).

From here it clearly follows that Samuel's testimony that the king would mobilize the people, would appoint from their midst officers of thousands and of hundreds with whose aid he would prepare instruments of warfare, would not have been construed by the people as an evil decree, but as the fulfilment of their wishes.[29]

Nor did Saul disappoint them. At the very time when the impotence of the Israelites had become common knowledge and aroused the derision of their enemies (*ib.* 2:3), he succeeded in mustering a national army and engaging in his war against Ammon (chap. 11). But he did not rest content with this spontaneous, single awakening. He gathered around himself "every mighty man and any valiant man" (*ib.* 14:52) and he provided his army with a permanent organizational core of 3,000 regular soldiers (*ib.* 13:2). These were

29. By overlooking the legal significance of "the Rule of King", Smith (*ICC*, 57) was led to a conclusion which decisively proves the falsity of his view: "The author counts on very small military ambition in Israel, a view which would argue for a later date."

divided into three sections. One was held in reserve, as it were, and was stationed in Giveat Benjamin, the seat of the government; it was under the command of Jonathan, the heir apparent. The second, commanded apparently by Abner, was stationed in Michmash,[30] while the third took up its position in the mountain of Bethel and was commanded by Saul himself. In time of war, the Bethel and Michmash units were to be combined in a single force and sent to the front, commanded by the king (*ib.*). Such an arrangement would allow Saul to close up any breach in his lines by concentrating his maximum force at the danger point, or else allow him to retreat in good order, when necessary, to the reserve area from which the forces could regroup and attack. This type of arrangement was to prove its worth in the first clash with the Philistines (chaps. 3, 14).

Neither the prospect of being appointed an officer over a thousand (1 Sam 17:18; 18:13), nor of being conscripted into the prestigious cavalry, nor of serving as an officer in the king's chariots could ever have deflected the people from its insistence upon a monarchy.[31] Even to "run before the king's chariot" was no degradation for a freeman, but rather an honor conferred by a ruler upon one of his subjects (Gen 41:43; 2 Sam 15:1; 1 Kgs 14:27–28; 18:46; Esth 6:9).[32]

We do not, however, hear of any established cavalry or charioteers corps either in Saul's or David's reign. The latter houghed the majority of the horses taken as spoil, leaving only 100 of them unharmed (2 Sam 8:4).[33] It fell to Solomon to create a corps of Israelite charioteers (1 Kgs 5:6, etc.). The biblical account of the Israelite occupation of Canaan does resound with an echo of the terror cast by enemy chariots upon the invaders. It was not possible to conquer the coastal plain and the valley of Jezreel, and these areas remained in the hands of the Canaanite nations "because they had chariots of iron" (Judg 1:19, etc.), against which the Israelite infantry was utterly helpless. These regions were the first to be overpowered by the Philistines.They subjugated the Canaanite population and so augmented their own military power by the addition of chariots, which alone had given the Canaanite enemy superiority over the disunited and poorly equipped tribes of Israel. The people understood and realized that no real change could be effected in their capacity to wage war unless they raised the standard of their weaponry to the level of the Philistine armaments. Chariots are group, not individual weapons. To operate a

30. Scripture is not explicit here. The facts emerge from the continuation of the narrative (*ib.* vv. 13: 4–5).
31. Cp. 1 Sam 22:7.
32. Ring, *Israels Rechtsleben* (1926), 187.
33. Cp. Josh 11:6, 9.

chariot required trained team-work, while throwing a group of chariots into battle as a unit needed intelligent co-ordination. To construct a chariot took money and skill, and these arts were not preserved by individuals or families. Cavalry-men and charioteers were forced to engage in constant time-consuming maneuvres. An entire complex of workshops, supply depots and barracks had to be established to maintain chariots and horses. All these items could only be provided by a strong central government authorized to levy duties upon the families and tribes. It followed, then, that the creation of a chariot corps was dependent, from the start, upon the introduction of a monarchy, and this was one of the main tasks devolving upon the king. Saul did not succeed in discharging this duty. He was compelled to wrestle with antecedent problems first, such as the organization of an infantry and its equipment with personal arms. His war was defensive – ranging over the mountain slope of Judah. He did not succeed in breaking through to the broad plains where alone chariot battles were feasible. These real deficiencies, however, do not gainsay our assertion that the idea of creating a chariot corps was one of the original motives behind the establishment of the Israelite kingdom.

We hear, already in Saul's time, of the emergence of a new class, the "servants". The term, "king's servant", is well known to us from the later days of the kingdom. This title was conferred on high officials. It is found inscribed on their seals.[34] Yet this specific sense of the word was already in use on Saul's day,[35] side-by-side with the use of the term as the normal, conventional manner of the person referring to himself while addressing the king, his master.[36] The "servants of the king" are those who obey his royal commands. They are his confidants, whose counsel he seeks (1 Sam. 18:22–24). Hence they are mentioned together, in the same breath, with the king and his heir (*ib.* 19:1).

It stands to reason that the appointment of such servants was a necessary concomitant of an order which was, by and large to base the government of the people on persons deriving their authority directly from the king. Theirs was an honored status – one which earned immediate reward (*ib.* 18:5). In his address, Samuel seized upon the generally accepted and predictable activities of kings – the appointment of officials – but inserted his note of sarcastic disapproval by associating this body with taxes and tithes, and by mentioning it in

34. Such as: שמע עבד ירבעם; אביו עבד עזיו; שבניו עבד עזיו; שמע עבד המלך; עבדיהו עבד המלך; יאזנהו עבד המלך; etc. See Diringer, *Semitic Inscriptions*. This title has been restored in one of the Lachish letters by Tur-Sinai. See his *Lachish Inscriptions* (Hebrew) (1940) 53 ff.
35. 1 Sam 16:15, 17; 18:5.
36. *Ib.* 16:16; 17:32–36. Cp. the corresponding development of the words *marechal* and *chamberlain*, first signifying household servants and later becoming titles of honor.

juxtaposition with actual male and female slaves (*ib.* 8:16–17).[37] This disparaging attitude could not distract the elders from bearing in mind the original significance of the term "servant" in the structure of the monarchical system.

(2) The responsibility of maintaining the army and royal officials naturally devolved upon the king,[38] since these persons had abandoned their gainful occupations for the king's service. But the king's resources were insufficient to defray the costs of his servants and so he would collect the required sums from the people whom he had liberated from the constant fear of mobilization. Levying taxes, in one form or another, is a *sine qua non* of a monarchical system and indeed of every social organization which includes functions that are non-productive but beneficial to society as a whole. Such services are the conduct of wars which become the responsibility of certain sections of the population. In an economy based, for the most part, on barter and which does not produce any appreciable surplus of basic necessities, taxes are collected in kind (*in naturalia*), ready for immediate consumption. At the beginning of the period of the monarchy, the Israelite economy had not yet developed into a money-based system of exchange. It consisted mainly of agricultural units producing their own necessities. Royal taxes were accordingly levied in the form of tithes of agricultural and animal produce.[39] This tax was imposed upon the "men of valor", the heads of families in accordance with a standard "key", and it was taken into account, from the outset, in the individual family budget.[40] As long as a fair balance was maintained between the number of royal servants and the number of producers, and as long as the needs of the state did not impose so heavy a burden of taxation as to endanger the economy, the people of Israel did not view their obligations as an infraction of the compact between them and their king. Rebellion only broke out when the royal yoke became unbearable. Even then, the population never demanded the abolition of all taxation, but only the alleviation of their heavy burden (1 Kgs 12:4).

The foundations of universal taxation were only laid in David's reign, once the population census had been taken (2 Sam 24). Tax collecting as such had already been introduced in Saul's time, however. This assumption throws light upon Saul's promise to the person who would smite Goliath, ". . . and make his

37. Goliath referred to the Israelite soldiers as "Saul's servants" (17:8) in similar sarcastic vein.
38. To them and especially to the best among them, the king would give "fields and vineyards" (1 Sam 22:7).
39. Amos 7:1; Cp. 1 Kgs 18:5.
40. 1 Kgs 4:7 12:1–12; 2 Kgs 15:20; 23:35.

father's house free in Israel" (1 Sam 17:25). Here, to be free meant to be exempt from taxation.

The commodities allocated by the people for the benefit of the royal household[41] served to sustain the army and officials.[42] As time passed, barns had to be built to store the produce.[43] Saul's income was not large, but his appointment of a "chief of the herdsmen" possibly indicates his possessing a considerable number of heads of livestock which he did not gain through any inheritance.[44] Apparently, then, in this area, too, Samuel's remarks were based upon actual economic facts, and were not projections from conditions prevailing in a later time to the early days of the monarchy.

(3) In Saul's time, features appearing in the later days of the monarchy had not yet developed. Giveat Shaul was not proclaimed a royal capital, nor did the king order the construction of a luxurious palace, as Solomon was to do later. Saul still assembled his servants under the tamarisk tree in Ramah (1 Sam 22:6) after the manner of the Judges (Judg 4:5). Indeed in Tell el-Ful the remains of a fortress dating back to Saul's reign has been uncovered, but its design is altogether functional. It served as a military stronghold for the king and his retainers.[45] It could not have satisfied any cravings for glory and splendor characteristic of the later kings, whose manifold activities were intended to demonstrate their enormous wealth and glory in the accepted manner of gentile rulers.

The Israelites were fully familiar with the institution of the king's household. They knew that it would sooner or later come into existence in their midst as well. In the enlarged economy of the king's household, people worked either for pay or in exchange for exemption from military service. Victory in battle brought the acquisition of new estates in its wake, and these became crown lands which would be cultivated by workers appointed by the king from among his subjects. The workers would plough the fields and harvest the crops. At times they would be required to supply their own oxen and donkeys to do the work. We reiterate that these practices had not yet developed in Saul's times, but it was possible even then to predict that they would eventually emerge. The people willingly submitted to such impositions as a necessary concomitant of

41. 1 Kgs 4:7.
42. Cp. Neh 5:15–18. Nehemiah appears here as the exception to the rule.
43. The pottery inscriptions למלך שוכה — ז(י)ף — ממשת — חברן indicate, according to one widely held opinion, that regional centers existed in these locations. See the summary of the various views in Diringer, "Royal Seals in Ancient Israel", *JJS* I, 4 161–170.
44. This office may perhaps be regarded as an earlier version of the office of "over the tax" (1 Kgs 4:6).
45. W.F. Albright, *The Archaeology of Palestine* (1949) 120–122.

the system in which they had placed their trust. Hence, during the whole history of Israel, there was never any attempt to replace the monarchy by some other form of government, even when it was at its weakest. To the extent that the people did revolt, they rebelled against excessive burdens. They demanded the right of supervision over the activities of the kings within the context of the rights conferred upon the rulers by the people.

The analysis presented here validates the view that "whatever was stated in the 'Rule of the King' was permitted to him." Samuel's speech deliberately distorted these practices, as well as many of the basic assumptions underlying the Israelite monarchy. It is almost certain that his description is not an exhaustive account of what constituted the system of monarchy. Other vestiges have been preserved in the "Commandment relating to the King" contained in the Book of Deuteronomy.[46] This law was widely known among the people and this possibly accounts for its not having been preserved in full in biblical literature. The assumptions underlying the "Rule of the King" served as the basis for the negotiations between the representatives of the people and the prophet Samuel, the founder of the Israelite monarchy.[47] And it was on these negotiations that the people were to base their arguments against their kings in later times.

Without delving into the problem of separating the chapters dealing with Saul's appointment into their various, literary sources,[48] we can assert that "the Rule of the King" reflects ancient, historical fact. Samuel's speech fits in logically with the portrayal of the sequence of events.[49] "The Rule of the King", described sarcastically in the narrative, depicts the beginning of the Israelite monarchy. It was intended to guide the course of this developing institution.

46. The relation between the two documents (Deut chap. 17; 1 Sam chap. 8) is a separate topic, requiring separate treatment.
47. "The relation between the Hebrew monarch and his people was as nearly secular as is possible in a society wherein religion is a living force", Frankfort, *op. cit.* 341.
48. An attempt to interpret the two as belonging to a basically single narrative was made by M. Buber, "Samuel and the Development of Government in Israel" (Hebrew), *Tarbiz* 22 (1951) 6–20; 65–84.
49. As against the view of A. Alt, *Die Urgestalt des Reiches Israel, op. cit.* (n. 23) 13.

THE JUDAEAN *'AM HA'AREṢ* IN HISTORICAL PERSPECTIVE

'Am ha'areṣ (in the singular) is found fifty-two times in bliblical literature. It is a collective noun which refers exclusively to a group of people, and never applies to an individual. Thirty-seven of the fifty-two occurrences of *'am ha'areṣ* are clustered in four biblical books: 2 Kings, 2 Chronicles, Jeremiah and Ezekiel, *i.e.* in books which record the history of the rival kingdoms of Judah and Ephraim, and especially the later phase of the history of Judah. For the sake of accuracy it should be stated that ten of these latter thirty-seven mentions are found in passages of the Books of Jeremiah and Chronicles which parallel records of events that are also related in the Book of Kings.[1] Thus the figure of thirty-seven may be reduced to twenty-seven independent single occurrences of *'am ha'areṣ* in those four books mentioned.

Outside these four it is extant nine times in the first four books of the Pentateuch: there are four occurrences in Gen 23:7, 12, 13; 42:6, three in Lev 4:27; 20:2, 4, and one each in Exod 5:5 and Num 14:9. The remaining six mentions of the term are spread over six books: Isa 24:4, Hag 2:4, Zech 7:5; Job 12:24, Dan 9:6, and Ezra 4:4, *'Am ha'areṣ* is never mentioned in Deuteronomy, Joshua, Judges, and Samuel, in the majority of the Minor Prophets, in Psalms and the Five Megilloth.

At this point a salient feature should be underlined: the conspicious absence of the term *'am ha'areṣ* from the Book of Deuteronomy and from the Book of Joshua, which is said to have been subjected to a farreaching deuteronomistic revision. This absence of the term from the hard-core of deuteronomistic literature appears to take the wind out of the sails of the school, headed by von Rad, that credited the *'am ha'areṣ* with a large share of responsibility for the Deuteronomy-centred reform that was carried out by Josiah.[2]

The preponderant majority of references to *'am ha'areṣ* pertain to the

1. Jer 52:6, 25a, b=2 Kgs 25:3, 19a, b; 2 Chr 23:13, 20, 21 = 2 Kgs 11:14, 19, 20; 26:21 = 25:5; 33:25a, b = 21:24a, b; 36:1 = 23:30.
2. G. von Rad, *Deuteronomium Studien* (Göttingen, 1948), 43ff; J.A. Soggin,"Der Judäische *'Am Ha'areṣ* und das Königtum in Judah", *VT* 13 (1963), 187–195.

Kingdom of Judah, and especially to the city of Jerusalem. All cases in which the term refers to non-Judahite groups are clustered in the Pentateuch and in the Hagiographa. Two of these are textually doubtful – Exod 5:5; Isa 24:4.[3] Altogether they may be subdivided into:

I. references to Israel as a whole, usually in settings of a cultic-legal nature Lev 4:27; 20:2, 4; Ezek 45:16, 22; 46:3, 9; also 39:13 and 33:2, which, though, pertain specifically to cultic traditions of the Temple in Jerusalem;

II. some references to non-Israelite ethnic groups: Egyptians – Gen 42:6; and possibly Exod 5:5; Canaanites – Num 14:9 and the בני חת – Gen 23:7, 12, 13;

III. and one or two to groups without any explicit ethnic or political affiliation – Job 12:24; and possibly Isa 24:4.

It should be stressed that not even once is the term *'am ha'areṣ* employed in a specifically Ephraimite setting. Therefore it is quite in order to present the issue at hand as 'the problem of the Judaean *'am ha'areṣ*'. In other words we are dealing with a term which is specifically connected with the Judaean body politic.

II

Scholarly endeavours to interpret the term *'am ha'areṣ* and to characterize the social group or groups so designated were, and still are, severely hampered by the apparent inconsistency in the employment of this term in biblical literature. Furthermore, no clear-cut lines could be established by which to delineate the semantic field of this term from that of other, comparable or synonymous expressions, such as זקנים, אנשים, כל העם etc. (in the present discussion I shall not apply myself at all to that latter aspect, an omission which I hope to remedy at a future occasion). It is for this and other reasons that the suggestions offered in explanation of the term *'am ha'areṣ* differ widely, and sometimes are diametrically opposed to one another.

Excepting Klamroth, who perceived in the *'am ha'areṣ 'die Volksmenge'*, that is to say the population of a country in the wider sense of the word,[4] all other opinions appear to concur in presenting the *'am ha'areṣ* as only one segment or stratum of a national society, in fact of Judah. But in the definition

3. In Exod 5:5 the Samaritan Version refers *'am ha'areṣ* to the Egyptians, the *MT* to the Israelites. In Isa 24:4 the word *'am* is not found in the basix text of $1QIs^a$ and was superscribed by a corrector, in conformity with the *MT* reading.
4. E. Klamroth, *Die jüdischen Exulanten in Babylon* (Leipzig, 1912), 99–101.

of this stratum a great variety of proposals were put forward, ranging from the top of the social ladder to its very bottom rung.

The *'am ha'areṣ* was put highest by Judge Sulzberger in his book *'Am ha'areṣ – the Ancient Hebrew Parliament*, published in 1909. To him, as to Elias Auerbach who developed the idea independently,[5] it is a 'great national council', the democratic representation of the nation *vis-à-vis* the king. Somewhat less enthusiastic was the German sociologist Max Weber, who rather would describe this group as an upper social class, the *'Landadel'*, a sort of landed gentry.[6] This definition was favoured also by R. Kittel, A.G. Barrois, R. Gordis and S. Daiches, who employed the rendition 'lords of the land'.[7] A. Menes, on the other hand, and similarly K. Galling, nevertheless could see in the *'am ha'areṣ 'die ärmeren Volksschichten'*, the proletariat that was opposed to the Judaean aristocracy.[8] The golden mean was struck by E. Gillischewsky: *'vollberechtigte Mitglieder eines politischen und kultischen Gemeinwesens'*.[9] It was put more succinctly by M. Noth: *'Die Gesamtheit der judäischen Vollbürger'*, and R. de Vaux: *'l'ensemble des nationaux'*.[10] With some adjustments and elaborations this is the definition which underlies the most recent and most detailed monographic discussion of the issue at hand, E. Würthwein's *Der 'am ha'arez im Alten Testament* (1936).

In view of this *embarras de richesses*, it can hardly come as a surprise that in the latest study of the term known to me, E. Nicholson can offer only a counsel of despair. He concludes his essay with the statement, 'the term has no fixed and rigid meaning, but is used rather in a purely general and fluid manner and varies in meaning from context to context'.[11]

It appears that the discussion of *'am ha'areṣ* has reached low tide. Therefore a renewed attempt at putting some order into this chaos may be justified. But it would be futile simply to follow the beaten tracks, trying to improve on the

5. E. Auerbach,"Am ha'areṣ"*Proceedings of the First World Congress of Jewish Studies, 1947* (Jerusalem, 1952, Hebrew), 362–366.
6. M. Weber, *Das antike Judentum* (Tübingen, 1921), 30ff.
7. S. Daiches,"The Meaning of am-haaretz in the O.T.",*JTS* 30 (1929), 245–249; R. Gordis, "Sectional Rivalry in the Kingdom of Judah", *JQR* N.S. 25 (1934/35), 237–259.
8. A. Menes, "Die vorexilischen Gesetze Israels im Zusammenhang seiner kulturgeschichtlichen Entwicklung", *BZAW* 50 (Berlin, 1928), 70f.; K. Galling, "Die israelitische Staatsverfassung in ihrer vorderoientalischen Umwelt", *AO* 28 (1929), 23.
9. E. Gillischewsky, "Der Ausdruck 'Am haareṣ im A.T.", *ZAW* 40 (1922), 137–142.
10. M. Noth,"Gott, König, Volk im A.T.",*ZThK* 47 (1950), 181 (repr. in *Gesammelte Studien zum A.T.* [München, 1950], p. 217); R. de Vaux, *Les institutions de l'Ancien Testament* (Paris, 1958), 111–113.
11. E.W. Nicholson,"The Meaning of the Expression עם הארץ in the O.T.",*JSS* 10 (1956), 66.

efforts of predecessors where flaws in their reasoning can be detected. Promise of success, though, could lie in choosing some other avenue of approach to the problem at hand.

III

Before presenting my own proposals, I must put in relief two features which are common to all the different views surveyed:

I. All seem to arrive at their proposed interpretation of the term by taking their departure from etymological considerations. By virtue of its components, the construct *'am ha'areṣ* is taken to designate an ethnically determined social group within the confines of a given territory.[12] Each commentator then elucidates further specifications of this group by using one or two of the variegated employments of the term in the Bible as his special launching pad.

Now, this is a rather dangerous procedure. The actual content of a term or a concept is often widely removed from its etymological basis, and cannot be adequately explained by it. The specific meaning of a word will be decided upon by its context, its literary and historical setting, much more than by its etymological derivation. By digging up the roots of a word, a pleasant pastime in itself, one has not yet unearthed the roots of its subject matter.

II. Practically all the suggested explanations of the term *'am ha'areṣ* conceive of it on a nation-wide scale, and set out to peg it into a convenient hole in a system of socio-political institutions. Here the impact of some fairly basic concepts in recent biblical research makes itself felt.

Scholars seem unanimous in agreeing that throughout biblical times 'democratic' forces or institutions played an important role in the Israelite body politic.[13] However the consensus completely breaks down when a more detailed analysis of the 'democratic' factors involved is attempted. Then the pendulum swings from their presentation as a mere *vox populi*, which in certain given situations, by the threat or the actual employment of physical force, gained an *ad hoc* ascendancy over the reigning monarch, to their definition as

12. See L. Rost, "Die Bezeichnungen für Land und Volk im A.T.", *O. Procksch Festschrift* (Leipzig, 1934), 125–138; and more recently: E.A. Speiser, "'People' and 'Nation' of Israel", *JBL* 79 (1960), 157–163.
13. The literature on this issue is fairly extensive. We shall make mention here only of the following items: M. Sloush, "Representative Government Among the Hebrews and Pheonicians", *JQR* N.S. 4 (1913), 303–310; R. Gordis, "Primitive Democracy in Ancient Israel", *A. Marx Jubilee Volume* (Philadelphia, 1950), 347–369; C.U. Wolf, "Traces of Primitive Democracy in Israel", *JNES* 6 (1947), 98–108. A dissenting opinion was voiced by P.A.H. de Boer: "Israel n'a jamais été une démocratie", *VT* 5 (1955), 227.

the spearhead of a legally constituted institution which by right took an active part in the administration of the realm. On the whole, the balance of the argument favours the assumption that the 'democratic' powers were constitutionally integrated into the Israelite monarchy. But the proper definition of the scope of their activities, the degree of their institutionalization, and the elucidation of their constitutional history yet remain a *desideratum.* Information in biblical literature on these democratic constituents of the Israelite society is extremely meager and lacks clarity. They are referred to by a variety of expressions which in some cases appear to be used interchangeably, while again in others they seem to be employed with different connotations. Nowhere does the Bible offer a systematic definition of the social forces which were active in the affairs of the body politic, or a circumscription of the political theory which served as the basis of the socio-political life of Israel. What is given is a purely descriptive account of a series of seemingly unconnected events in the history of the Israelite state in which the impact of non-monarchic agencies on the fate of the monarchy became especially obvious.

As a result of the above trends of thought, the attempts to define the *'am ha'areṣ* remain altogether on the plane of typology, and leave aside specifically historical considerations. Yet it appears that one indeed should probe into the genesis of the *'am ha'areṣ*, whatever its definition be, and into its subsequent historical developments. This task becomes especially urgent if proper attention is given to the fact already mentioned that the term never is used in a purely Ephraimite setting, but, with respect to Israel, is exclusively applied to Judah. The explanation of this phenomenon must be sought in some specifically Judaean historical experience which was not shared by the tribes that constituted the Northern Kingdom, and which had been conducive to the emergence of the 'Judaean *'am ha'areṣ*'.

I cannot offer here a detailed presentation of my lines of thought, and therefore shall state my case in a series of working hypotheses. In view of the apparent inconsistency in the employment of the term *'am ha'areṣ* in biblical literature, considerations of method lead us to base the ensuing analysis on the most salient occurrences, and then to explore whether the remaining cases, or some at least, can subsequently be fitted into the emerging frame of reference.

Let me first turn to the admitted variety of connotations which attach to the term *'am ha'areṣ* in the Bible. I propose to explain this phenomenon by assuming a semantic division of the term which resulted in diverse synchronic employments:

a. as a general noun which refers to a variety of human groups;

b. as a technical term which can be applied only to a specific entity in the Judaean body politic.

Such a semantic duality can be observed in other biblical words, *e.g.* עבד and נער.

Being historically and sociologically circumscribed, the technical term *'am ha'arlṣ* was always used as a collective singular, and was never accompanied by a plural form. On the other hand, the general connotation, which in the singular also could relate to Israel, or for that matter to Judah, did have a complementary plural form – עמי הארץ or עמי הארצות – which was applied exclusively to non-Israelite ethnic groups, such as the native inhabitants of Canaan (Deut 28:10; 1 Chr 5:25), or the motley population of Palestine that was encountered by the returning exiles (Ezra 9:2). Further, the employment of the technical connotation was virtually discontinued after the disintegration of the body politic to which it specifically pertained, *i.e.* after the destruction of the Kingdom of Judah. The general connotation, on the contrary, experienced a diachronic semantic development which resulted in its preponderance in post-exilic literature, especially in the plural form עמי הארצ(ות) which is used synonymously with גויי הארצות. There and then it became saturated with the opprobrium which attaches to the singular *'am ha'areṣ* in post-biblical Hebrew, already in early rabbinic literature.[14]

IV

Now an elucidation of the history and the character of the *'am ha'areṣ* in the technical sense can be attempted.

As already stated, our information on the Judaean *'am ha'areṣ* derives almost wholly from the historiographies Kings and Chronicles, and from the prophetic books of Jeremiah and Ezekiel. Irrespective of the fact that these books were finally edited only after the destruction of Judah, their reports on the actions of the *'am ha'areṣ* presumably are contemporaneous with the events recorded.

Explicit references to the *'am ha'areṣ* are spread over a period from about the middle of the ninth century B.C.E. to the beginning of the sixth.

The earliest mention, put on record in 2 Kgs 11 (cp. 2 Chr 23), relates to events of the year 836 B.C.E. We learn that the *'am ha'areṣ* was instrumental in the overthrow of Athaliah who had usurped the throne of Judah. In the wake of the rebellion, the *'am ha'areṣ* restored to the throne the crown-prince Joash,

14. Cp. the classical monograph by A. Büchler, *Der galiläische 'Am-ha'areṣ des zweiten Jahrhunderts* (Wien, 1906).

the rightful heir of the murdered King Ahaziah.

The last reference to the *'am ha'areṣ* in a distinctly historical context is set in the detailed description of the conquest of Jerusalem by the Babylonians. Among the civic leaders who were captured in Jerusalem, and then were executed by Nebuchadnezzar at Riblah, together with King Zedekiah's sons, sixty members of the *'am ha'areṣ* figure prominently, as well as the סופר of the *'am ha'areṣ* (2 Kgs 25:19; Jer 52:25).[15] These two, chronologically speaking widely removed events in the recorded history of the *'am ha'areṣ* clearly illustrate that in weal and in woe this body was aligned with the Davidic dynasty, and ultimately shared its unfortunate fate. The first impression is fully substantiated by a survey of the other historical incidents in which the Judaean *'am ha'areṣ* was involved.

On three further occasions this body safeguarded the uninterrupted succession of Davidic kings on the throne of Judah. King Amaziah met with the same fate as his father Joash (2 Kgs 12:21–22). In 769 he was assassinated in Lachish by some of his courtiers who had plotted against him in Jerusalem (*ib.* 14:19). Again partisans of the Davidic dynasty intervened, and made Amaziah's son and heir Uzziah, King of Judah (*ib.* 14:21; 2 Chr 26:1). True, in this case the faction is referred to as עם יהודה. Therefore, in order to prepare the ground for the inclusion of this incident in a discussion of the *'am ha'areṣ*, I wish to state provisionally that *'am ha'areṣ* as well as עם יהודה may be considered two different abbreviations of the same full designation of that body עם הארץ לבני יהודה. I shall tie in this proposition with my argument at a later stage of the inquiry.

It would appear that in the period which we have covered so far, *i.e.* the second half of the ninth century and the first half on the eighth, the Davidic dynasty repeatedly was threatened by internal rift, and that for this reason the *'am ha'areṣ* time and again had to put into effect its protective power. From the inception of the Kingdom of Judah until Athaliah's *coup d'état*, the Davidic line never had been in tangible danger. This statement includes even Jeroboam's rebellion which resulted in the very creation of a separate Northern Kingdom. During that period the *'am ha'areṣ* lay dormant, so to speak, yet kept a watchful eye on the affairs of the realm. Thus may be explained the silence of our sources with respect to this body until Athaliah's seizure of power. It may

15. When the title הסופר המצביא את עם הארץ was no longer properly understood, the interpretative gloss שר הצבא was infused into the text of 2 Kgs 25:19. The resulting syntactical difficulty, הסופר שר הצבא, was subsequently eased in the parallel reading in Jer 52:25 by the elimination of the determinative article before סופר.

well be that the recurrent assassinations of Davidic kings between 842 and 769 B.C.E. – Ahaziah, Joash, Amaziah – necessitated a regularized and continuous association of the *'am ha'areṣ* with the royal house, more so than in the past, or, as we yet shall see, in the future. Therefore, when, as a result of his illness, Uzziah was unable to control the realm effectively, but yet did not relinquish power, his son, the crown prince Jotham, took charge of state affairs and at the same time appears to have assumed direct control of the *'am ha'areṣ*: ויותם בן־המלך על־הבית שפט את־עם הארץ (2 Kgs 15:5).

The next mention of the *'am ha'areṣ*, the last before the apprehension and subsequent execution of sixty of its members by the Babylonians, pertains to the year 640 B.C.E. Again a king of Judah, Amon, is murdered by his courtiers. Again the *'am ha'areṣ* quickly reacts, and restores order by inflicting the death penalty on the plotters, and by putting Amon's son Josiah on the throne (2 Kgs 21:23–24). In this, as in virtually all the other cases mentioned, we find a similar constellation of opposing forces. The *'am ha'areṣ* intervenes to counteract an imminent threat to the continuity of the Davidic dynasty, a threat which was brought about by regicides from among the royal courtiers who hatched their plots in the metropolis. This recurring constellation indeed may disclose an underlying tension between the *'am ha'areṣ* and the city, or the acropolis of Jerusalem. This point will call for some further elaboration at a later stage of our inquiry.

At this juncture we can offer some provisional conclusions which follow from the foregoing survey:

Not once in its recorded history did the *'am ha'areṣ* serve in an advisory capacity, as do the זקנים, *e.g.* at Rehoboam's invitation. *Ergo*, the *'am ha'areṣ* is not an institution of deliberation, but rather an instrument of action. Any attempt to describe it as a 'national council' of some sort or other therefore is completely misleading.

The *'am ha'areṣ* never was formally convened, or called upon by the king or some other agent, although it apparently was headed by a functionary designated סופר. It follows that this body was not an institution at all, but a fairly loosely constituted power group within the Kingdom of Judah. This characteristic is further put in relief by the fact that the *'am ha'areṣ* does not function continuously, but always goes into action *ad hoc*, when extraordinary political conditions make action imperative.

The deployment of the *'am ha'areṣ*, apparently in full force, in the overthrow of Athaliah, within the confines of the Temple precincts, indicates that this body was comprised of a comparatively small number of individuals, running into not more than a few hundred. This supposition is borne out by the explicit reference to 'sixty' members of the *'am ha'areṣ* who were executed after the conquest of Jerusalem. Therefore it is unlikely that in the *'am ha'areṣ* were incorporated all full-fledged citizens of Judah.

Our sources do not permit us adequately to describe the socio-economic composition of the *'am ha'areṣ*. The exclusive concentration of all its actions within the city of Jerusalem, in fact within the confines of the acropolis, militates against its definition as a stratum of landed nobility.

The only recognizable *raison d'être* of the *'am ha'areṣ* is the *de facto* championing of the house of David which lacks any *de jure* circumscription in the political framework of the Judaean kingdom. Accordingly the *'am ha'areṣ* can not be defined in terms of a constitutional-legal nature.

V

At this stage we have to broaden the scope of our investigation, in order to work in a set of references to an *'am ha'areṣ* outside the political limits of Israel or Judah. We refer to the *'am ha'areṣ* of the בני חת in Hebron that plays such a central role in the sale of the Machpelah to Abraham (Gen 23).

The very existence of the בני חת in Hebron, and their identity, is a vexing problem on which I cannot elaborate here. Neither can I go into a detailed analysis of this episode. But some comments which bear directly on the problem under discussion are in order:

I. The Abraham traditions reflect motifs and concepts of the late premonarchic and the early monarchic period. In fact, I would maintain that Abraham's meetings as an equal with Melchizedek, King of Salem, *i.e.* Jerusalem (Gen 14), and with the *'am ha'areṣ* of Hebron (Gen 23) are prefigurations of David's future relations to and claims on these two cities, each of which served as the metropolis of his realm, at different stages in his career. It is in this light that the portrayal of Abraham as a monarch-like figure may be explained. The honorific title נשיא אלהים bestowed upon him by the *'am ha'areṣ* of the בני חת in the Machpelah episode (Gen 23:6), recalls the equally honorific comparison of David to a מלאך האלהים, by the wise woman of Tekoa (2 Sam 24:17, 20), and by Mephibosheth (2 Sam 22:28), with its late echo in Zach 22:8, ובית דוד כאלהים כמלאך ה' לפניהם.

II. As the old name Qiryat 'Arba' suggests, and as was shown by B. Mazar,[16] the population of this city was of a heterogeneous composition. The different ethnic groups occupied different quarters of the city, each of which may have

16. B. Maisler (Mazar), "חברון — קרית ארבע", *B. Dinaburg Jubilee Volume* (Jerusalem, 1949, Hebrew), 310–325, where previous literature on the subject is quoted; and *id.*, *Encyclopaedia Biblica* III, 16–20 (Jerusalem, 1958, Hebrew).

maintained some sort of autonomy within the wider city organization. This may explain why Abraham addresses his request for the acquisition of a plot of land to the *'am ha'areṣ* of the בני חת and not to the אנשי העיר. It is worthy of note that in the Dinah incident, Shechem and his father Hamor refer their proposal to enter into an alliance with the house of Jacob to אנשי עירם (Gen 34:20), the equivalent of the Mesopotamiam *puḫrum*, or *'alum*. True, the sale of the Machpelah is finally ratified by Efron in the presence of כל באי שער עירו (Gen 23:18; cp. also 25:10). But in the preceding negotiations only the *'am ha'areṣ* of the בני חת is involved.

It seems to follow that the term *'am ha'areṣ* in the Machpelah episode designates one segment of the population of Hebron, namely the בני חת, which as such has no formal legal power. This legal power rests with the אנשי העיר. In other words, although the *'am ha'areṣ* has some standing in the city community, and does have some influence on one component of its population, namely the בני חת, this influence is not legally or constitutionally circumscribed, but rather appears to be derived from common interest and group cohesion.

Let us now return to the Judaean *'am ha'areṣ*. Is it a mere coincidence that the term *'am ha'areṣ* can be shown to apply almost exclusively to the city of Jerusalem and to the city of Hebron, the two successive capitals of the Davidic realm? Should we not rather assume that in the process of the transfer of the capital to Jerusalem some components of the Hebronite population and some of its civic concepts and terminology were infused into the new metropolis? The answer to this question without doubt must be in the affirmative. Biblical evidence clearly indicates that David rebuilt Jerusalem after having conquered it, and repopulated it, settling there his גבורים, former Hebronites and other elements of the tribe of Judah. In fact he had previously done so also with respect to Hebron, immediately after he had chosen this city as his first seat of government: ואנשיו אשר־עמו העלה דוד איש וביתו וישבו בערי חברון – 'And his men that were with him did David bring up, every man with his household; and they dwelt in the cities (rather boroughs) of Hebron' (2 Sam 2:3). It is probable that some of these new Hebronites at a later stage again followed David, becoming part of the population of Jerusalem. The comparison of Hebron with Jerusalem in respect to the *'am ha'areṣ* and its functions is especially meaningful in view of the fact that the population of Jerusalem was of as composite and heterogeneous a character as that of Hebron. *Vis-à-vis* the autochthonic Jebusites, and the foreign mercenaries in the service of the king, with their fickle allegiance to the royal house, the Judahites, the עם הארץ לבני יהודה constituted a hard core of staunch defenders of the Davidic dynasty. The confrontation of these two antagonistic factors in the citizenry of Jerusalem helps in explaining the fact on which we have already remarked, namely, that in recurrent historical situations the *'am ha'areṣ* is found in open opposition to the royal courtiers.

The infusion of Judahite followers of David into his new capital and its citadel is reflected in two ecological terms which pertain to the city-plan of Jerusalem: בית הגבורים – 'the house of the mighty men (of David)' which is mentioned as late as the times of Nehemiah (Neh 3:16); and בית העם, which I propose to take as an apocopated reading of בית עם הארץ – 'the house of the *'am ha'areṣ*'. This latter was obviously a building of some prominence and was burned down by the Babylonians after the capture of Jerusalem, together with the king's palace (Jer 39:8) and the Temple (Jer 52:13; 2 Kgs 25:9).

In fine, I should like to review some of the conclusions which arise from the preceding analysis:

I. The *'am ha'areṣ* is a social phenomenon which is rooted in city life in the territory of Judah, *ergo* in the structure of a sedentary society. In the early stages of the Davidic monarchy it was assimilated into the emerging socio-political framework of the empire, which thus can be shown not to be solely derived from axiomatic tribal-amphictyonic institutions.

II. Contrary to the institutionalizing tendencies which haunt recent biblical research, the *'am ha'areṣ* of Judah can not be viewed as a democratic or otherwise constitutionally circumscribed institution. Rather is it a body of Judaeans in Jerusalem that rose to some power and importance which was ultimately derived from their loyalty to the Davidic dynasty. The *'am ha'areṣ* in fact constitutes a sociological phenomenon that belongs to and illustrates a power structure which appears to be typical of a hereditary monarchy without clearly defined constitutional foundations. The readily given support of a group like the *'am ha'areṣ* helps in maintaining the political equilibrium by counteracting the possible eroding impact of an ascending class of courtiers and ministers. Unwavering loyalty arising from kin ties balances a pragmatic allegiance rooted in vested interests.

However at the very same time the support given by the *'am ha'areṣ* to the king entails a dependence of the king on the *'am ha'areṣ* which effectively circumscribes the king's power. Thus, although lacking a constitutional definition, the *'am ha'areṣ* is a supportive yet restrictive force which prevents the deterioration of the monarchy into an absolutist regime.

III. Viewed in historical retrospect, the *'am ha'areṣ* served as an important means for the implementation of an ideology inspired by the Davidic dynasty which took the form of a prophecy from the mouth of Nathan 2 Sam 7:16: וְנֶאְמַן ביתך וממלכתך עד־עולם – 'And your house and your kingdom shall be made sure for ever'.

THE NEW HEBREW LETTER FROM THE SEVENTH CENTURY B.C.E. IN HISTORICAL PERSPECTIVE*

A

The circumstances of discovery of the "Hebrew Letter From the Seventh Century B. C.," and foremost the fact that it was found in a guardroom in the town gate,[1] make it exceedingly probable that this ostracon is a juridical document. It is a plea entered by an unnamed plaintiff, henceforth X, with an authority whose seat was the fortress in which the letter was found,[2] to annul the fine or punishment which had been imposed upon him by one Hoshaiah ben Shobay (or Shobi), who appears to have been an official of lower rank than that of the *śār* to whom the letter is addressed. The somewhat awkward style of the letter, which is in glaring contrast to the practiced penmanship, suggests that its contents were dictated by the plaintiff to a professional scribe. The drawing up of the complaint in writing is to be accounted for by the absence of both X and Hoshaiah from the fortress, rather than by the assumed failure of the plaintiff's previous oral remonstrations with the *śār*, as Naveh suggested.[3] Both men had obviously remained in *Ḥaṣar 'Asam* where the incidents had occurred which resulted in the lodging of the complaint. The fortress presumably was the seat of a district governor, the *śār* under whose superior jurisdiction also came the locality *Ḥaṣar 'Asam*, where Hoshaiah seems to have been in charge. It is likely that *Ḥaṣar 'Asam*, as its name implies, was an unfortified settlement south-east of the fortress, which again was located about a mile south of Yabneh-Yam (Mînat Rūbîn). The relationship of the fortress to *Ḥaṣar 'Asam* may be likened to that of Ashdod, Ekron, etc. to their respective *ḥaṣērîm* (cp. Josh. 15:32-62, especially vv. 45-47). *Ḥaṣar 'Asam* was probably situated in the traditional territory of the

* My sincere thanks go to Prof. Frank M. Cross, Jr., with whom I have discussed in detail the issues dealt with in this paper. Prof. Cross also read a draft of it *in toto*. His criticism and comments have been extremely helpful. The responsibility for views expressed and for faults that there may be lies with the author.

[1] J. Naveh, "A Hebrew Letter From the Seventh Century B. C.," *Israel Exploration Journal* 10 (1960), pp. 129-139.

[2] Naveh, *op. cit.*, p. 129, reports that the Israeli Government Place Names Committee named the site Meṣad Ḥashavyahu. This name cannot be derived from the document under review. F. M. Cross correctly reads the official's name, mentioned in the letter, Hoshaiah (BULLETIN 165 [Feb., 1962], pp. 42-43). This, by the way, is also the name of another high Judean official who is mentioned in the Lachish Letters (3, 1. Cp. H. Torczyner, *Lachish I. The Lachish Letters* (London, 1938), pp. 51-52). Furthermore, nothing indicates that the official actually lived in the fortress. In fact we shall propose that this was not the case, and that he was connected with Ḥaṣar 'Asam, where the incidents described in the letter took place. However, the designation *Meṣad Ḥashavyahu* may be kept on the basis of the broken sherd, also found at the site, on which the name *ḥšbyhw* was undoubtedly inscribed.

[3] "A Hebrew Letter . . .," p. 136.

tribes Judah and Simeon, in which were found a number of localities whose names contained the component *ḥṣr*.[4]

A detailed analysis of the legal situation reflected in the document led us to conclude that the plaintiff was not necessarily a poor man who had hired himself out to his creditor, apparently the *śār*, in payment of a debt, nor "one of many reapers employed in the governor's service."[5] He was, rather, a *corvée* laborer who claimed that he had adequately discharged the duties incumbent upon him.[6] In the light of this proposition the terms employed in the document will be explained and their specific legal connotations elucidated. This then will lead to some further proposals with regard to the historical background of the document under review.

The basic facts stated in the letter are the following: Hoshaiah impounded the garment of X for an unspecified reason, while the latter was engaged in harvest activities in *Ḥaṣar 'Asam*. X maintains that Hoshaiah acted without justification. Therefore he appeals to the *śār* for a review of the case and for the return of his garment. In order fully to understand X's arguments, it is imperative to reconstruct from his recital the events which had led to his punishment.

These events are described in the first part of the letter, after the introductory formula: *yšmʿ. 'dny. hśr 't dbr ʿbdh. ʿbdk*. In conformity with epistolary style the *śār* is addressed in the introduction in the 3rd person sing., whereas in the main part of the letter he is referred to in the 2nd pers.[7] The combination *ʿbdh ʿbdk* (l. 2) is a transition phrase which closes the introductory formula and leads on to the subject matter. One might compare 2 Sam. 9:11: 'according to all my lord the king has commanded his servant (*ʿbdh*), thus your servant (*ʿbdk*) will do.'

X had been harvesting in *Ḥaṣar 'Asam*. This fact is first described by the expression *qṣr hyh ʿbdk* (lines 3-4). Thus the locale and the time-setting for what is to come have been established. Then the general term *qṣr* is broken down into a more detailed description of the activities in which X had been engaged. In this context three verbs are employed: *wyqṣr* .. *wykl w'sm*, "(your servant) reaped . . . measured and stored" (ll. 4-5). This triad is again referred to, with some variation, in lines 6-7, and in lines 8-9. The repetitive employment of *qṣr*, *k(w)l* and *'sm* appears to indicate that all three have some bearing on the ensuing situation,

[4] *Ḥaṣar-gaddah* (Josh. 15:27); Ḥaṣar-shu'al (Josh. 15:28; 19:3; 1 Chr. 4:28; Neh. 11:27); Ḥaṣar-'addar (Num. 34:4); Ḥaṣar-susah/susim (Josh. 19:5; 1 Chr. 4:31). Also Ḥaṣor (Josh. 15:23) and Ḥaṣor-ḥadattah (Josh. 15:25). See further Is. 42:11; 1 Chr. 4:32.—For Hebrew *ḥāṣēr* cf. H. M. Orlinsky, "*Ḥaṣer* in the O. T.," JAOS (*Journal of the American Oriental Society*) 59 (1939), p. 22 ff.; A. Malamat, "Mari and the Bible." JAOS 82 (1962), p. 147; M. Noth, *Die Ursprünge des alten Israel im Lichte neuer Quellen* (Köln 1961), p. 37.

[5] Naveh, *op. cit.*, p. 135.

[6] We note with satisfaction that our conclusion, arrived at independently, concurs with I. Mendelsohn's interpretation of the legal situation which is reflected in the document (BULLETIN 167 (Oct., 1962), pp. 33-34). Basically this is also the view of F. M. Cross, who presents X as a farmer in a military colony, or a sharecropper who had failed to render his full obligation (*op. cit.*, pp. 45-46).

[7] *Cf.* e. g. 1 Sam. 26:19.

namely the impounding of X's garment by Hoshaiah, which is reported in lines 7-8: "there came Hoshaiah the son of Shobay and took your servant's garment." We further learn that this happened when X was about to quit work—*lpny šbt.*

The terms *wykl* and *lpny šbt* call for some clarification. For orthographic reasons,[8] *wykl* must be derived from *kwl*—'to measure' or 'to weigh,' rather than from *klh.* In Is. 40:12 *kwl* is paralleled by *mdd* and *šql.* S. Ronzevalle who compared arab. *kyl,*[9] and again independently Tur-Sinai,[10] find this verb also in the Gezer Calendar, as a component of the term which indicates the (end of the) harvest-season: *yrḥ qṣr wkl*: 'the season of harvesting and measuring.' The proposed interpretation ties in better with the argumentative tone of the letter. It appears that it had been X's obligation to deliver to the granary (*w'sm*) a specific amount of reaped grain (*wyqṣr*), the exactness of which was verified by measuring or weighing (*wykl*). There and then Hoshaiah turns up, obviously in order to supervise the delivery of produce by the laborers. The verb *wyb'* by which Hoshaiah's arrival is described may indicate that he arrived at that very time in *Ḥaṣar 'Asam.* It would seem that he turned up only at the end of the *corvée* period in order to ascertain that the laborers delivered the required amount of grain, and subsequently to authorize their release. He may have been a district supervisor in charge of several localities and of several gangs of conscripted laborers. His status could be compared to that of one Semakyahu, a military man of whom the Lachish letters (4:4-13) tell us that he had been in a certain place, possibly Bet Hareped, on his inspection tour—*btsbth bqr,* but had already moved on at the time when an inquiry on his whereabouts was received by the commandant of that locality. The nature of his mission may have been similar to that in which Hoshaiah was engaged, i. e., the supervision of men who were in the king's service (ib. 13:1-2).[11]

Hoshaiah apparently decided that the amount of grain delivered by X was short of the assigned quota. Therefore he impounded X's garment. Against this implied accusation X defends himself by stating three times in a row that he had delivered to the granary *kymm.*[12] This term obviously indicates a full and adequate measure. A comparable term is found in Jud. 17:10. There Micaiah pledges his newly appointed priest, to give him *layyāmîm* ten pieces of silver, one suit of clothes and full board. Here *layyāmîm* certainly denotes a fixed period, and may be translated 'per annum.' In an Aramaic ostracon *kymn* carries the meaning 'regularly, periodically.'[13] Again we find a similar term in a South-Arabian document (RES 3854/3-4) which reads *ymmyw ymmyw bwrḫm b'stnm ḏfr'm wsḏtm ḏfqḥw bwrḫm wrḫm.* In the view of A. F.

[8] See F. M. Cross, *op. cit.*, p. 44, n. 42.

[9] *Palestine Exploration Fund. Quarterly Statement* (1909), p. 109.

[10] *Lashon wa-Sefer*, vol. *Lashon* (Jerusalem, 1948), pp. 44-46.

[11] H. Torczyner, *Lachish I*, pp. 76-79; further infra, n. 36.

[12] Thus with Cross and against Naveh's reading *kynm.*

[13] *Cf.* A. Dupont-Sommer, "L'ostracon araméen d'Assour," *Syria* 24 (1944/45), p. 45, n. 44; now quoted also by F. M. Cross, BULLETIN 168 (Dec., 1962), p. 23, addendum.

L. Beeston, this document refers "to a specific ordinance requiring the performance of corvée duties 'on each of two days in a month, namely on the first of the first decade and on the sixth of the second decade, month by month,' that is to say on the 1st and the 16th of every month, i. e. 24 days in the year at half-monthly intervals." [14]

We may conclude that in our ostracon *kymm* specifies the time-span for which X, or possibly all *corvée* laborers were conscripted. This conclusion bears on the interpretation of the expression *lpny šbt* in line 5. Indeed the term may say only that X completed his chores before taking his rest (Naveh). However, this appears to be unlikely. If mere 'resting' were implied, Hoshaiah could have compelled X to continue work, instead of impounding his garment. Much better is Albright's suggestion to translate 'before the Sabbath.' [15] The approaching weekend would have made the continuation of work impossible, and the impounding of the garment would become an especially severe punishment. Yet in view of the *corvée* setting we tend to interpret *lpny šbt* as a technical term, meaning 'time off' (cp. Ruth 2:7; Ex. 21:19; and especially Ps. 127:2), [16] or 'dismissal.' The verb *šbt* is thus employed in Ex. 5:5 in a comparable *corvée* context, where Pharaoh accuses Moses and Aaron of stopping the Israelites from executing their enforced labor duties: 'you detain them from their *corvée* labor'— *wᵉhišbattem 'ôtām missiblôtām.* It thus indicated the complete cessation of work in this specific harvest-period in *Ḥaṣar 'Asam*, and affected either all the *corvée* laborers in X's gang or X alone (cp. Gen. 2:1-3). In this technical connotation Hebrew *šbt* equals Aram. *bṭl.*[17] Onkelos translates MT *šibtô* in Ex. 21:19 correctly *buṭlānēh*, (whereas in Gen. 2:2-3 he renders *wᵉnāḥ*). In Ezra 4:21-24 the complete stoppage of work at the temple, caused by the interference of local adversaries, is again expressed by *bṭl.*

We have no means of defining the length of the *corvée* period covered by the term *kymm*, nor the intervals at which one was conscripted for *corvée* duties.[18] By inference from Jud. 17:10 we may assume that *kymm* specifies the *annual corvée* quota incumbent upon X and possibly also on his co-reapers. This time-quota could not have been more than a few days, as appears to be the case also in the South-Arabian text. Detaching farmers from their own fields for an extended time during the harvest season would have had disastrous consequences for the national economy. In order to prevent the *corvée* laborer from wasting his

[14] A. F. L. Beeston, *Epigraphic South Arabian Calendars and Dating* (London, 1956), pp. 6-7. We are not concerned here with the specific problems of the terminology used in this document, which is differently interpreted by other scholars.

[15] *Apud* Cross, BULLETIN 165 (Feb., 1962), p. 45, n. 45.

[16] The context makes it quite clear that the Psalmist has in mind the over-zealous, who starts early and quits late, erroneously assuming that diligence ensures success, even when divine protection is absent. For the situation implied cf. Neh. 4:15.

[17] Dr. B. Levine reminds me that also Akk. *baṭālu(m)* often refers to the cessation of work. See: W. v. Soden, *Akkadisches Handwörterbuch, sub voce.*

[18] The probable reference to conscription for the *corvée* in 1 Sam. 8:16 does not specify its length. The *corvée* imposed upon Israel by Solomon, one month out of every three (1 Kg. 5:28), presumably exceeded the norm.

allotted time, and to make sure that the legally circumscribed period was fully utilized, a quota of grain to be reaped had been established. Therefore, when at the time of measuring the laborers' produce Hoshaiah finds X's amount to be short of the quota required, he impounds his garment in order to keep him from returning to his home (which was probably not in *Ḥaṣar 'Asam*) as his fellow conscripts were allowed to do. He deferred X's release and in fact put him under open arrest, until X made up the missing amount. Instead of bowing to this decision, X lodged a complaint with the district governor, who was probably one of the *śārê meleʼket hammelek* (1 Chr. 29:6), and asked for an investigation, maintaining that he had handed in the full quota.

In view of the foregoing analysis we suggest that *kaph* in *kymm* should be explained as a prefixed *kaph veritatis*,[19] and not as a *comparative kaph*. In the case under review here the *kaph* is used to heighten the effect of the recurrently employed *ymm*, and not to weaken it as the comparative *kaph* would do.[20] This same *kaph* asserts, e. g., the exactness of a number in 1 Sam. 9:22 (and possibly also in Judg. 20:31). There *kišelōšîm 'îš* designates a representative group of exactly thirty Israelites to whom Samuel presents Saul, the king elect. 'The thirty' as a designation of a circumscribed body of public functionaries is known from the Bible [21] and also from Egyptian sources.[22] The same *kaph veritatis* may have been employed in Ruth 2:17 to stress the exactness of a quantity. Having threshed her gleanings, Ruth discovers, probably after having measured her grain, that she had gathered *keʼêpāh śeʻōrîm*. The similarity of the setting in the harvest situation makes the comparison of the ostracon with the Book of Ruth especially meaningful. (See also Neh. 5:11, 7:2).

The notion of 'exactness' which is inherent in the *kaph* of *kymm* appears again to be stressed in line 9 where *kaph* is replaced by *zh* (*ymm*). Syntactically this word may be compared with the somewhat doubtful *zeh* in Jud. 5:5. In both cases it could be taken as a relative pronoun which introduces a qualifying statement. Thus in the ostracon *zh ymm* would circumscribe the quantity of the previously referred to 'harvest'—*qāṣîr*.

[19] See Ḳimḥi's comment on Josh. 3:4 and 1 Sam. 9:13. For examples found in West-Semitic inscriptions consult Ch.-F. Jean and J. Hoftijzer, *Dictionnaire des inscriptions sémitiques de l'ouest*, Leiden, 1960, p. 114, *s. v. kaph* (4). To the examples adduced there the following may be added: A. Cowley, *Aramaic Papyri of the Fifth Century B.C.* (Oxford 1923), 7, 8 (p. 20): *kḥsn bbytk (l') 'lt.*

[20] There is some basic similarity between the *kaph veritatis* and the *asseverative kaph*. For a discussion of this latter see: C. R. Gordis, "The Asseverative Kaph in Ugaritic and Hebrew," *Journal of the American Oriental Society* 63 (1943), pp. 176-178.

[21] It may suffice to mention David's 'thirty' (2 Sam. 23; 1 Chr. 11); the reference to Samson's 'thirty companions' who engage him in a riddle contest (Jud. 14:11 ff.), and who, like the 'thirty' sages, possibly referred to in Prov. 22:20, may reflect an Egyptian tradition. See B. Mazar, *Gibbōrê Dāwîd. Encyclopaedia Biblica* (Jerusalem, 1959), pp. 398-400; K. Elliger, "Die dreissig Helden Davids," *Palästinajahrbuch* 31 (1935) pp. 29-75.

[22] The relevant material is quoted by B. Mazar and K. Elliger (see n. 21 above). Further: K. Sethe, *Von Zahlen und Zahlwörtern bei den alten Ägyptern* (Strassburg, 1916), p. 40.

Heb. *zeh* as a particle which stresses a quantity or a number is found e. g. in Gen. 27:36 *wayya'qebēnî zeh pa'amayim.*[23] *zeh* may indicate exactness in Gen. 31:38, 41—*zeh* (*lî*) *'eśrîm šānāh.*[24]

The temporal *k'šr* which opens the clause 'after I had measured my grain,'[25] seems to have overtones of 'although,' as probably also in Gen. 26:29. Thus X would indignantly reiterate what he already had stated previously (l. 6-8): "Although I had measured my reaping, the exact quota, did he take thy servant's garment."

In order to substantiate his claim X offers to call as witnesses his fellow-reapers who are referred to as *'ḥy . . hqṣrm 'ty* (l. 10). The suggested socio-political setting of the document under review leads us to believe that also the term *'ḥy* in this context has a more technical connotation than is implied in the translation "my brethren." In a number of instances in the O. T. *'ḥ* is employed to indicate a fellow-soldier, a comrade-in-arms with a specific unit. The leader of a gang of freebooters in the days of 'Abimelek, Ga'al ben 'Ebed, enters Shechem at the head of *'eḥāw* (Jud. 9:26). The combination *ga'al ben 'ebed we'eḥâw* is used twice more in that story (Jud. 9:31, 41). Similarly David addresses his soldiers, the men of the *gedūd*, as *'eḥāy* (1 Sam. 30:23). Elisha delegates a prophet to call Jehu from *'eḥāw* and to anoint him king over Ephraim (2 Kg. 9:2). The term clearly refers to his fellow-officers in the detachment stationed in Ramoth-Gilead (2 Kg. 9:5). In a post-exilic setting this technical term is used with regard to Nehemiah's soldiers (Neh. 4:17; 5:10, 14) as well as with regard to the men of his adversary Sanballat. In this latter case it is further clarified by the expression *ḥêl šōmerôn* (Neh. 3:34).[26]

The invitation to give evidence is expressed by: *y'nw ly* (l. 10-11). Again we are concerned with a juridical term. When followed by the preposition *be* the evidence is expected to be detrimental to the accused (1 Sam. 12:3; Deut. 31:28; 1 Sam. 8:9; 2 Sam. 1:16; Hos. 5:5, Mic. 6:3), whereas if followed by *le* it is expected to be in his favor.

y'nw ly in the ostracon is a pregnant expression and does not require a direct object. A comparison with Ruth 4:10-11 makes it probable that initially, the full formula may have been *y'nw ly*: *'dm*, i. e. 'we are prepared to be witnesses.' Accordingly we presume that *'mn* in line 11 opens a new sentence. It introduces the accused's declaration: 'not guilty,' and should be compared with the biblical introductory formula *'omnāh* or *'omnām*,[27] rather than with the affirmative response *'āmēn*

[23] Cf. Gen. 43:10; Num. 14:22; 22:28, 32, 33; 24:10; Job 19:3.

[24] Cf. Gen. 45:6; Ex. 22:8; Deut. 2:7; 8:2, 4; Josh. 14:10; Jer. 25:3; Esth. 4:11.

[25] Cf. Jud. 16:22.

[26] Cf. Gen. 31:32, 37, 46, 54, and Levitic terminology, e. g. in 1 Chr. 15-16. *'ḥ* has this specific technical connotation also in the Bar Kokhba documents, both Hebrew and Greek. See e. g. the excerpts quoted in the first report: *Bulletin of the Israel Exploration Society* 25, 1-2 (1961), pp. 57, 59, 66-68, 71, and the remarks of B. Lifschitz on pp. 72-73.

[27] Prof. Cross has suggested to me that this usage may be reflected in some of Jesus' sayings which open with the formula: "Amen, I say to you" (e. g. Matt. 5:18, 26; 8:10; also 6:5; Luke 23:43; John 1:52; 3:3). It is of interest to note that "this specific use of 'Amen' by Jesus is not followed by any apostle or prophet

(Num. 5:21-22; Neh. 5:12-13 etc.).[28] The perfect parallel to X's declaration of innocence, *'mn nqty*, is Achan's confession of guilt: *'omnāh . . . ḥāṭā'tî* (Josh. 7:20). One may further compare Gen. 20:12 and Ruth 3:12 where *'omnāh* and *'omnām* introduce assertions of a legal nature and could be translated: 'I testify . . ." (cf. also 2 Ki. 19:17 = Is. 37:18; Job 19:4-5; 34:12; 36:4; Ps. 58:2).

Since we are dealing with the specific issue of *corvée* obligations it is probable that *nqty* here has the technical meaning "I have absolved myself of the *corvée* duty," rather than "I am innocent" (Cross), or "I am free of g(uilt)" (Naveh). Again the O. T. presents some instances of this specific employment of *nqh*, in the sense of 'exempted' or 'discharged' from *corvée* or military obligations. The connotation of 'exemption' is inherent in Deut. 24:5—*nāqî yihyeh lᵉbêtô šānāh 'eḥāt*— in a law which frees the newly wed husband from military duty for one year. An opposite case is stated in 1 Kg. 15:22: Asa excuses no one— *'ên nāqî*—from *corvée* obligations which he imposes upon Judah. The term carries the notion of 'discharge' in Num. 32:22. Moses promises to the two and the half tribes that settled in Transjordan that they will be discharged of their military obligations after they have assisted the other tribes in the conquest of Cis-Jordan: *wihyîtem nᵉqîyîm mi-yhwh ûmî-yiśrā'ēl.*[29]

In view of this interpretation one doubts whether the word following *nqy* should in fact be restored *m'(šm)*, as proposed by Naveh and accepted by Cross. We should rather expect to find here a word which describes the obligation from which X claims to have discharged himself. What comes to mind is *'lh* which in Gen. 24:41 refers to an imposed obligation, in a context in which *nqh* is also employed: *'āz tinnāqeh mē'ālātî . . . wᵉhāyîtā nāqî mē'ālātî.* Accordingly, one might wish to restore line 12 of the ostracon: *'mn nqty m'(ltk)*[30] *wyqḥ bgdy.*—'I testify that I had discharged myself of what you had imposed on me (lit. your imposition), and he (Hoshaiah, nevertheless) did take my garment.'

In order to clinch the argument X seems to ask for a recount, or a remeasuring of the quantity which he had delivered. This appears to be implied in the expression *w'ml' lśr* (l. 12)[31] Naveh felicitously compares 1 Sam. 18:27, where a similar sentence structure is employed. That passage—*waymal'ūm* (better: *waymallᵉ'ēm*) *lammelek*—certainly should be translated 'and he counted them (the foreskins) out for the king.' X does not offer "to pay whatever may be demanded of him" (Naveh), but rather continues to maintain that he can prove his faultlessness. The missing phrase at the beginning of line 13 therefore again may have

of the early Church" (*Interpreter's Dictionary of the Bible*, I [Philadelphia, 1962], *s. v.* Amen.)

[28] Thus both Naveh and Cross.

[29] *nqh* as a legal term meaning 'to clear (from obligation),' is often found in sales documents. See the recent discussions of the term by J. J. Rabinowitz, *Biblica* 35 (1954), pp. 202-203; Y. Kutscher, *Journal of the American Oriental Society* 74 (1954), p. 247, n. 131; R. Yaron, *Bibliotheca Orientalis* 15 (1958), pp. 17 ff.

[30] Or, possibly, *m'(lty)*.

[31] Thus Naveh. Cross reads *w'm l'*.

told of the full quota which he had delivered. Accordingly, it may have ended with (*kym*) *m*.[32]

The restoration of the concluding passage is altogether conjectural, since many possibilities are open. We suggest the reading:

13 *kym*]*m* *'lw rḥ*
14 [*mt lhšb bgd* ']*bdk wl' tdḥnw*[33]
15 [*mpnk*]

(13) Pray, be merc[iful (14) and return your se]rvant's garment, and do not drive him away (15) [from before you].

B

On the basis of palaeography and the stratigraphy of the site, both Naveh and Cross concluded that the ostracon must be dated in the last third of the seventh century B. C., i. e. in the reign of King Josiah. Thus the letter would provide welcome information on events unknown from other sources, namely " that Josiah had established a coastal fort far south of Megiddo,"[34] obviously as an outpost against Egypt. So far we had lacked any proof of a military and economic expansion of Judah under Josiah to the southern coastal area, except for one reference in 2 Chr. 34:6 to Josiah's imposing his cultic reform also on Simeon, a reference which is not corroborated by the parallel account in 2 Kings. Nowhere is Josiah credited with the establishment of a *corvée* system which, as was suggested here, is the setting of our document. It is for this reason that we have to turn to other biblical evidence, pertaining to other periods, in order to fill in the picture.

The political and economic situation which appears to be reflected in the new ostracon may be compared, to some advantage, with the conditions brought about by Uzziah and Hezekiah, kings of Judah who preceded Josiah.

In his attempt to restore the Davidic empire by reuniting Ephraim with Judah, Hezekiah fortified Jerusalem and strengthened the national economy of Judah. He expanded grain-storage facilities, possibly in expectation of an Assyrian attack, and considerably increased livestock in Judah. At the same time he built the required enclosures. He provided " store-houses for grain, wine and oil, and enclosures for animals and flocks. And he prepared for himself settlements, and abundant flocks and cattle. . . ." (2 Chr. 32:28-29, cp. 2 Kg. 20:13; Is. 39:2). Now the traditional area for such operations is the northern Negeb, where two generations prior to Hezekiah Uzziah had carried out similar plans: "And he (Uzziah) built towers in the grazing-land (*midbār*), and hewed out many cisterns for he had much cattle " (2 Chr. 26:10). Thus " his name spread into Egypt " (2 Chr. 26:8).

[32] Both Naveh and Cross identify the letter, of which only traces are left, as a *nun*. However Cross admits that " *mem* is possible " (*op. cit.*, n. 38).

[33] Reading thus with Cross, and not *tdhm.n*, as proposed by Naveh.

[34] Cross, *op. cit.*, p. 42. Similarly Naveh, *op. cit.*, p. 139; *Israel Exploration Journal* 12 (1962), pp. 27-32.

Such economic expansion must have entailed recruitment of a labor force, based on a nucleus of permanent settlers in the king's service. Thus it is reported of Uzziah that he had "farmers in the lowlands and in the plains, and terrace-farmers in the foothills (*karmel*)[35] and in the mountains" (2 Chr. 26:10). This skeleton force most probably was strengthened by conscripted *corvée* laborers in seasons of intensified agricultural activities, such as sowing and reaping.[36] A prerequisite for conscription is a census. Now 1 Chr. 4:41 records that Hezekiah had registered the population of Judah, or possibly only the population of the southern districts of his realm. It appears likely that this census was preparatory to the resettlement of Judahites in the territory which Hezekiah had reconquered from the Philistines (2 Kg. 18:8), after it had been lost to them in the days of Ahaz (2 Chr. 28:18; cf. Is. 14:28-32). It cannot be established for certain that this expansion triggered the movement of the Simeonites into the deep south, which is reported in proximity to the census account (1 Chr. 4:41-43). However such a connection seems likely.[37]

We may assume that Josiah followed a similar policy, foreseeing an open conflict with Egypt. The dating of the ostracon in Josiah's reign may throw some additional light on the writer's insistence that he had delivered his grain according to an exact quota. It appears that neither he nor Hoshaiah intentionally misrepresented facts, but rather that their dispute arose out of a genuine difficulty, namely a difference between the weights or vessels employed by them which resulted from the non-existence of standard measures. Now in the second half of the seventh century there appear in Palestine, in appreciable measures, stamped jar-handles.[38] They come from different sites in Judah, and probably belonged to vessels which had been especially manufactured in royal potteries or wineries.[39] The majority of these standard jars are connected with administrative centers in southern Judah: Hebron, Ziph, Sokoh, *Mmšt*, which either were the places from which they came or to which they were sent.[40] It has been conjectured that these vessels were

[35] We follow here a suggestion made orally by Prof. B. Mazar, that *krm* (noun and verb) in O. T. Hebrew, and also in other West Semitic languages, often do not refer to vinegrowing, but have the wider connotation of terrace-agriculture.

[36] 1 Sam. 8:14.16 See: I. Mendelsohn, "Samuel's Denunciation of Kingship," BULLETIN 143 (Oct., 1956), pp. 17-22; S. Talmon, "*Mišpāṭ Hammelek*," *Sefer Biram, Publications of the Israel Bible Society* (Jerusalem, 1957), pp. 45-56. We surmise that a reference to the *corvée* is also contained in Lachish Letter 13, 1 where the words *l'št ml'kh* are followed by the name of Semakyahu who apparently was in charge of such activities, as may be implied by the reference to him in letter 4, 6 (see also *supra*). For *ml'kh* in the specific connotation of 'king's labor' cf. 1 Chr. 4:23; 26:30. The very combination *'šh ml'kh* in this context is found 27:26.

[37] See B. Maisler (Mazar), "Sennacherib's Campaign in Judah," *Eretz Israel* II (Jerusalem 1952), pp. 170 ff. (Hebrew).

[38] Y. Yadin, "Ancient Judean Weights and the Date of the Samaria Ostraca," *Scripta Hierosolymitana* 8 (1961), pp. 17-22.

[39] A discussion of these stamps is presented by P. W. Lapp, "Late Royal Seals in Judah," BULLETIN 158 (Apr., 1960), pp. 11-12. There the relevant earlier literature is quoted.

[40] See: *Encyclopaedia Biblica* (Jerusalem 1954-58) vol. II, p. 912, *s. v.* "Ziph"; vol. III, p. 81, *s. v. ḥōtām*.

commissioned by the Judean kings of that period, especially by Josiah, but possibly already by Manasseh (and Hezekiah), in an attempt to introduce standard measures which would be commonly accepted and would curb dishonestly in the payment of taxes. It is therefore extremely suggestive that at the site of the fortress a number of ostraca were found which may bear witness to the assumed endeavor to establish standard measures.[41] Two ostraca (nos. 3 and 4) are inscribed with four vertical strokes; no. 4 adds *shin,* i. e. 4 shekels. No. 5 has *šq*, which may be completed to read 'shekel'; no. 6 has, in addition to the inscription 'four (shekels of) silver' the two signs which are known on weights as the designation of 4 shekels. Naveh's conclusion that "four shekels were used at Meṣad Ḥashavyahu as a common unit of weight is altogether convincing. This is further substantiated by the discovery, near the doorway, of "a dome-shaped stone weight of 44, 82 gr., bearing the same signs as the four-shekel weights known from other Judean sites." It stands to reason that disagreements between tax collectors and taxpayers over the accuracy of the amounts delivered in kind would frequently arise in the initial period of the introduction of new standard measures. Against this background the controversy mirrored in our ostracon—especially the demand for re-measuring—has an exceedingly realistic ring.

[41] All references are to J. Naveh, "More Hebrew Inscriptions From Meṣad Ḥashavyahu," *Israel Exploration Journal,* 12 (1962), pp. 27-32. Cf. R. B. Y. Scott, "The Shekel Sign on Stone Weights," BULLETIN 153 (Feb., 1959), pp. 32-35.

THE GEZER CALENDAR AND THE SEASONAL CYCLE OF ANCIENT CANAAN*

A fixed Calendar, Emile Duerkheim once wrote, "expresses the rhythm of the collective activities while at the same time its function is to assure their regularity."[1] By virtue of these characteristics an analysis of the calendar of a given society, or even an investigation into a specific and detailed calendar problem will often reveal aspects of social and economic life that surpass the mere "calendaric" nature of the initial enquiry. The present paper illustrates this point. An attempt to clarify the meaning of a technical term in the Gezer Calendar (henceforth: G.C.), by means of comparing it with similar Hebrew expressions in the O.T. and in the literature of the Judean Covenanters, as well as with pertinent Akkadian and South-Arabic terminology, leads to some general remarks on the relative importance of flax-growing and grass-cropping in Palestinian agriculture. The emerging economic factors are then shown to be actually mirrored in O.T. narratives and also in biblical imagery. The resulting new insight into the seasonal cycle of Canaan provides a key for the better understanding of the "calendaric realism" underlying some prophetic oracles. It further reveals the widespread and continuous employment of some technical agricultural terms which were perpetuated in the Near East since the second millennium B.C.E.

Palaeographically, and orthographically, the G.C. is a product of the tenth century B.C.E.,[2] as a comparison with the Phoenician inscriptions from Byblus shows.[3] Archaeological and historical considerations further help to limit this

* The author's thanks are due to Prof. B. Mazar who read a typescript of this paper, and offered many valuable comments which then were incorporated in the final draft.

1. *The Elementary Forms of Religious Life*, Transl. from the French (London 1911), p. 11.
2. Cp. W.F. Albright, "The Gezer Calendar," *BASOR* 92 (1943), pp. 16–26. There also previous discussions of the G.C. are reviewed. Cp. further: D. Diringer, *Le Inscrizioni Antico-Ebraiche Palestinesi* (1934), pp. 1–20; the article "Gezer" in *Encyclopaedia Biblica*, II (1954); W. Wirgin, "The Calendar Tablet from Gezer," *Eretz Israel* 6 (1960), pp. 9–12 (Hebrew).
3. See: B. Maisler (Mazar), "The Phoenician Inscriptions of Byblus and the Development of the Phoenician-Hebrew Alphabet," *Leshonenu* 14 (1946), pp. 166–181, esp. pp. 178–180

time-span and enable us to ascribe the G.C. to the reign of Solomon. In all probability the writing of this document did not precede the rebuilding of Gezer as an Israelite fortress by Solomon in the latter part of his reign (1 Kgs 9:15–17), and it cannot be dated later than the destruction of that city by Pharoah Shishak in the fifth year of Rehoboam's reign (1 Kgs 14:25–26; and esp. 2 Chr 12:2–3), *ca.* 918 B.C.E.[4] Accordingly, it may be assumed that the calendar was written by an Israelite in approximately 950–925 B.C.E. This proposed dating may give an indication of the purpose for which the G.C. was composed. Under Solomon's reign Gezer was a provincial center in which were settled Levites who served the king in an administrative capacity.[5] One may surmise that the G.C. is an official document which presents in proper chronological sequence the main farming seasons in the district of the lowlands of ancient Palestine. Most probably it was drawn up for the purpose of tax-collections on behalf of the royal administration.[6] The importance of such a document may explain the fact that its writer saw fit to sign it with his name, which, unfortunately, is only partially preserved. To us the G.C. presents a true picture of an Israelite farmer's occupations throughout the year.

As is well known, the calendar enumerates eight periods starting with the "ingathering of summer fruit," *i.e.* roughly before the beginning of the rain-season. Four of the seasons are designated by the term *yrḥw*, which Albright explained as a dual form indicative of a two-months span of time.[7] The remaining four seasons are apparently of only one-month duration and are called *yrḥ*.[8] Consequently the G.C. encompasses practically a twelve-month year.[9]

(Hebrew); W.F. Albright, "The Phoenician Inscriptions of the Tenth Century B.C. from Byblus," *JAOS* 67 (1947), pp. 153–160, esp. p. 160.

4. On Shishak's campaign see: B. Mazar, "The Campaign of Pharaoh Shishak to Palestine," *Suppl. to VT*, IV (1957), pp. 57–66.
5. W.F. Albright, "The List of Levitic Cities," *L. Ginzberg Jubilee Volume, English Section* (1945), pp. 49–73; B. Mazar, "The Cities of the Priests and the Levites," *Suppl. to VT*, VII (1959), pp. 193–205.
6. For other interpretations see Albright, *op. cit.*, p. 19; Wirgin, *op. cit.* There also the new proposal is made to regard the G.C. as an incantation tablet.
7. Cp. H.L. Ginsberg, in: *BIES* 2 (1935), p. 49; J.B. Segal, "*Yrḥ* in the Gezer Calendar," *JSS* 7 (1962), p. 221, who, though, takes the sign after ירח as a numerical symbol for two, and not as the letter *waw*.
8. Albright, *ib.*, pp. 22–23 reads *yarḥo* and *yarḥew*, assuming that the possessive pron. sing. and plur. respectively were appended to the noun (cp. Num 28:14; 1 Kgs 5:7; Isa 66:23). A comparable form appears to be extant in Sabaean where a decree can be dated by "its month" – *wrḫhw-ḏ-X.* Quoted according to A.F.L. Beeston, *Epigraphic South Arabian Calendars and Dating* (London 1956), p. 1 and note 2.
9. Some earlier opinions assumed that the G.C. mentions only eight months. Cp.

If indeed the calendar is connected with a system of tax-collection, it would be admirably appropriate in Solomon's reign. In 1 Kgs 5:7–8 are recorded the major types of victuals which were delivered as taxes by the populace to the royal storage houses: provisions for the king and his entourage, and fodder for the royal cavalry. It may be assumed that the former kind of tax was paid during the seasons of אסף, קצר וכל, possibly זמר and קץ. The latter tax which was composed of שעורים and תבן (*ib.* v. 8), *i.e.* of barley and (green) fodder (cp. Isa 11:7; 65:25 and Gen 24:25, 32; Jud 19:19: תבן and מספוא), most probably would have been paid in the seasons לקש, עצד פשת and קצר שערם. גזי המלך (Am 7:1) "the king's cutting" is probably another term which pertains to taxes levied on green fodder.

The underlying intent to record taxation-seasons may explain why in the G.C. ירחו זרע was not given a line by itself, but was appended to ירחו אסף. The "season of sowing" certainly is not an appropriate time for the collection of taxes.[10] Thus, the roster would enumerate altogether seven seasons in which seven types of taxes were collected.

Following Albright's suggestion that both ירחו[11] and ירח (defective writing) contain the poss. pron. pl. (dual) and sing. respectively (see n. 8), I would propose that the pronouns refer to items of taxes which may have been recorded on the now missing right-hand part of the tablet. Thus a complete line would have read:

[tax X] – its period [literally: one month] is the [time] of barley harvest
[tax Y] – its period [literally: one month] is the [time] of grape harvest
[tax Z] – its period [literally: two months] is the [time] of fruit harvest

From among the specific names of the eight agricultural seasons enumerated in G.C. it is ירח עצד פשת which has caused difficulties to interpreters. The noun עצד as such so far is not known from any other Hebrew source. However, another word from the same root – מעצד – is employed twice in the O.T., albeit in doubtful context (Isa 44:12; Jer 10:3).[12] The root עצד was equated

W. Lidzbarski, *PEFQ* (1909), p. 28; G.B. Gray, *ib.*, p. 30; S. Daiches, *ib.*, p. 117; G. Dalman, *ib.*, p. 119; Joh. Lindblom, "Der Sogenannte Bauernkalender von Gezer," *Acta Academicae Aboensis. Humaniora* 7 (1931), pp. 1–25.

10. The combination of וזרעיכם with וכרמיכם in 1 Sam 8:15, paralleling ואת שדתיכם ואת כרמיכם in the preceding verse, shows that the king will collect a tenth – יעשר – from the "seed crops and vine crops" or "grain fields," not from the "seeds". See: P.K. McCarter, Jr., *I Samuel, AB* 8 (New York 1980), p. 153; H.P. Smith, *The Books of Samuel, ICC* (Edinburgh 1912), p. 57 *et alii*.
11. Grammatically the form would be comparable to חדשו in 1 Kgs 5:7, as suggested by Albright (*ib.*), but in content the two are different.
12. It has been suggested to read in Isa 10:33 במעצד for MT: במערצה (see BH *ad loc.*).

with Acc. *eṣêdu*, Aram. חצד and Arab. *ḥáṣada* – "to reap (grain)." This equation shows clearly in Jer 5:13 where MT קצירך is rendered by TJ חצדך. L. Finkelstein discovered the verb עצד in a quotation from the Tannaitic work *Torat Kohanim* (or *Sifra*ʾ), preserved in a commentary that is ascribed to Rabbi Samson of Sens. In the majority of mss. of *Torat Kohanim* other words, such as חוצד and קוצר, all meaning "to reap," are substituted for עוצד in that quotation.[13]

The other constituent word of the designation of that season, פשת, was explained as a defective spelling of biblical פשתה – "flax." This, more than independent philological considerations, may explain Albright's preference for the equation of עצד with Arab. *ʾáḍada* – "to lop off" or the like, over any other derivation, since this verb would best describe the harvesting of flax.[14] Accordingly, ירח עצד פשת is generally taken to mean "the season of flax-hoeing."[15]

This explanation encounters serious difficulties. The first of these is of a philological nature. None of the semitic verbs with which Hebr. עצד was compared actually refers to "the hoeing of flax," with the one possible exception of Arab. *ʾáḍada*. Aram. חצד[16] and Arab. *ḥáṣada*[17] indicate activities pertaining to grain-crops. They describe the "cutting" of the standing grain with an instrument, usually a sickle. The same can be said of Akk. *eṣêdu*.[18] S. Daiches, sensing this difficulty, therefore proposed to render *eṣêdu* simply by "ingather," thus giving it a meaning wide enough to include also the reaping of flax.[19] Furthermore, in the quotation from *Torat Kohanim* already referred to, עצד describes a manner of reaping (plucking) grain, in a comment on Lev 19:19, a passage that again deals with the sowing of grain. The flax-plant is not mentioned in that context, though flax-yarn is implied in the concept of שאטנז.

13. L. Finkelstein, "A Talmudic Note on the Word for Cutting Flax in the Gezer Calendar," *BASOR* 94 (1944), pp. 28–29.
14. *BASOR* 94 (1944), p. 28, n. 2.
15. Cp. Lidzbarski, Gray, Daiches, Dalman, *op. cit.*; Albright, *BASOR* 92 (1943), p. 22 and many others.
16. Thus this verb is employed in Onq. to translate קציר in Gen 45:6, and in the Targum of Isaiah in 18:4. Cp. further: M. Jastrow, *Dictionary etc.*, I (1943), *s.v.* חצד.
17. G. Dalman, *Arbeit und Sitte in Palästina* (1924), I, p. 6; II, pp. 135, 157 and glossary p. 321; P. Haupt, "Der Korngrünfutterschnitt-monat," *OLZ* 18 (1915), p. 301.
18. *CAD s.v. eṣêdu*; B. Landsberger, "Jahreszeiten im Sumerisch-Akkadischen," *JNES* 8 (1949), pp. 248–297.
19. S. Daiches, "Notes on the Gezer Calendar," *PEFQ* (1909), p. 116. Cp. also G.B. Gray's remarks, *ib.*, p. 31; H.P. Müller, "Notizen zu althebräischen Inschriften I," *UF* 2 (1970), pp. 229–231.

Hence we have as yet no evidence for the use of עצד in Hebrew literature with the specific connotation of "flax-hoeing" or "flax-plucking."[20]

To these purely philological comments may be added the following note. By inference from the seasons preceding and succeeding it, it can be established that ירח עצד פשת approximately coincided with the months Adar–Nissan of the Hebrew lunar calendar and with March–April in the Julian solar year. Now this season cannot be considered a suitable time for the ingathering of flax which in Babylonia, at least in one case, was only sown in the month of Adar (bTal Meg. 5b). This, however, may have been exceptionally late.

In Palestine flax was sown somewhat earlier. Again according to Talmudic evidence, flax could be sold on the stalk by Purim, *i.e.* in the month of Adar, since at that time the plants were already developed enough to allow for an estimate of the expectable crop.[21]

Of even more weight than these considerations is the fact that not once in O.T. literature the actual cultivation of flax in Palestine is mentioned. In contrast to the complex legal system affecting all other field- and tree-products – "tithe" (Lev 27:30; Num 18:21, 26; Deut 14:23–26), "*pēʾāh* and gleanings" (Lev 19:9–10; 23:22) and "leftovers" (Deut 24:19–22) – we observe a surprising lack of legal prescriptions dealing with the flax-plant and its crops, though flax can be grown, and in antiquity actually was grown for the production of edible oil.[22] The only law pertaining specifically to flax – כלאים or שאטנז – is not concerned with the plant as such, but forbids the interweaving of already spun flax-yarn with wool-thread (Lev 19:19; Deut 22:11; cp. further, Hos 2:7, 11).[23]

20. Cp. further S. Lieberman's comments in: *Tosefta Kifshutah Zeraʿim*, pp. 139–140; *Peʾah*, p. 46. However Lieberman quotes jTal. Meg. IV, 1 (74b): זרע דכיתן וזרע ליה וחצר ליה, equating חצד and עצד, to show that עצד can apply also to flax. He concurs with the explanation of ירח עצד פשת in the G.C., as "the month of flax-hoeing."
21. jTal Bab. Meṣ. V, 9 (10c); J. Felix, *Agriculture in Eretz-Israel in the Times of the Mishnah and the Talmud* (Jerusalem 1963), pp. 149, 197 (Hebrew). In Egypt flax was sown "by the middle of November and could be pulled within 110 days", R.J. Forbes, *Studies in Ancient Technology*, IV (1956), p. 29. See further O. Heer, *Flachs und Flachskultur im Altertum* (1872), pp. 4, 19; G. Horst, "The Plagues of Egypt," *ZAW* 70 (1958), p. 49.
22. Cp. I. Löw, *Aramäische Pflanzennamen* (1881), p. 406, no. 44; p. 411, no. 90; A. Lucas, *Ancient Egyptian Materials and Industries*, 3rd edition (1948), p. 385; R.J. Forbes, *op. cit.*, p. 28: "The seed capsules were used as food (in Egypt) even before the fibres of the plant were utilized." It is this fact which is reflected in the comparison of the taste and the external appearance of the "mannah" with that of flax-seed cakes (Num 11:7–8). See further F.E. Zeuner, "Cultivation of Plants" in Ch. Singer–E.J. Holmyard–A.R. Hall, *A History of Technology*, I (1964), pp. 358, 372; T. Grant, *ib.*, p. 448.
23. In a written communication to the present author, Miss Louisa Bellinger of the Textile

This lack of 'flax-laws' is matched by the conspicuous absence of references to flax-growing from O.T. narratives and from biblical imagery. Seventeen out of twenty instances in which the term פשתה or פשתים is mentioned either deal with the already processed weaving-material (Lev 13:48, 52; Hos 2:7, 11; Prov 31:13), or with a finished product: a garment (Lev 13:47, 59; Deut 22:11; Jer 13:1; Ezek 44:17, 18²), a wick (Isa 42:3; 43:17), a rope (Jdg 15:14; Ezek 40:3). Linen cloth – בד – is mentioned more than twenty times. בוץ, another term for a linen-fabric, occurs eight times, all of them in late biblical writings (Ezek 27:16; Esth 1:6, 8:15; 1 Chr 4:21, 15:27; 2 Chr 2:13, 3:14, 5:12), where it replaces the earlier שש.[24] It is probable that these terms pertain to varieties of fine linen which in Israel were used almost exclusively by royalty and cultic personnel, evidencing a possible Egyptian influence on Israelite customs.[25] פשתים, on the other hand, in biblical language seems to refer to a cheaper kind of linen, more commonly used (Lev 13:47, 49; Deut 22:11; Jer 13:1), although Ezekiel employs the terms with reference to priestly garments (Ezek 44:17, 18). Only once is the flax-plant and once the processing of flax brought up, and, most significantly, both times in literary compositions with an Egyptian setting (Ex 9:31²; Isa 19:9). Flax-growing in Egypt is abundantly attested in extra-biblical, especially in Egyptian sources, epigraphic and visual.[26] Against all these we find only one instance in which "flax-stalks" that had actually grown in Canaan are mentioned (Jos 2:6), if the term פשתי העץ employed there may be identified with עצי הפשתים, as was done already in G: ἔω τῇ λινοκαλάμῃ, and in rabbinic literature (bTal Shab. 27b).[27]

Museum in Washington considers the possibility that the biblical injunction proscribes the "spinning" together of wool and linen-fibers. Such threads as yet have not been found in the Ancient East, whereas materials "woven" of wool and linen threads are not infrequent.

24. Cp. J. Vergote, *Joseph en Egypte* (Louvain 1959), p. 119. That בוץ is of late Hebrew word-stock may also be deduced from the reading במעיל בוץ in 1 Chr 15:27, as against בכל עוז in 2 Sam 6:14.
25. בוץ – "byssos" was already identified as linen by Herodotus who reports that Egyptian priests used to dress in byssos garments (II, 86).
26. Cp. W. Wreszinski, *Atlas zur altägyptischen Kulturgeschichte* (1923–26), pls. 189, 193, 432; H.F. Lutz, *Textiles and Costumes Among the Peoples of the Ancient East* (1923), pp. 10 ff.; O. Heer, *op. cit.*, pp. 2–5; A.S. Moore, *Linen* (n.d.), pp. 1–4; A. Lucas, *op. cit.*, pp. 166–168; J.B. Pritchard, *ANEP* (1954), pls. 92, 142, 143; R.J. Forbes, *op. cit.* and additional bibliography quoted there. The prominence of flax in the economy of Egypt was also well known in later times. A midrash in Ber. Rab. (ed. Theodor-Albeck, p. 142) connects the name of the antediluvian river פישון (Gen 2:16) with פשתים. Then it goes on to identify this river with the Nile whose waters nourish the flax and make it grow (Isa 19:9).
27. The presence of flax-stalks on the roof of Rahab's house may indicate that the plants had been left there to dry (Forbes, *op. cit.*, p. 32) or else to be dew-retted (L. Bellinger). The

The assumed absence of flax from among Palestinian crops is also suggested by the following observation. As already mentioned the only reference to פשתה as a plant in the O.T. has an Egyptian setting, and therefore should not be adduced as evidence for flax-cultivation in biblical Palestine.[28] The author of Exod 9:22–26 purports to give a plastic description of the afflictions that the hail, one of the ten plagues, brought upon Egypt. Man and beast that were in the open were slashed by the hailstones. So were all the plants. This latter category is represented by the two main divisions of agricultural growths: "the hail smote all the field herbs and broke all trees" (*ib.* v. 25). Then this somewhat general statement is amplified in what could well be an editorial comment. In an annalist-like fashion we are told in detail which field crops actually were destroyed by the hail and which escaped damage: "The flax and the barley were damaged because the barley was (already in the) אביב (stage, *i.e.* ripe) and the flax was (already in the) גבעול (stage)," *i.e.* probably in its bloom, and therefore was adversely affected by the hail. However, "the wheat and the spelt were not damaged because they are a late growth" (cp. Mishnah *Shebíᶜít* 6, 4), and therefore could yet recover. The Palestinian writer of Exodus obviously took "flax" to represent, together with "barley," "wheat" and "spelt" (*kussemet*), the most important and most typical cultivated crops of Egypt, which, in fact, was the case.[29] For this reason it is rather striking that in the only two other instances in the O.T. in which "barley, wheat and spelt"[30] are mentioned in this combination, and in which, together with other grain varieties, they are representative of characteristic Palestinian crops, "flax" — פשתה — is most significantly omitted (Isa 28:23–29;[31] Ezek 4:9). One could actually say that in listing the main activities pertaining to field cultivation for the purpose of prophetic imagery the author of Isa 28:23–27 may have paraphrased some Israelite farmer's manual, which to a certain degree is reminiscent of the G.C. The recurring omission of flax can hardly be explained as a mere coincidence. Rather it appears to be indicative of local conditions.

stems of the flax-plant are used for basketry (R.J. Forbes, *op. cit.*, p. 28; T. Grant, *loc. cit.*, *supra* n. 22).

28. K. Galling, *Biblisches Reallexikon, HAT* (Tübingen 1937), col. 300.
29. See: A. Erman–H. Ranke, *Aegypten* (Tübingen 1923), p. 522, 72; G. Hort, "The Plagues of Egypt," *ZAW* 70 (1958), pp. 49 ff.
30. Prof. Mazar informs me that "spelt," dating from the time of the United Monarchy, was found in considerable quantities during the excavation at ᶜEn-Gedi.
31. For a discussion of this pericope see L.J. Liebreich, "The Parable Taken from the Farmer's Labors in Isaiah XXVIII, 23–29," *Tarbiz*, XXIV (1955), pp. 126–128 (Hebrew).

It is of interest to note that also in Ugaritic texts, published to date, *pšt* or *pštm* refer exclusively to linen-cloth, or to finished linen garments and never to a plant.[32] We tend to conclude that into Ugarit too linen was imported, possibly from Egypt, already processed. This assumption most certainly would apply to Tyre and probably to the whole of Phoenicia. Thus in the eleventh century B.C. Wen-Amon reports that at his request the Egyptian officials Ne-su-Ba-neb-Ded and Ta-net-Amon sent to the Prince of Byblus, among other merchandise, "10 pieces of royal linen (and) 10 *kherd* of good Upper Egyptian linen," in partial payment for timber which was to be shipped to Egypt. Wen-Amon himself received inter alia "5 pieces of clothing in good Upper Egyptian linen (and) 5 *kherd* of good Upper Egyptian linen."[33]

Phoenicia always has been dependent on her *Hinterland* for agricultural products. This fact is vividly depicted in Ezekiel's detailed description of Tyre's middle-man economy. The main victuals were imported from predominantly agricultural Judah and Israel (Ezek 27:17; cp. 1 Kgs 5:23–25; 2 Chr 2:14). Wool came from Aram (Ezek 27:18). Other weaving materials, and woven or spun cloth, were brought from Mediterranean countries (*ib.* vv. 16, 19, 20), and embroidery linen (שש ברקמה) from Egypt (*ib.* v. 7).[34] These served as raw-material for a flourishing Phoenician finishing-industry. The materials were dyed and expertly made into garments which then became an export item, and were also included in tribute payments.[35] These facts probably were well-

32. Ch. Virolleaud, *Le Palais Royal d'Ugarit*, II (1959), *texts* 112, 1, 4 (p. 146); 113, 8, 9 (p. 147); 115, 3 (p. 148); 106, 8, 25 (p. 137); 107, 11 (p. 142); 114, 4 (p. 147).

33. "The Journey of Wen-Amon to Phoenicia," translated by J.A. Wilson, *ANET*, p. 28a. See further: A.S. Moore, *op. cit.*, pp. 4–5; A.J. Warden, *The Linen Trade – Ancient and Modern* (1867), pp. 176–177.

34. B. Mazar, convincingly argues that the "Oracles against Tyre" in Ezek 27–28 reflect conditions which prevailed in Phoenicia in the tenth or the beginning of the ninth century B.C. They are in fact, a paraphrase on a Phoenician national epic. This dating would enhance the relevance of that document for the problem under discussion. See: B. Mazar, "The Philistines and the Rise of Israel and Tyre", *Proceedings of the Israel Academy of Sciences*, Vol. I (Jerusalem, 1964).

35. They are always mentioned in the reports on booty or on tribute received by Assyrian kings from Upper Mesopotamia and Palestine, *e.g.* in the annals of Ashurnasirpal II (*ANET* 275–276), Shalmaneser III (*ib.*, p. 280a), Adad-Nirari III (*ib.*, 282a), Tiglath-Pileser III (*ib.*, pp. 283–284), and Sennacherib I, in the version published by D.D. Luckenbill, *The Annals of Sennacherib* (1924), p. 61. The enumeration given there of "multicoloured garments, linen garments, purple (dyed) wool" among other items is replaced in the final edition of the Annals by the summary "all kinds of valuable treasures". Thus in the Oriental Institute Prism, published by A.L. Oppenheim in *ANET* (1950), pp. 287–288, and in the Taylor-Prism, published by H.G. Rawlinson, *The Cuneiform Inscriptions of Western Asia* vol. 1 (1861), pls. 37–42. See further A.L. Oppenheim's remark in *ANET*, 275, n. 6.

known in antiquity. In the list of tributes which he received from the kings of Syria and Palestine, Tiglath-Pileser III expressly differentiates between "garments of their *native* (industries) (being made of) dark purple wool" and "linen garments with multicolored trimmings" which apparently he did not consider to be native in these parts.[36]

Solomon employed a Tyrian craftsman for the artistic finishing of objects in his temple (2 Chr 2:12–13; cp. 1 Kgs 7:14 where the art of working in fabrics is not mentioned among the many accomplishments of this artisan). In the description of the building of the Tabernacle the very same tasks were performed by two Israelites, Beṣalel of the tribe of Judah and Oholiab of the tribe of Dan. This appears to be significant. The continuous tradition of such workmanship in Judah is attested by the important note in 1 Chr 4:21 which tells of fine-linen manufacturers in Judean Mareshah. For Dan it is indicated by the fact that Solomon's head-artisan descended on his mother's side from the district of Naftali (1 Kgs 7:14), or more precisely, from the town of Dan-Laish (2 Chr 2:13) which was situated in this district.[37] No final conclusion can be drawn from these isolated bits of information. However they seem to point to the import of materials and of technical skill into Dan-Naftali from their northern neighbor Phoenicia, and into Judah from its southern neighbor Egypt.

Linen was an important export-article of the Egyptian industry. It is also mentioned as an item of tribute paid to Esarhaddon by Egypt: *sa(d)-din bu-u-ṣi*.[38] It stands to reason that in Palestine centers of linen-manufacture would develop preponderantly in the south due to its proximity to Egypt. The families of traditional fine-linen (בוץ) manufacturers in Mareshah, who were in the service of the king (1 Chr 4:21; cp. 1 Chr 26:30, 32), therefore cannot be adduced in evidence for the actual cultivation of flax in biblical Palestine.[39] This would have been economically futile in view of the inferiority of flax retted by dew – which would have been the prevalent technique in Palestine – to the easily accessible Nile-watered-retted Egyptian flax[40] which was of a much superior quality.[41]

36. Building inscription, translated by A.L. Oppenheim, *ANET*, p. 282.
37. See: B. Mazar, "The Cities of Dan," *IEJ* 10 (1960) 65–77, esp. 71.
38. S.R. Borger, *AFO Beiheft* 9 (1956) 101; *ANET*, p. 293b, n. 1.
39. Dalman, *op. cit.*, V 23, 29; R.J. Forbes, *op. cit.* 32. In Egyptian sources an "overseer of the king's flax" is mentioned. See: Erman–Ranke, *op. cit.* 98.
40. Traditional exegesis of Gen 2:11 betrays a knowledge of this fact. Explaining the name of the river Pishon, *Gen. Rab.* (ed. Theodor-Albeck, p. 142) says: "the name of the first [river] is Pishon which grows flax and its waters run smoothly." Sam Targ, Rashi, Ibn Ezra and Saadya *ad loc.* identify Pishon as the Nile.
41. Communicated to me by Miss L. Bellinger who was led to conclude that the waters of the

Though fully aware of the pitfalls entailed in an argument *e silentio* we feel that it can be stated provisionally that in biblical times flax was not cultivated to an extensive measure, if at all, in Palestine (or on the Mediterranean coast to its north). The evidence in favor of this conclusion cannot be outweighed by the discovery of remains of flax-seed in fifteenth century B.C.E. pits at Tell Beit Mirsim,[42] or by the disputable עצד פשת in the G.C., as R.J. Forbes would have it: "the recently excavated Gezer Calendar points to the importance of flax cultivation in the Jordan Valley (*sic*!) which did not decline before the fourth century A.D."[43]

It is worthy of remark that the picture emerging from the analysis of the biblical sources is corroborated by the fact that flax is not usually grown in modern Palestine. All authorities are unanimous on this count. In his classic book *Die Flora der Juden* (1929), I. Löw states categorically: "heute ist der Flachsbau in ganz Palästina ausgestorben" (vol. I, p. 212). The same was observed by G. Dalman who adduces also other authorities to bear out the statement: "linum usitatissitum von mir nie in Palästina angebaut gesehen."[44] Macalister who endeavoured to illustrate the agricultural basis of the G.C. by comparing its arrangement with the order of agricultural activities in Abu Šûše, an Arab village adjoining the site of ancient Gezer, failed to mention flax altogether (*Gezer* II 24 ff.). Dalman again explains this remarkable omission by stating that flax-growing has disappeared completely from modern Palestine (*op. cit.* I 8). The same holds true for modern Syria[45] and Persia.[46] This disappearance cannot be considered accidental. True, flax is mentioned fairly often in rabbinic literature (*e.g. b Tal. Bab. Bat.* 84b, 86b; *Meg.* 5b; *jMeg.* 4,1

Nile contained ingredients which made the flax retted in them turn out soft and pliable.

42. This information was given to me by Prof. W.F. Albright.
43. R.J. Forbes, *op. cit.*, p. 32; K. Galling, *loc. cit.* states with laudable accuracy: "Der in stark bewässertem Land anbaubare Flachs . . . ist in Pal. *vereinzelt* geflanzt worden."
44. *Dalman, op. cit.*, II, p. 298; V, pp. 19–20, 23; cp. also R.P.H. Vincent, "Un calendrier agricole Israélite," *RB* 6 (1909), pp. 261, 269 *post scriptum*.
45. The British Naval Intelligence Report on the Economy of the Middle East has no entry whatsoever under "flax" as a modern commodity with regard to Syria. As against this several paragraphs in the reports on Egypt and Iraq deal with the amounts of flax produced in these countries and with its relative importance in their economies. I am indebted for this information to Prof. I.J. Gelb to whom it was given and to Prof. E.F. Campbell, Jr. of McCormick Theological Seminary who passed it on to me. Also A. Lucas says: "There is still a considerable flax cultivation in the country" (*op. cit.*, p. 166). However Miss L. Bellinger informs me that flax is not grown in modern Egypt.
46. See: J.B. Knight, *The Existing State of Persian Agriculture* (1927) (mimeograph, Harvard University Library).

74d) and there is sufficient evidence to prove that it was grown in Palestine in Roman times.[47] Now, this discrepancy with regard to the issue under discussion, between the Canaanite-Israelite and the late Turkish-Arab periods on the one hand, and the Roman on the other hand, may have resulted from a decisive change in relative water-supply and irrigation techniques. Flax is grown under irrigation, except where ample rainfall makes this unnecessary. Especially the processing of flax into yarn and the manufacture of linen-cloth require considerable quantities of water which hardly could be set aside for this purpose in ancient or in modern Palestine until most recent times. The alternative process of dew-retting produces harsh and brittle flax of inferior quality. It appears that in Nabatean and Roman times the situation was somewhat more favorable thanks to comparatively highly developed systems of water preservation. But even in the literature of that period the bulk of references to flax in Palestine mainly concern the manufacturing of linen garments and other finished flax products (Mish. Kilʾayim 2, 3; 9, 1; bTal. Jom. 71b; Zeb. 18b) from imported flax-fibers (Tos. Sheb. 4, 19) or even from imported woven flax cloth (linen).

The upshot of this investigation seems to be that while the cultivation of the flax-fiber plant was widespread in ancient Egypt which "was verily the land of linen in antiquity,"[48] and probably also was common in Mesopotamia, where however it "was completely overshadowed by wool,"[49] flax began to be cultivated in Palestine to an appreciable measure only in the second half of the first millennium B.C. This process may be reflected in the content shift of the terms פשת and עצד. While, as was shown, פשת—פשתה—פשתם in Ugaritic and O.T. literature predominantly is used to indicate flax products, its assumed Punic transcript φοιστ appears to designate a plant in the compound noun ζεραφοιστ = זרע פשת,[50] and possibly also in χουρφοιστ.[51] Similarly it is only in post-biblical Hebrew that the verb עצד pertains to the plucking of flax.[52]

The absence of information from our sources on flax-growing in Canaan–Israel is in striking contrast to the abundant and detailed accounts of

47. References are given by Löw, *op. cit.*, II, p. 208; Dalman, *op. cit.*; Forbes, *op. cit.*; cp. further S. Kraus, *Talmudische Archäologie* I, pp. 138, 156; further J. Felix, *loc. cit.* (*supra* n. 21).
48. J.E. Forbes, *op. cit.* 42; F.E. Zeuner, *op. cit.*, pp. 372–373.
49. J.E. Forbes, *op. cit.*, p. 33.
50. Could זרע פשת be a late substitute for זרעגד in Num 11:7?
51. I. Löw, *loc. cit.* (*supra* n. 22); Guil. Gesenius, *Scripturae Linguae Phoeniciae Monumenta Quotquot Supersunt* (1837), p. 389.
52. See note 20.

all the other agricultural activities enumerated in the G.C.: ,אסף, זרע, קצר שערם קצר (וכל?), זמר, קץ, with the possible further exception of לקש which precedes עצד פשת in the list. (These two are actually intimately related as will be shown below.) It goes to demonstrate that flax was not a major asset to Canaanite–Israelite economy and that we cannot expect it to have played an important role in a farmer's life in biblical times. Therefore a reference to a "season of flax-hoeing," as to one of eight annual agricultural periods, would be rather surprising, to say the least. Hence some further thought should be given to Tur-Sinai's suggestion to explain עצד פשת as the "cutting of sundry herbs and grass" that grow after the spring rains.[53] This suggestion now can be substantiated by a comparison of the G.C. with some calendaric terminology found in the literature of the Judean Desert Covenanters.

The proposed comparison calls for an apology. In spite of their comparative lateness the Judean Desert Scrolls in certain instances have preserved ancient Hebrew words and usages. Especially in matters with which the Covenanters' minds were exceedingly preoccupied, their writings may add to our previous knowledge of the Hebrew vocabulary. For these reasons it seems to be permissible to fall back upon Judean Desert material where we may expect it to present means for clarification of an obscure expression in O.T. writings, or even in an ancient inscription such as the G.C.

At the very end of a list of "ordained times", the author of 1QS enumerates the main four seasons of the year in the following order: מועד קציר לקיץ ומועד זרע למועד דשא (10:7) – "the season of reaping, (the season) of summer (fruits), the season of sowing, (the season) of vegetation."[54]

Two of these seasons – קציר and קיץ – are also mentioned in a similar, albeit probably fragmentary context in Aeth. En 82:16–19: "And these are the signs of the days which are to be seen on the earth in the days of his dominion (of the angel Malchiel): sweat, and heat, and calm (the winds); and all the trees bear fruit, and leaves are produced on all the trees, *and the wheat is ripe for harvest*, and the rose flowers, and all the flowers which come forth in the field, but the trees of the winter season become withered . . . and these are the signs

53. *BIES* 7, pp. 4 ff.; הלשון והספר I (1948) 44. His attempt to find פשת also in the ʿ*zrb*ʿ*l* inscription, reading there in lines 4–5 *mpšt* and *mpštk* was proved wrong by Albright, *JAOS* 67 (1947), p. 18, who established the readings *mgštk* and *mgšt*. Cp. now the reconfirmation of these readings by S. Iwry who, however, gives the word a different meaning from that proposed by Albright, namely: divining implements (*JAOS* 81 [1961], p. 32).

54. M. Burrows, *The Dead Sea Scrolls of St. Mark's Monastery*, II, Fasc. 2: *Plates and Transcriptions of the Manual of Discipline* (1951).

of the days (of the angel Elimelech) on the earth: glowing heat and dryness, *and the trees ripen their fruits and produce all their fruits ripe and ready*, and the sheep pair and become pregnant, *and all the fruits of the earth are gathered in*, and everything that is in the field and the winepress." In contradistinction to the author of the Manual of Benedictions who used short, concise terminology, the language of the author of Enoch is paraphrastic. Nonetheless, this fact does not hide the similarities between both lists.[55]

A subdivision of the year into four seasons appears to underly Solomon's corvée system. According to 1 Kgs 5:27–28, three contingents of 10000 men each were called up in turn for one month of work in the Lebanon, followed by a two-month period "at home" during which time the men could tend to the seasonal requirements of their own farms. Thus, the corvée quota for each man would amount to four months *per annum* in a staggered arrangment (see table on next page).

Similarly, a four-season division of the year appears to be reflected in the "mourning rites", observed for four days annually, referred to in the tradition concerning Jephtah's daughter (Jdg 11:40). The reference should be understood as saying that one day of mourning was observed in each quarter of the year.[56]

A juxtaposition of the Qumran list of seasons with the G.C. shows that while the Calendar starts off with the annual fruit-harvests – אסף,[57] – the Qumran document lists the grain-harvests first – קציר, and in the Book of Enoch the first season is that of the flowering and the fructification of the trees, which coincides with דשא in the Qumran calendar, and לקש, עצד פשת in the G.C. This matter will have to be considered separately. However, the internal

55. I dealt with these passages in a wider calendaric context in: "The 'Manual of Benedictions' of the Sect of the Judean Desert," *RQ* 8 (1960), pp. 486–487. It is possible that the same seasons are also referred to in a liturgical fragment (1Q 34 bis), published by J.T. Milik in *Qumran Cave* I (1955), pp. 152–153; cp. also the Aramaic text 1Q 24, *ib.*, p. 99.

56. The combined evidence for a division of the year into four seasons of three months each in ancient Israelite practice, appears to outweigh the evidence adduced by F.S. North for his theory of "Four-Month Seasons in the Hebrew Bible," *VT*, XI (1961), pp. 446–448.

57. אסף originally was not a specific designation of the olive-harvest (Albright, *BASOR* 92, p. 22, n. 30), but rather an overall connotation of fruit harvest (Exod 23:16), similar in meaning to, and partly coinciding with ירח בול (1 Kgs 6:38). When a more specialized terminology emerged which designated the grape and fig-gatherings by בציר and קיץ respectively, אסיף could be applied preponderantly to the remaining fruit-crops, among them olives (cp. Isa 32:10 where for אוסף, אסיף should be read).

	Contingent 1		Contingent 2		Contingent 3		
	Lebanon	at home	Lebanon	at home	Lebanon	at home	
1. Quarter	I			I		I	Months
		II	II			II	
		III		III	III		
2. Quarter	IV			IV		IV	
		V	V			V	
		VI		VI	VI		
3. Quarter	VII			VII		VII	
		VIII	VIII			VIII	
		IX		IX	IX		
4. Quarter	X			X		X	
		XI	XI			XI	
		XII		XII	XII		

sequence of the seasons is obviously the same in both catalogues and in the Book of Enoch, with this difference that against every two seasons mentioned in the G.C. the Qumran author lists only one:

Gezer Calendar	Qumran List	Am 7:1–8:1[58]	Enoch
ירחו אסף			אסיף
ירחו זרע	זרע		
ירחו לקש		לקש	
ירח עצד פשת	דשא	עשב הארץ	עלים (עשב)
ירח קצר שערם			
[59]ירח קצר וכל	קציר	(אש)	קציר
ירחו זמר			
ירח קץ	קיץ	כלוב קיץ	קיץ

58. The relevance of the Amos passage for the problem under review will soon become apparent.

59. This reading, rejected by Albright, *BASOR* 92, p. 23, seems to derive new support from a

The designation of the period between זרע – "sowing" and קציר – "harvesting" by דשא in 1QS obviously proves that the Covenanters considered this the "grass season" par excellence.[60] Now, this very same season, sandwiched in, together with לקש, between ירחו זרע and ירח קצר שערם is called in the G.C. ירח עצד פשת. Is it too farfetched to assume that פשת and דשא should be considered identical, or synonymous, and that consequently עצד פשת must refer to "cropping verdurous growths"?[61]

The argument can be clinched by additional biblical evidence which sustains the proposed equation of דשא–פשת. In the G.C. the פשת season follows immediately upon ירחו לקש. This term indicates the late-rain vegetation rather than the "late planting (of grain)," as was suggested by Albright.[62] In Am 7:1–2 the very same term לקש is followed by a synonym of דשא, namely עשב הארץ (Gen 1:11–12).[63] This is not a mere coincidence. In the cluster of four oracles, each of which is introduced by the recurring phrase – כה הראני (Am 7:1, 4, 7; 8:1), the individual prophetic utterances obviously are arranged in accordance with the progress of the agricultural seasons to which the prophet alludes.[64] The group is headed by a vision of locust, observed at the

recently discovered Hebrew inscription. There the same word is employed several times (lines 5, 6, 8, 10) in connection with harvesting activities. See: J. Naveh, "A Hebrew Letter From the Seventh Century B.C.," *IEJ* 10 (1960), pp. 129–140; S. Talmon, "The New Hebrew Letter from the Seventh Century B.C. in Historical Perspective," in this volume pp. 79–88. The word can be derived either from *klh* "to terminate, to end," or from *kwl* "to measure." This latter derivation proposed by S. Ronzevalle for the G.C. (*PEFQ* [1909], p. 109) may actually be preferable. A somewhat similar situation to the one underlying the "Seventh Century B.C. Letter" may be reflected in Ruth 2:17 and 3:15, where the measure אפה and the verb מדד respectively are employed.

60. There is no justification for P. Wernberg-Moeller's reticence to invest the term מועד, used in this passage, with the meaning "season" (*The Manual of Discipline* [1957], p. 114, n. 23).

61. G. Hoffmann, "Versuche zu Amos," *ZAW* 3 (1883), p. 116; Cp. also *BDB, s.v.* לקש; R.P.H. Vincent, *RB* 6 (1909), pp. 247–248; 260. H.P. Müller (*loc. cit.*) considers this assumption to be "unwahrscheinlich."

62. *BASOR* 92, p. 22. In this interpretation he is followed by Koehler-Baumgartner, *Lexicon in Veteris Testamenti Libros* (1958), *s.v.* לקש. In Palestinian Arabic this season is often called *er-rabīʿ*, probably connected with רביעה which is a designation of the rain periods in rabbinic literature (H. Vogelstein, *Die Landwirtschaft in Palästina zur Zeit der Mishnah*, Teil I [1894], pp. 1–4; Dalman, *op. cit.*, I, p. 125). *ʾEr-rabīʿ* is the period of the new vegetation which provides abundant fodder for farm animals (Dalman, *op. cit.*, I, pp. 22, 45 ff.).

63. There is little to commend Vincent's (*op. cit.*, p. 247) proposal to read in Job 41:20 *leqeš* for MT: *ḳqaš*, paralleling תבן in the preceding verse.

64. Here we find ourselves in agreement with A. Weiser, *Die Prophetie des Amos* (1923), pp. 13–14.

incipient growth of late-rain herbs (לקש), immediately after the first crop had been harvested for the king, as was the custom (*ib.* 7:1). The second growth fell to the individual farmer who also grew livestock, to some extent. Now this new "grass of the land" – עשב הארץ (*ib.* v. 2) – will be devoured by the locust, a matter evidently considered by the prophet as being of considerable consequence for the livelihood of the people. The expected loss of the "grass of the land" evokes his woeful question and entreaty: "O Lord God, refrain, how shall Jacob survive" (*ib.*). At this juncture, in the months Adar–Nissan (March–April), the locust causes double and three-fold loss to the farmer. It spoils not only the already ripened grass and herbs, but also the nearly fully developed barley, then in its אביב stage (Exod 9:31, 23:15, 34:18; Deut 16:1). The season involved would be in babyl. terminology *pan šatti*. It begins some two months before the barley harvest and is characterized by the sprouting of green grass (*dīš pan šatti*), the appearance of locust swarms, and ample rainfall.[65] With the termination of the grass-season, the barley harvest begins. And soon the grains will be in danger of suffering from the summer-heat or from sudden fires which often ruin the crops just before harvest-time.[66] This, it would appear, is the content of the second vision (*ib.* vv. 4–6) which presumably is set in the קציר season.[67] Thus the mention of the fire (אש) which consumes "the farmer's patch of land" (חלק, *ib.* v. 4) has a very realistic background (cp. *ib.* 4:7; Isa 18:4) and it is gratuitous to invest the passage with some undefinable and obscure mythological meaning.[68]

While the 'season' explanation of the second vision was arrived at mainly by inference, the fourth oracle, in which the cluster culminates, demonstrably presupposes the late summer season as its setting. The "basket full of summer-fruit" – כלוב קיץ (*ib.* 8:1–2) – is clearly a symbol of the season ירח קץ which closes the G.C. The very same season is presumably alluded to also in Jer 24:1–2 in a vision which may be directly dependent on Am 8:1–2.

In view of the foregoing discussion we conclude that ירח עצד פשת of the G.C. preceded by ירחו לקש, and עשב הארץ of Am 7:2 preceded by לקש respectively, are but synonymous designations of the late-rain vegetation and the season of its cropping (cp. below the discussion of Ps 12:6).

65. Cp. B. Landsberger, *op. cit.*, p. 258.
66. Cp. Joel 1:17–20, 2:5 where the same sequence locust–fire, found in Am. ch. 7, is maintained.
67. See A. Weiser, *loc. cit.*
68. As do, *l.g.* Th.H. Robinson–F. Horst, *Die zwölf kleinen Propheten, HAT* (1954), p. 99. See my remarks on this passage in *Tarbiz* 35 (1966), pp. 301–303 (Hebrew).

The terms were evidently thus understood by the Aramaic translators of Deut 32:2:

MT: כשעירים עלי דשא וכרביבים עלי עשב
TO: כרוחי מטרא דנשבין על דתאה וכרסיסי מלקושא דעל עסבא
PsJ: כרביעות רוחי מטרא דמינתבין על דיתאין בירח מרחשון
וכרסיסין לקושין דמרווין צמחוני ארעא בירחא דניסן
FrgT: וכרוחיא דמנשבין על עשבא
וכרסיסי דמלקושא דנחתין ומרווין צימחא דארעא בירחא דניסן

Some further remarks on this subject may be appropriate. In the O.T. the term דשא always indicates "(spring) grass" and never "spring time," as it does in the, to date, only instance of its employment in Qumran literature 1QS 10:8. The apparent shift of meaning could be easily explained by the factual coinciding of spring and grass-growth in nature. Moreover these, in Hebrew literature non-combined, connotations can be derived from one common Akk. source.[69] Akk. *dišu, diš ʾu, daš ʾu* refers to "spring grass, pasture" as well as to the "spring-season."[70] On the one hand we find expressions which are completely parallel with figures of speech employed in the O.T. Compare *e.g.*[71] *ellâmma di-i-šum* (BBR no. 100:17) – "(Adad makes rain fall and) the spring grass shoots up," with 2 Sam 23:4 ממטר דשא, מארץ or *ina di-še u-ḫabbūrī šurušat tamirtu* (TCL 3 229 Sar.) – "the common was planted with spring grass and shoots," with Prov 27:25 גלה חציר ונראה דשא. Again *kīma watmū irtanappudu i-di-ši-im* (Gilg. O.I. rim 2) – "they will run around in the spring grass like chicks," with Mal 3:20; Jer 50:11. On the other hand an expression such as *ištu da-aš-e adi harpē* (JSOR 11 117 no. 11:11) – "(from) spring to harvest time," could be rendered in Hebrew: מועד דשא למועד קציר and is actually paralleled by מועד קציר לקיץ ומועד זרע למועד דשא in 1QS 10:7.

The *diš ʾu* season would extend roughly from the month of *Ṭebetu* throughout *Adaru*, or maybe *Nissanu*. Now *Adaru* has the ideographic ascription *araḫ ŠE-KIN-KUD*, "month of reaping" – *maškan[āt ṣē]ri imallâ ina ugārī rabbūti niggallu ul isêt*, when, in B. Landsberger's translation, "die Tennen der Ackerflur füllen sich, in den grossen Ländereien bleibt keine Sichel

69. See: *CAD*. W.v. Soden, *Akkadisches Handwörterbuch* (1959); R.C. Thompson, *A Dictionary of Assyrian Botany* (1949), *s.v. dišu*; B. Landsberger, *op. cit.*, pp. 258, 287 ff.
70. I am indebted to Prof. A. Malamat, for drawing my attention to this fact during the discussion that followed the reading of this paper at the ninety-seventh meeting of the Society of Biblical Literature, St. Louis, Missouri, December 1961.
71. The following quotations are taken from *CAD*.

(ungenützt)."[72] It is also called *araḫ eṣêdu*, of which (פשת) ירח עצד would be a mere transcription. Pinches[73] and Haupt[74] have shown that both these terms refer to the mowing of green fodder, and not to the reaping of grain. It is however debatable whether this crop was constituted of "green wheat and barley before the ear forms."[75] In fact *ŠE-KIN-KUD* is preceded by a season in which "allerlei Pflanzen spriessen gleichzeitig auf der Ackerflur" – *šammū* [*ma ʾdūtu*] *mith*[*āriš ina ṣēri uṣṣûni*], a description which is remindful of בתחלת עלות הלקש in Am 7:1, just as ירח עצד פשת is preceded by ירח לקש in the G.C. The succession of a "month of mowing" upon a period of "sprouting" would suggest that a crop of non-cultivated grain varieties and verdurous grass is involved.[76]

In fact the somewhat differentiated, although interrelated connotations of Akk. *dišʾu* which underlie the Hebrew usages discussed so far, are also retained in Ancient South Arabic calendaric nomenclature. This nomenclature is known from documents and inscriptions which, chronologically speaking, fall into two rough categories. For reasons of method we propose to deal here only with terms which are extant in the earlier documents, prior to 300 C.E., to the exclusion of terms which are attested only in materials pertaining to the period from 500 C.E. onwards.[77] In one Sabaean inscription (Fakhry 71, 13 f.) *dṯʾn* describes ample rain which fell in the, as yet only tentatively identified, month *ʾlʾlt: wšqy hwʾ dṯʾn bwrḫ ḏ-ʾlʾlt.* At the same time, in Sabaean as well as in Minaean, *wrḫ ḏ-DṮʾ* is the proper name of a month in which spring-rains fall, *i.e.* in the season which in the G.C. and in Am 7:1 is denoted by לקש. This makes it plausible that the South Arabic *wrḫ ḏ-MḪẒDM* – the month of "(Grass)ernten"[78] is to be equated with (פשת) ירח עצד of the G.C. Accordingly

72. See: S. Daiches, "Notes on the Gezer Calendar and some Babylonian Parallels," *PEFQ* (1909), pp. 113–118; B. Landsberger, *op. cit.*, pp. 274–275.
73. S. Pinches, *PSBA* 35, 20, 23, p. 127. W. Muss-Arnolt who referred the name to the reaping of corn, could not help finding it "rather strange" (*JBL* 11 [1892], p. 173).
74. P. Haupt, *JBL* 32 (1913), pp. 139–141, 273–274; *OLZ* 18 (1915), Sp. 359–361.
75. P. Haupt, *JBL* 33 (1914), p. 298.
76. The author is indebted to Prof. Th. Jacobsen for checking and correcting the references to the Akkadian material.
77. The ensuing discussion of some pertinent South-Arabic material is based on the presentation of these matters by A.F.L. Beeston, *Epigraphic South Arabian Calendars and Dating* (London 1956) and by Maria Höfner, "Die Altarabischen Monatsnamen," *Festschrift für V. Christian* (Wien 1956), pp. 46–54. The number of names preserved, 19 for the older, and 8 or 9 for the younger period, make it plausible that some months had several names which pertained to different calendaric systems and which may have been employed by different social groups (cp. M. Höfner, *op. cit.*, p. 49).
78. The derivation of *mḫẓd* from *ḥáṣada*, in spite of phonetic difficulties, and its interpretation as

one surmises that *wrḫ ḏ-DṮ*ʾ and the month of *MḪẒDM* constitute the spring-season proper, *i.e.* coincide with ירחו לקש and ירח עצד פשת of the G.C. Further, just as in some Akk. sources and in the Hebrew document from Qumran *dišu – diš*ʾ*u* and דשא respectively designate the spring-season, taking the name from its most prominent month, also in Ancient South-Arabic *dṯ*ʾ sometimes carries the same connotation. A further significant development is found among the Kabyles. Here *diṯa*ʾ can be used as an overall name of the early harvest-period, the later being called *qiyaẓ*.[79]

Thus some basic agricultural terms which are employed in the G.C. can be shown to have been perpetuated to the first millennium C.E., in an area which extends from Mesopotamia via the Mediterranean coast to South Arabia.

The results of this linguistic analysis are actually reflected in agricultural reality. Though *linum usitatissitum*, the cultivated variety of flax, which is grown as a fibre crop, was comparatively rare in ancient and in modern Palestine, as shown, wild varieties of this plant, especially *linum augustifolium Huds.*, are very common (jTal. Kil 9.1–31d; bTal. Joma 71b; Zeb. 18b).[80] Wild flax, as most other non-cultivated plants, shoots up with the onset of the rain-season and ripens in the early spring. It often invades cultivated fields, there topping the barley shoots which attain full growth somewhat later.[81] This situation is recaptured in the saying of the Sages: "In which month is the earth full of grass (דשאים) and the fruits of the trees begin to form? In Nissan." (bTal. R.H. 11a). Under these specific conditions it would be dangerous to drive cattle into open pasture, since it would be next to impossible to keep them from roaming into the grain-sown fields. Therefore green fodder had to be cut and be brought to them, a practice which usually was adhered to only with regard to animals kept for fattening. Accordingly ירח עצד פשת should be translated "the season of green-fodder cropping." Moreover "grass-harvesting" was imperative, if indeed the farmer had to deliver fodder as a tax to ṭhe king (1 Kgs 5:8; Am 7:1).

The foregoing study makes it probable that פשת of the G.C. and biblical פשתה have different meanings and possibly are to be derived from different roots.

"mähen (Gras) ernten" is favored by M. Höfner, *op. cit.*, p. 51; and by Beeston, who translates "month of reaping" (*op. cit.* cp. 17, n. 40). Its equation with Akk. *eṣêdu* was already proposed by Muss-Arnold, *JBL* 11 (1892), p. 173, n. 103.

79. E. Glaser, "Die Sternkunde der südarabischen Kabylen," *SBWA Math.-Nat. Kl.* 91 (1885), pp. 89 ff., as quoted by M. Höfner, *op. cit.*, p. 50; Beeston, *op. cit.*, pp. 16; 19–20.
80. Löw, *op. cit.*, II, pp. 208 ff.; Dalman, *op. cit.*, I, pp. 335 f., 363 f., 369; II, p. 310; Heer, *op. cit.*, pp. 1–2, 14.
81. Dalman, *op. cit.*, II, pp. 308–310, 323–328.

Before going further into this matter, some comments on the derivation of Hebrew פשת-פשתה from an assumed Akk. *pištu–piltu* as proposed in Koehler–Baumgartner, *Lexicon in VT Libros*, seem to be in order. This derivation in fact is unfounded. In the yet unpublished files of *CAD* not one single entry for *paštu–pištu–piltu* meaning "flax" could be found. Bezold's entry on which Koehler apparently relied, and which was tentatively accepted by Forbes,[82] has been discredited and has been differently translated in the several places where it occurs.[83] The only possible exception is a reading in one text (*MDP* XIV 90 Reverse), cited by I. Gelb.[84] There a sheepskin was reportedly filled *b/pašt/du*. Gelb's translation "flax" was proposed on grounds of the similarity with Hebrew פשתה, and can not be substantiated from the Akk. vocabulary.[85] Also R.C. Thompson's Dictionary of Assyrian Botany (1949) has no entry under *pištu–piltu*.[86] Thus biblical פשתה – "linen" to date cannot be derived from any traceable non-Hebrew source.

On the other hand פשת of the G.C., carrying the connotation of "verdurous growth," could be connected with biblical פשה–פוש – "to grow, to spread."[87] The connotation seems to underlie Mal 3:20 "You shall go forth and feed upon abundant grass – ופשתם," and Jer 50:11 "While (?) you feed – תפושי – like a heifer on (abundant) grass."[88]

It could well be that also פשתה – "flax" was derived from the same root, if we assume that the generic term פשת included "wild flax" from which the cultivated yarn-plant was developed.

This common source of פשת – "grass" and פשתה/ן – "flax" may be reflected in an interesting Midrash preserved in Sifre 4, 43 (ed. Friedmann, p. 80b). Elaborating on the words "and I will give the grass of your fields – עשב (ב)שדיך – unto your cattle" (Deut 11:15), Rabbi Simeon b. Yoḥay offers two interpretations:

82. *Op. cit.*, p. 71, n. 43.
83. My thanks are due to Prof. E.F. Campbell Jr. who supplied this information at my request.
84. I. Gelb, *Glossary of Old Accadian* (1957).
85. Cp. v. Soden, *op. cit.*, *s.v.* [piššu]: "[pištu] m.W. unbelegt."
86. Thompson gives *kitû* the connotation of *linum usitatissitum*. But the word presumably designates only processed linen. This illustrates Forbes' words: "None of the Semitic languages has so full a vocabulary of linen goods or other textiles (as has the Egyptian language)," *op. cit.*, p. 43.
87. Tur-Sinai, *op. cit.*, reads פֹּשת in the G.C., deriving the word from the biblical פשׂה which also has the connotation "to grow, to increase." The two roots פסה and פשׂה could well be related.
88. MT reads דשה, deriving the word from דוש "to thresh." This does not fit the context. G and V mirror the correct reading דשאה. And indeed, Mss Ken. 30 (sm) 93 96 150 have דשא.

"You will cut — גוזז — and throw to your cattle in the rain-period and will abstain from it (your field) thirty days before the (barley) harvest. And it (the field) will (then) continue to produce and will not depreciate its grain."

"Another explanation for 'I will give the grass of your field etc.': This is פשתן (flax). That is what the psalmist says: 'He (God) makes *hay* grow for the cattle and *grass* for a man's flocks (לעבדת האדם),[89] so that bread may be won from the earth' (Ps 104:14)."

Here, and similarly in other midrashic literature,[90] we find side by side the two possible explanations of the "green-fodder crop." It is either constituted of the green shoots of cultivated grains which are expected to grow again after the first cutting; or it is conceived as a period of the ingathering of wild grass and herbs.

However, there can be no doubt that Rabbi Simeon b. Yoḥay took פשתן, a word that usually has the connotation "flax/linen," to be synonymous with עשב and חציר, the verdurous growth on which cattle feed.

Assuming a mutation פשׂה/פשׁה, for which other illustrations can be adduced from biblical Hebrew (*e.g.* Jdg 12:6 שׁבולת/סבולת; Isa 13:4 שׁאן / 9:4 סאן), one is inclined to find a counterpart to פשת of the G.C. in פסת of Ps 72:16. What we have there is a series of images from the plant-world by which the psalmist depicts [the blessings of] a righteous king. The images in the first metaphor are derived from the description of the blessing of rain (v. 6);[91] ירד כמטר על גז[92] כרביבים זרזיף ארץ. The images in the second metaphor are taken from the abundance of growth following the rain (v. 16): יהי פסת בר בארץ בראש הרים ירעש כלבנון פריו[93] ויציצו מעיר כעשב הארץ. This passage is admittedly the most difficult in the psalm.[94] Specifically problematic are the two expressions

89. Thus, instead of MT: לעבודת האדם. The proposed reading is corroborated by G: τῇ δουλείᾳ, and may be compared with Gen 26:14 MT: ועבדה רבה, G: ἔργα; Job 1:3 MT: ועבדה רבה מאד, G: ἔργα.

90. See Sifrē ʿ*eqeb* 43, ed. Friedmann, p. 60.

91. Ps 72:6 presents a parallelism of members in which the verb ירד and the particle על are also understood as referring to the second member. In order to balance the meter, the poet expanded the synonym of כמטר: כרביבים זרזיף.

92. Cp. 1 Kgs 5:8; Am 7:1.

93. In Biblical Hebrew פרי sometimes means "leafage." See: H.L. Ginsberg, "Root (שרש) below and leafage (פרי) above, and related matters," *Sefer Hanoch Yalon*, Jerusalem 1963, pp. 167–170 (Hebrew). Accordingly, Ps 72:16$^{\alpha\beta}$ should be rendered: "his boughs shall rustle as the boughs of the cedar of Lebanon," G.R. Driver connected ירעש with the Arabic رغس = "increase, wealth" (*JThS* 33, 1931–32, p. 43).

94. H.L. Ginsberg, "Some Emendations in Psalms," *HUCA* 23 (1950–51), p. 101; R. Tournay, "Le Psaume 72, 16 et le Réveil de Melquart," *Ecole des Langues Orientales Anciennes de*

פסת בר and ויציצו מעיר. None of the proposed emendations have proven helpful. However, it is possible that the verse can be understood in its present form. As has been pointed out above, פסת equals פשת of the G.C. בר here indicates uncultivated land, as in Job 39:4: יחלמו בניהם ירבו בבר (of the ibex) יצאו ולא שבו למו. Consequently, פסת בר means "grass" or "hay", as Rashi and H.L. Ginsberg, *loc. cit.*, correctly explained, and not "crop", as is the view of most modern commentators.[95] Thus פסת בר would refer to the "abundance of grass on the mountain tops,"[96] in correct parallelism to the expression עשב הארץ at the end of the verse (in biblical literature mountain tops are known for their grass crops — cp. Isa 42:15). This synonymous usage is strengthened by an exactly similar parallelism in biblical Aramaic: בדתחא די ברא . . . בעשב ארעא (Dan 4:12).[97] In other words, דתחא די ברא of Dan 4:12 equals פסת בר of Ps 72:16 equals פשת of the G.C., and all these terms are synonymous with עשב הארץ in Ps 72:16, Am 7:1 and עשב ארעא in Dan 4:12.

The synonymity of יהי כפסת בר בארץ and יציצו (*lege:* יציץ) כעשב הארץ indicates that בראש הרים and מעיר have a similar relationship. Therefore, by its rare parallel, the undefined מעיר must be interpreted to mean "mountain" or "hill." Possibly, we are here dealing with a homonym. This assumption gains credence if viewed against the background of Ugaritic literature, where we find *ǵr* paralleling *gbᶜ*. While battling with his enemies, Baal invites Anat to come *btk.ǵr y.il ṣpn b qdš b ǵr. nḥlty bnᶜm. bgbᶜ. tliyt.* (3[ᶜnt]. 3. 26–28).[98] addition, in a parallel phrase (10 [76].3.32) *ǵr* is substituted for *gbᶜ* in relationship to *tliyt*. The proposed identification of *ǵr* with *hr*[99] is re-enforced

l'Institut Catholique de Paris, Memorial de Cinquantenaire (Paris 1964), pp. 97–104. This article contains a review of recent studies of this Psalm; M. Dahood, *Psalms II, AB* (New York 1970), pp. 178–185, esp. comment *ad loc.*

95. Tournay, *op. cit.*, pp. 98 ff. I am indebted to Prof. N. Sarna for bringing to my attention that G.R. Driver explained פסת in Ps 72:16 as meaning "lot" and then "plenty," connecting it with Judeo-Aramaic פיסא, and Syrian *psh-psth*, acknowledging at the same time that "the origin of the root appears to be quite unknown" (*HThR* 29, 1936, pp. 185–186; see also *Canaanite Myths and Legends*, Edinburgh 1956, p. 163, n. 2).
96. There is no need to emend בראש to דשא, as Ginsberg suggests, *op. cit.*
97. I am indebted to Prof. A. Hurvitz for having brought this parallelism to my attention.
98. References to Ugaritic texts are given here according to R.E. Whitaker, *A Concordance of the Ugaritic Literature* (Cambridge, Mass. 1972).
99. It is probable that the word *ǵr* has this meaning also where Ginsberg contrasts it with *gbᶜ*, and translates it as "valley" (*e.g.* 4 [51]5.77, 93, 100; 5 [67].6.26; 6 [49].2.16). See: H.L. Ginsberg, *The Ugaritic Texts* (Jerusalem 1936), pp. 31, 33, 56, 61 (Hebrew). This fact disavows Tournay's opinion concerning מעיר: "il ne peut s'agir évidemment des montagnes" (*op. cit.*, n. 99).

by Ex 15:17: תביאמו ותטעמו בהר נחלתך . . . מקדש אדני כוננו ידיך, and by Ps 74:2 where the conflated expression הר נחלתך is broken up in a parallelistic structure:[100] זכור נחלתך קנית קדם גאלת שבט נחלתיך הר ציון זה שכנת בו (here the word קדש serves in the succeeding verse — כל הרע אויב בקדש). It should be emphasized that this passage concerns the battle between God and his enemies, just as the term in Ugaritic comes at the end of the description of the battle of Baal and Anat with their enemies.

The proposed interpretation of ויציצ(ו) מעיר[101] as יציץ מהר supports our claim that Psalm 72 describes the blessing of the king in the image of the blessing of the growth of green-fodder on mountain-tops:[102]

יהי [כ]פסת בר בארץ בראש הרים
ירעש כלבנון פריו
ויציצ(ו) מעיר [=מהר] כעשב הארץ

"May he [the king] be [like] abundant grass on mountain-tops in the land,
may his foliage rustle like [that of the cedars of] the Lebanon,
may he [MT: they] sprout from the mountain like the grass of the earth."

This image is a literary reflection of a farmer's life experience in the biblical period. The abundance of green vegetation and its harvesting are an important facet of farming, and its success is dependent on them: "When the grass is gone, and the new growth appears, and the herbage of the mountain is gathered, the lambs will provide your clothing, and the goats the price of a field; there will be enough goats' milk for your food, for the food of the household and maintenance of your maidens" (Prov 27:25–27). Just as grass is a symbol of blessing and good fortune (Gen 1:30, 9:3; Deut 11:15, 32:1–2; 2 Sam 23:4; Isa 66:14; Mic 5:6; Zech 10:1; Job 5:25; Prov 19:12, 27:25), so too, failure and downfall are often depicted in terms of its destruction (Exod 10:12, 15; 1 Kgs 18:5–6; 2 Kgs 19:26; Isa 15:6, 37:27, 42:15; Jer 12:4, 14:5–6; Joel 1:18; Ps 102:5, 12, 105:35).

The synopsis of the G.C. with some biblical passages, Qumran material, rabbinic sayings and ancient South-Arabic documents clearly suggests that a

100. In reference to this system, see: E.Z. Melamed, "Break-up of Stereotype Phrases as an Artistic Device in Biblical Poetry," *Scripta Hierosolymitana* VIII (Jerusalem 1961) 115–153; S. Talmon, "Synonymous Readings in the Textual Traditions of the Old Testament," *ib.*, pp. 335–343 *et alii.*

101. Concerning צי/ץ meaning פרח (flower), cp. Ps 132:17–18; and in synonymous parallelism with "grass", Ps 92:8: בפרח רשעים כמו עשב ויציצו כל פעלי און.

102. With the elimination of the meaning of מעיר as referring to a city, one may also eliminate the mythological interpretation given by Tournay to Ps 72:16 (*op. cit.*, pp. 102–104).

definite "season of grass-cropping" or "hay-making" was recognized in Palestine in the early Israelite (Canaanite) period and in rabbinic times, as well as in South Arabia. This is readily explained by the economic importance of grass crops in stock breeding. They serve as a welcome source of fodder in the interval between the fruit-tree harvests and the grain harvests, when leaves, cuttings and spoiled fruit, or stubbles respectively, are not available. It is for this reason that "grass" and the "grass-season" are mentioned so often in biblical narratives and are employed frequently, and with many variations, in biblical imagery.

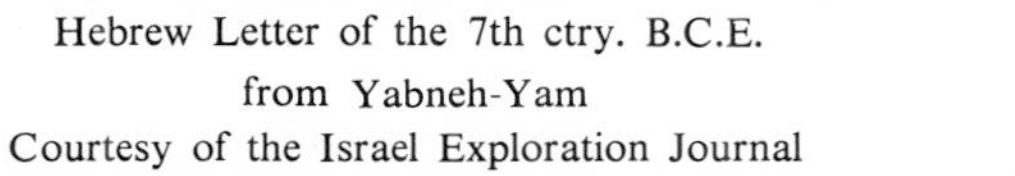

Hebrew Letter of the 7th ctry. B.C.E.
from Yabneh-Yam
Courtesy of the Israel Exploration Journal

The Gezer Calendar
Courtesy of the Israel Department of
Antiquities and Museums

The Cultic Area – *beth bamoth* – at Tel Dan
Courtesy of the Nelson Glueck School
of Archaeology, Jerusalem

Four-horned altar from Tel Dan
Courtesy of the Israel Department of
Antiquities and Museums

Four-horned altar from Tel Dan – *in situ*
Courtesy of the Nelson Glueck School
of Archaeology, Jerusalem

Small altar of the 13th ctry. B.C.E. from
Assyria, with relief showing King Tukulti Ninurta I
in two positions before an altar, kneeling and standing up
Reichsmuseum Berlin

THE CULT AND CALENDAR REFORM OF JEROBOAM I

This essay deals with alterations in calendar-reckoning effected by Jeroboam I, as reported in 1 Kings xii. It will be shown that the changes introduced helped to bring about the separation of Ephraim from Judah in matters social and religious. Jeroboam's apparent innovation grows in importance when seen in relief against actions ascribed to Hezekiah and Josiah, kings of Judah; this entails a re-interpretation of certain passages in the books of Kings and Chronicles.

Jeroboam's actions can fully be explained only in the light of David's policy. In order to avoid an imminent struggle for supremacy between the champions of the two rival towns Sichem and Hebron, capitals of the Ephraimite and Judaean territories respectively, king David had set up the newly-conquered Jebusite town of Jerusalem as the metropolis of the united kingdom. David's son Solomon followed in his father's steps, who had transferred the ark to Jerusalem, when he proclaimed the temple which he erected there the focal sanctuary of Yahweh worship. To enhance the unifying force of this temple Solomon bestowed exclusive rights to the priesthood upon the family of Zadok (1 Kings ii 35), who may have been previously connected with a local cult, as has been conjectured [1]. At the same time he expelled rival priests, such as the house of Ebiathar (ibid. vv. 26-27).

It is accepted by the Biblical historiographers that in the time of Solomon Jerusalem was the pivot around which rotated the main aspects of public life in Israel:

1) Being the seat of the ruling dynasty the claims of Jerusalem

*) This paper was read in part to the Second International Congress for the Study of the Old Testament, held at Strasbourg in August, 1956.

1) A. Bentzen, in: Festskrift of the University of Copenhagen. vol. X (1931), as quoted by J. Pedersen, *Israel*, vol. III-IV. p. 155. 1940 — H. H. Rowley, "Zadok and Nehushtan", *JBL* LVIII (1939) pp. 113-141.

to supremacy in the state were uncontested. Around it centered the network of administration and judicial organization. (2 Sam. xv 2; 1 Kings iii 16ff.).

2) Worship was concentrated in the temple in Jerusalem and was supervised by the sole representatives of the cult of Jahweh, Zadok the high priest and his family. The central position of Jerusalem was visibly manifested in the annually-recurring three festivals of ascent to the Temple, events which were the culmination of the Israelite farmer's life.

One is therefore justified in saying that by the end of Solomon's reign Jerusalem constituted one of the most unifying elements in the social structure of the Hebrew nation.

These considerations must perforce have influenced the thoughts and actions of Jeroboam I, who was called upon by the house of Joseph to reduce the Davidic dynasty that symbolized the supremacy of the tribe of Judah in national affairs. It has been repeatedly pointed out that Jeroboam's actions were explicitly directed towards the restoration of political, social and religious conditions which had been prevalent in Israel before the establishment of a united kingdom under David.

One of Jeroboam's first acts of sovereignty, following closely upon his open revolt against Rehoboam and his election as king over the northern tribes, was the break with Jerusalem and the re-establishment of Sichem as the capital of the new kingdom. This stroke shattered the centralized administration of public affairs, carefully built up by Solomon.

But Jeroboam knew that further steps were required to cement the recently-won independence. In order to estrange the Ephraimites from Jerusalem, which latter was bound up with the dynasty of David, a break with Solomon's temple was imperative. The custom of sacrificing in Jerusalem had to be abolished. Above all there had to be found a means of cutting off the northern tribes from the contact with Judah and its capital, which manifested itself again and again in the time-honoured institution of ascent to the Temple.

Scripture tells us that "Jeroboam said in his heart: "Now shall the kingdom return to the house of David. If this people (i.e. the northern tribes) go up to offer sacrifices in the house of the Lord at Jerusalem, then shall the heart of this people return again unto their lord, even unto Rehoboam king of Judah; and they shall kill me, and return to Rehoboam King of Judah" (1 Kings xii 26-27).

We are confronted here with what we may well call the actual considerations of Jeroboam couched in the language of a Judaean writer. The author goes on to describe Jeroboam's actions resulting, quite naturally, from those reflections: "whereupon the King took counsel and made two calves of gold, and he said unto them (i.e. the people). It is too much for you to go up (or: Ye have gone up long enough) to Jerusalem; behold thy gods [1]) O Israel, which brought thee up out of the land of Egypt. And he set the one in Bethel and the other put he in Dan" (ibid vv. 28-29).

It must be stressed in this context that dissenters, political and religious alike, will as a rule not proclaim themselves innovators. They will, on the contrary, always try to appear as champions of time-honoured ideas and institutions that, according to their contentions, have been desecrated by the leaders of the community from which they strive to detach themselves. Jeroboam is no exception to the rule. It is for this very reason that he reverts to the calf-cult established in Israel from ancient times [2]) and chooses the ancient cultic centres of Bethel and Dan as substitutes for Jerusalem, which presumably had no roots in Hebrew tradition prior to the days of David.

One surmises that similar considerations guided his choice of priests for the restituted sanctuaries. Quite logically the Jerusalem priesthood was discarded and Jeroboam "made priests" — according to the Hebrew text מקצות העם — a term which the AV translates, not

[1]) Thus the RV. But actually the apparent plural אלהיך should be translated here, as in similar passages, as a singular: Behold thy God O Israel. (cp. Gen. xx 13 MT and Sam.; Ex. xxxii 4 etc.). The two calves were conceived of as images of the one god (A. Šanda, *Die Bücher der Könige* I, p. 343, 1911). In this fashion the author of Neh. ix 18 interprets our passage. — There is no reason to assume with Montgomery-Gehman (*Kings*, *ICC*, p. 255. 1951) (and similarly with Šanda) that "the present text is a development of the original tradition that he (Jeroboam) set up a calf at Bethel concerning which he would have proclaimed 'This is thy God who brought (reading sing. verb) thee' etc." — For the same reason it is gratuitous to charge the authors of Ex. xxxii 4, 8 and of Hos. x 5 with a wilful alteration of the sing. into the pl. (Montgomery, ibid.).

[2]) Against the views of Eissfeldt (*ARW* 1930) and T. J. Meek (*Hebrew Origins*, p. 160ff.), who hold that Jeroboam introduced a new religion, — cf. Y. Kaufmann, *Toledoth Ha'emuna Hajisraelith*, vol. III, p. 682; IV, pp. 261, 276. — It would appear that even the Chronicler did not consider the calf-cult in itself a foreign institution. He saw fit, therefore, to qualify Jeroboam's action by complementing the statement of the author of Kings: " . . . for the high places, *and for the he-goats*, and for the calves which he had made" (2 Chr. xi 15). — Jehu the "Baʿal Baiter" did not consider Bethel and Dan places of idolatrous worship and saw fit to spare them (2 Kings x 29). The same holds true for Joram (ibid. iii 3).

without bias, "of the lowest of the people" (ibid v. 31 [1]). But the term should be translated either "from among all the people" (cp. ibid. xiii 33; 2 Kings xvii 32) without any specifying adjective [2]), as done in the RV, or else should be given a positive connotation: "from among the outstanding men of the people" [3]). This latter meaning is required in Judg. xviii, 2, where מקצותם refers without doubt to heads of the Danites who were sent out to discover new territory for their tribe [4]). — It seems to be appropriate as well in Ez. xxxiii 2. — In this positive sense is the equivalent מקצה employed in Gen. xlvii 2: ומקצה אחיו לקח חמשה אנשים ויצגם לפני פרעה [5]). — The technical term קצין „leader-ruler", carries similar connotations [6]).

It is worthwhile to point out that the Chronicler recorded his account of this story in rather careful words. We are told in 2 Chr. xi 13-14 that "the priests and the Levites that were in all Israel resorted to him (Rehoboam) out of all their borders. For the Levites left their suburbs and their possession, and came to Judah and Jerusalem: for Jeroboam and his sons cast them off, that they should not execute the priest's office unto the Lord". This departure resulted from the fact that Jeroboam discarded the traditional priesthood and that "he appointed him priests for the high places". But these priests are not belittled in any way [7]). The author quite obviously did not interpret

[1]) This interpretation is to be found, quite naturally, in early rabbinic literature, e.g. Jer. Gittin i. 5 (43d) אמר ר׳ אילא מן הקוצים שבעם מן הפסולת שבעם. — Ab. Zarah i 1 (39 b); Bab. Kid. 75 b.

[2]) F. Burney, *Notes on the Hebrew Text of Kings*, 1903, p. 178. Similary Montgomery, ibid.: "from the whole range of the people". Cf. Gesenius, *Handwörterbuch* 17, p. 721; Koehler, *Lexicon in VT Libros*, p. 847.

[3]) Rabbah bar bar Chana (ca. 300) in the name of R. Johanan (ca. 100) interprets the term מקצותם (2 Kings xvii 32) "from the worthiest" (מן הבחירים שבעם). The negative attitude to those priests was caused by transgressions at a later stage of their career.

[4]) With the task of reconnoitring were entrusted usually chieftains and valiant warriors. cf. Num. xiii; Judg. vii 9 ff; 1 Sam. xiv 1 ff. etc.

[5]) Against traditional Jewish interpretation, which tends to ascribe to the passage a negative meaning (Rashi ad loc.; Ber. Rab. ad loc).

[6]) According to some texts Rabba bar bar Chana equalled מקצותם with מן הקצינים שבהם (Bab. Kid. 75b).

[7]) It is interesting to observe that in 2 Chr. xiii 9, in a passage which is usually ascribed to the Chronist and mirrors his conception of his sources (M. Noth, *Überlieferungsgeschichtliche Studien* I, pp. 161; 177), a new note is subtly introduced. In Abijah's famous "sermon on the mount" the northerners are accused of having made priests כעמי הארצות. This seems to be a definite anachronism which shows the influence on the mind of the writer of occurrences during the period of the Return. This allusion is lost in the translation of the RV: "and have made

מקצות העם in 2 Kings as a derogatory term, as is the fashion of later interpreters [1]).

We cannot help but assume that Jeroboam's new priests were men of considerable social prestige. And this assumption seems to be borne out by Biblical tradition. — According to the apparently original Hebrew text of the Book of Judges (xviii 30), "Jonathan, the son of Gershom, the son of Moses, he and his sons were priests to the tribe of the Danites until the day of the captivity of the land" [2]). This priestly family officiated in הר אפרים, in "the hill-country of Ephraim" (ibid. ch. xvii), before they were brought to the town of Lajish-Dan [3]) during the migration of the Danites — or rather of a part of that tribe — to northern Galilee. Now this term, "hill-country of Ephraim", is most probably identical with the town of Bethel [4]), since, according to the historical traditions embedded in Judg. i, 22-26, Bethel was the only town in the central hills of Canaan to be captured by the Hebrews at this stage of their settlement [5]).

It stands to reason that the priests installed by Jeroboam were but remnants of the family of Moses who had already officiated

you priests after the manner of the peoples of other lands." — It would appear that in the Hebrew text כ and מ have been interchanged and that the verse read originally — מעמי הא׳ (cf. G). This constitutes a wilful and malignant interpretation of — מקצות העם (2 Kings xii 31).

[1]) R. Akibah, who cannot be considered pro-Samaritan, accepted the view that the priests who were installed at the Bamoth in Samaria after the destruction of the country were כשרים. And there (2 Kings xvii 32) the same term is applied: "and made unto them from among themselves (מקצותם) priests of the high places". Says R. Akibah (Bab. Kid. 75): "כותים גרי אריות היו וכהנים שנטמעו בהם כהנים כשרים היו, שנא׳ ויעשו להם מקצותם כהני במות".

[2]) Kaufmann (op. cit. I p. 172) accepts this tradition but contends that this priestly family officiated during two generations only, until the destruction of Siloh (ibid. vol. IV, p. 377 n. 27), so that they would have no connection with Jeroboam and his priests. This necessitates the acceptance of Houbigant's emendation of הארץ to הארן (Judg. xviii 30).

[3]) For the sake of this reference alone the name of Dan cannot be excised from the report of Jeroboam's actions, as suggested by Montgomery, *ibid.*

[4]) Bethel served as a sanctuary during the first period of the settlement in Canaan, as we may learn from Judg. xx 26. It would appear that from the occurrences at Bethel during the war against the Gibeonites, when the people "wept" there before God, the name בכים for this town was derived (cf. Judg. ii 1. 5).

[5]) We accept the order of events, outlined already in the Talmud und again by Jewish mediaeval commentators, according to which the migration of the Danites occurred at the beginning of the period of the Judges and definitely before the days of Gideon and Abimelech. It appears to us that the historical happenings reported in Judg. xviii-xxi were originally outlined at the head of the present second chapter of Judges.

previously at the central shrines in Ephraim [1]). Descendants of this family were attached as Levites to the temple in Jerusalem at the time of David (Solomon) according to the lists preserved in 1 Chr. xxvi 23-26; xxiv 20-22; xxv 20.

The emphatic statement by the Judaean author of Kings that the priests at Dan and Beth-El "were not of the sons of Levi" (ibid. xii 31) [2]) must obviously be taken with a grain of salt, though it has been accepted — sometimes with reservations — by modern writers [3]).

It appears therefore that Jeroboam strove to substitute specific Ephraimite values and traditions for pan-Israelite institutions innovated by David and by Solomon [4]).

II

Along these lines one more of Jeroboam's actions should be viewed. In order to gain the upper hand over Jerusalem it was apparently not enough to divert the northern tribes from their adherence to Solomon's temple and to re-direct them towards the hallowed shrines of Bethel and Dan. The reversion from Jerusalem in the south to Dan in the far north would, so it seems, not achieve a complete break with the Temple which had been associated with popular worship for nearly two generations. There was yet some danger that at the Festivals of Ascent the people "may go up to sacrifice in the house of the Lord at Jerusalem" (1 Kings xii 27) as was their custom, and turn again "unto Rehoboam, king of Judah" (ibid).

Apprehensive of this danger, Jeroboam introduced one more radical change into the public life of the northern tribes. The author

[1]) Kaufmann arrives at the conclusion that Jeroboam's calves were made according to plans prevalent among Aaronide priests who officiated at the great shrines in northern Palestine (*op. cit.* IV, pp. 261; 264). The connection of Aaron with the calf-episode in the desert (Ex. xxxii; Deut. ix 11 ff.) points in this direction. — But another tradition outlined above (Judg. xviii) reports that priests descending from the house of Moses served at Dan — and most probably at Bethel as well — where the calf-cult prevailed. It seems therefore that the calf-tradition was the common heritage of the house of Amram.

[2]) This may be a direct allusion to 1 Kings viii 4 where we are told that in Solomon's temple officiated "the priests the levites" as one may prefer to read here on grounds of comparison with 2 Chr. v 5.

[3]) J. Pedersen, *op. cit.* pp. 173-74, introduces an unwarranted differentiation between the levitic priesthood at Dan and the priesthood at Bethel that supposedly was not levitic. He seems to have overlooked the obvious ties between the functionnaries of those two shrines, indicated by the author of Judg. xviii. — cf. Šanda's remarks on this point, *op. cit.* pp. 344-45.

[4]) Cf. Montgomery, *loc. cit.*

of Kings twice reports that "Jeroboam ordained a [1]) feast in the *eighth* month on the fifteenth day of the month, like unto the feast that is in Judah and he went up unto the altar" (ibid. v. 32). (This happened probably in Dan, since Bethel is explicitly mentioned in the parallel reading in v. 33. Its name has been inserted into v. 32 as well — "so did he in Bethel").

The O.T. evidently attributes to Jeroboam manipulation of the calendar. In order to upset the synchronization of cultic and therefore of public life in Ephraim and Judah [2]), he allegedly did not even stop short of the deferment of the Feast of Tabernacles by one whole month. This feast which follows close upon the grape and fruit harvest and in the agricultural calendar is identical with the "feast of the ingathering" — חג האסיף (Ex. xxiii 16; Lev. xxiii 33-34) [3]), was now transferred from the seventh month to the eighth. The author of Kings, or else a redactor, wishes to suggest to the reader that Jeroboam fixed the festival on a date "which he had devised of his own heart" (ibid. v. 33) [4]). Bearing in mind, however, the predominantly "pro-tradition" character of Jeroboam's other actions, the authenticity of this statement deserves to be questioned [5]).

Before exploring this point in detail, we must give more attention to the question whether the Biblical report really has any historical background. To the modern mind the calendar is scientifically defined. It is fixed objectively on grounds of astronomical observations and mathematical calculations uninfluenced by social or other considera-

---

[1]) Actually "the feast", i.e. Tabernacles. cp. MORGENSTERN, *HUCA* I. p. 68 n. 92.

[2]) The social impact of calendar-revisions has been illustrated by the present author in his paper "Yom Hakkippurim in the Hab. Scroll" (*Biblica* 1951, pp. 549-63). — J. MORGENSTERN had previously drawn attention to a possible interpretation on similar lines of Dan. vii 25 where the "fourth king" is charged with intentions "to change the times".

[3]) We need not enter here into the question whether Tabernacles was originally an agricultural festival. On this point consult J. WELLHAUSEN, *Prolegomena*[6], p. 97; *Reste Arabischen Heidentums*[2], pp. 94-101; and now N. H. TUR-SINAI, "Tabernacles, Passover and the Matzoth Festival", (in: *Halashon Wehasefer*, vol. III. pps. 78-86. 1956). Suffice it to say that in the period of the First Commonwealth agricultural affinities constituted the outstanding feature of the feast.

[4]) Cp. Jer. Aḥ. Zarah i 1 (39 b); Tanh. Pinhas xvii (ed. BUBER, p. 156); Bam. Rab. xxi 23.

[5]) The Talmud (Sanh. 102a) ascribes to R. Nahman (ca. 300) a most interesting midrashic interpretation of the verse (1 Kings xi 29) "Now he had clad himself with a new garment". Turning the ב = 'with' into כ = 'as', "R. Nahman said: As a new garment: just as a new garment has no defects, so was Jeroboam's scholarship (תורתו = teaching?) without defect".

tions. The mere possibility of trifling with the calendar and of adjusting the seasons to what appear to be political needs is inconceivable to us.

But the attitude of the ancients was different. Calendar-reckoning was not considered to be dependent upon abstract calculations. The calendar was subject to events which could be directly perceived, such as the appearance of the new moon. These observations were often inaccurate [1]) because of alterable conditions, such as a clouded sky [2]), which affected different regions diversely. The framework of the calendar was provided by the agricultural seasons which gave rise to festivals connected with the main features in the annual cycle of the farmer's life.

These climaxes, such as sowing and harvesting, cannot be objectively determined, as can the rotation of the sun or of the moon. Their appropriate time will differ from year to year and from region to region [3]). Especially is this so in Palestine, where climatic differences between the valleys and the mountaineous parts, between the subtropical south and the moderate north, are greatly accentuated. As a result of these conditions, which favour an earlier ripening in the south, the average Judaean farmer would have completed the harvest of his main crops when the harvest in the north was yet at its height. The agricultural calendar was therefore not concurrent with the astronomical division of the year into twelve, more or less equal, stretches of time. It was governed by considerations of agricultural seasons which lent themselves to a division into eight periods, as we may learn from the Gezer Calendar [4]). There is no need to enter here into a discussion of this calendar, which is usually dated in the ninth century B.C. Suffice it to draw attention to the fact that four out of the eight periods enumerated are designated ירח, while the remaining four are called ירחו. The suffix — ו is most probably to be explained as an archaic indication of the dual, or of the plural [5]), so that ירחו would stand for a period of approximately two months. Now the

[1]) Jer. Taanith iv 11 (69c).

[2]) R. H. ii 7-8.

[3]) On these lines should the controversy over the date of the "new year of trees" most probably by explained. While Beth Shammai fixed the date on the first day of Shebat, Beth Hillel, whose ruling prevailed, fixed it on the fifteenth (R. H. i 1).

[4]) A convenient summary of views on this calendar is given in the *Encyclopaedia Miqraith*, vol. II. cols. 471-474.

[5]) For discussion on this point consult N. H. Tur-Sinai, *op. cit.* vol. I. pp. 40-47.

first season to be mentioned in that calendar is אסף, the agricultural counterpart of the Feast of Tabernacles. It appears in combination with the term for a double-month, namely ירחו מסף. This seems to bear out the contention that the fruit-harvest festival was originally not fixed definitely, but would fall at some time during the latter part of this period [1]) with some alterations from region to region [2]). This is corroborated by the fact that in Ex. and in Deut. this festival is set, rather loosely, at "the end of the year (Ex. xxiii 16) or at the termination of harvests (Deut. xvi 13). A fixed date "on the fifteenth day of this seventh month" is introduced only in the probably later sources of Lev. xxiii 34; 39.

In the pre-monarchic era agricultural festivals were not celebrated at one and the same time in all parts of Palestine. Barring the levelling influence of social and cultic agents — such as a common government and a central sanctuary (which were not in force before the establishment of the united kingdom) — harvest ceremonies may have been spread over a certain period in the year. They were, most probably, not observed merely as local feasts fixed by each locality individually (Judg. xxi 19ff.). For one may assume that partial synchronization was achieved already during the first stages of settlement of the Israelites in Canaan. This synchronization would have been effected in communities in which climatic conditions differed to moderate degrees only, e.g. in the villages of Judah, Simeon and Benjamin on the one hand and in the mountaineous settlements north of Bethel on the other hand [3]). But a full-scale synchronization, affecting all Israel and going counter, in a sense, to climatic conditions and agricultural requirements, could have been established only by centralizing forces as were inaugurated by David and by Solomon. The har-

[1]) J. MORGENSTERN, *HUCA* III (1926) p. 87: "As it is it begins with that agricultural operation, viz. the ingathering which took place, speaking broadly, during the sixth and seventh month of Calendar II." — Cp. S. AALEN, *Die Begriffe 'Licht' und 'Finsternis' im A.T.* etc., p. 48. 1951 — TUR-SINAI, *ibid.* p. 43.

[2]) These conditions have not changed basically until this day. I am indebted to Dr. P. SPIEGEL of the Ministry of Agriculture of Israel for the following information: Grapes of the same variety will ripen in the hill-land of Ephraim approximately one month later than in the Judaean Shephelah. This holds true especially for local varieties, such as Dabouki. — While in Sichem olives will usually not be harvested before the end of November, the olive harvest in the district of Lydda-Ramleh will take place between mid-September and mid-October.

[3]) PEDERSEN, *op. cit.* p. 417. — cp. MORGENSTERN's remarks on Passover, *HUCA* III (1926) p. 80.

vest-feast, as other ceremonies, was then divorced from its direct and immediate relation to the family and to rural norms and became a more or less royal undertaking [1]).

Now, as stated before, Jeroboam aimed at dissolving the ties binding Ephraim to Judah by emphazising exclusive Ephraimite traditions. One may therefore be justified in assuming that in deferring the Feast of Tabernacles by one month he reverted to an established northern calendar [2]). This calendar is obviously alluded to in 1 Kings vi 38 where we are told that Solomon's temple was completed in the month of Bul, the eighth month [3]). In viii, 2 on the other hand, it is reported that the dedication took place in the month of Etanim, the seventh month, during "the Feast", i.e. during Tabernacles. The most plausible explanation for these contradictory statements is to be found in the assumption that the two dates given are based on two different calendars. — Jeroboam readjusted the time-reckoning to actual climatic and agricultural conditions prevalent in the north of Palestine. He thus put to his use basic principles determining the life of the rural population of Ephraim in a not unprecedented combination of cunning and good faith.

These considerations will explain the ready acceptance of Jeroboam's action by the northern tribes. Without giving regard to the political machinations involved, though not unaware of them, the Ephraimite peasant acclaimed the change which brought the cultic festivals again into focus with the agricultural seasons.

These deliberations prompt us to conclude that Jeroboam's decree should not be thought of as merely a temporary measure, as implicitly understood by ancient and modern scholars alike [4]), but that it should be considered a standing order [5]).

---

[1]) This characteristic of the festival was finally established under the influence of the reforms of Hezekiah and Josiah.

[2]) Kaufmann tends to assume that this date for Tabernacles was bound up with the calf-cult and was part of an Aaronide tradition prevailing in the north (*op. cit.* IV. p. 262).

[3]) The remark was significantly dropped from the parallel version in 2 Chr. v, while the date "in the seventh month" is retained (v 3) though without mentioning "the month of Etanim". This can hardly be explained as a mere omission of ancient names which were of no significance to the contemporaries of the Chronicler (Brunet, *RB* LXI, 1954. p. 363). The disconcerting date "in the month of Bul which is the eighth month (1 Kings vi 38) has been scrapped altogether in Chr.

[4]) Cf. Morgenstern, *JQR* VIII (1917) p. 54.

[5]) Kaufmann does not take a definite stand in this question though he surmises that differences in cultic customs between the north and the south were bound to arise (*op. cit.* IV. p. 262).

The added month did not affect the Feast of Tabernacles exclusively. This feast was chosen as a starting point for the new calendar not for any intrinsic reason, but because it happened to be the first of the festivals of ascent to occur after Jeroboam's rebellion. Jeroboam synchronized the dedication of the new sanctuaries in Bethel and Dan with the dedication of the Temple in Jerusalem by Solomon, which was celebrated בחג (1 Kings viii 2) [1]). His evident intention was to cling to established traditions [2]) and to emphasize the equivalence in importance of his holy places with the Jerusalem Temple.

Since, as shown, the deferment depended upon natural phenomena, it actually indicated an all-out adjustment in calendar-reckoning bringing the seasonal feasts into proper correlation with climatic conditions of northern Palestine. — It would appear that this cleavage was perpetuated until well after the conquest of Ephraim by the Assyrians. But since it had been accepted as normal it was not mentioned anymore in the historical books of the Bible.

III

The destruction of Samaria ended the political independence of the northern tribes. But it did not reconcile them either with the south or with the Davidic dynasty. This reconciliation was attempted by some Judaean rulers who were backed up by certain groups in the northern population. The Bible reports at length on two efforts by Judaean kings to incorporate the remnants of the northern tribes into the southern kingdom.

The first to attempt this, shortly after the conquest of Ephraim, was Hezekiah. He found himself beset by a two-fold problem:

1) An agreement had to be reached with the Ephraimites inducing them to accept again Jerusalem as the religious centre and as the capital of the nation.

[1]) According to Rabbinic tradition the ceremonies took place on the 10th of the 7th month, which was a day of rejoicing (Mish. Taanith iv 8). — These questions in their complexity are treated by J. Morgenstern in papers already cited (*JQR* VIII; *HUCA* I).

[2]) Cp. Ezra iii 6; iii 8; 1 Kings vi 1; 2 Chr. iii 2. — cp. Brunet's pertinent remarks on this point with a view to Solomon's Temple (*op. cit.* p. 364). — There is no reason whatsoever to ascribe the prominence in historical events connected with the cult of the seventh month to just a "schriftstellerische Gepflogenheit von Chr." as M. Noth (*Überlieferungsgeschichlische Studien*, p. 159, 1943) would have it. The combination of cultic reforms with the New Year festival is in itself plausible and became a fixed pattern after the dedication of Solomon's temple. — Cp. S. Aalen, *op. cit.* p. 48.

2) It was essential to restore the synchronization of the calendar-reckoning in order to co-ordinate the march of events in the lives of the two populations.

The Chronicler reports that, after having cleansed the temple, Hezekiah sent messengers to Ephraim and Manasse and that he "wrote letters . . . that they should come to the house of the Lord at Jerusalem to keep the passover unto the Lord, the God of Israel" (2 Chr. xxx 1). His summons met with refusal. The people did not agree to come to Jerusalem (v. 3). And since "the priests had not sanctified themselves in sufficient number" (ibid.) the king and his nobles decided to "keep the passover in the second month" (v. 2).

At first sight it appears that Hezekiah — or else the Chronicler — based the deferment on the law of the "Second Passover", prompted by his awareness of the ritual uncleanliness of the priests. Translators and interpreters of the passage under review have therefore repeatedly drawn attention to Num. ix where this law is outlined [1]). But there is actually no connection between that law and Hezekiah's action. We may note that the author of Chr. does not invoke that ordinance explicitly, though it must have been known to him [2]). The later Rabbis as well did not generally apply this obvious interpretation to Hezekiah's decree. There are numerous comments on this action to be found both in the Babylonian Talmud (Ber. 10b; Sanh. 12 a-b) and the Palestinian Talmud (Pes. ix 1 36c), in the Tosseftah (Pes. viii 2; Sanh. ii 6) and in Midrashic collections (Teh. c. 108; ed. BUBER, pp. 463-464). Hezekiah's action evoked the disapproval of the Rabbis. The gist of their reasoning is given in Bab. Pes. 56a: "Our Rabbis taught: Six things King Hezekiah did; in three they agreed with him, and in three they did not agree with him . . . he cut (the gold off) the doors of the Temple and sent them to the King of Assyria (2 Kings xviii 16) and they did not agree with him; he closed up the water of the upper Gihon (2 Chr. xxxii 1-4) and they did not agree with him; and he intercalated the month of Nisan in Nisan (ibid. xxx 1-3) and they did not agree with him". The Rabbis deny here implicitly any connection between the deferment of

[1]) MORGENSTERN, *JQR* VIII, p. 63; J. BENZINGER, *Die Bücher der Chronik*, p. 123, 1901. — E. L. CURTIS, *Chronicles* (*ICC*) p. 472, 1910. etc.

[2]) Even if one accepts a post-exilic date for the inception of this ordinance which is considered a part of P (J. WELLHAUSEN, *Die Composition des Hexateuchs*, pp. 173-74, 1855; PEDERSEN, *op. cit.* III-IV, p. 414) it was already observed in the Chronicler's times.

Passover by Hezekiah and the Second Passover and attribute the alteration to wrongly employed intercalation. The issue is raised again in Bab. Sanh. 12a and there we find an explicit dissociation of Hezekiah's ordinance from the law of the "Second Passover". They posed the question whether Hezekiah was justified in changing the date of Passover because of uncleanness and were divided over this issue. We read: "Our Rabbis taught: We may not intercalate a year because of uncleanness". This ruling was contested by R. Judah who said "We may intercalate" and who based his opinion on the incident under review. R. Judah observed: "It once happened that Hezekiah King of Judah declared a leap year because of uncleanness, and then prayed for mercy". R. Simon queries this statement with some justification: "If the intercalation was actually on the grounds of uncleanness it holds good (in the view of R. Judah). Why then did Hezekiah implore Divine mercy?" The reason given at first is, that he "intercalated a Nisan in Nisan" which cannot be done. But it appears that the Rabbis hit upon the actual cause of Hezekiah's action which prompted their disapproval. R. Simon b. Judah said on behalf of R. Simeon, that they disagreed with Hezekiah "because he had persuaded — עישה or העשה — Israel to celebrate a Second Passover (unduly)". (Cp. Jer. Ned. vi 13, 39 d; Sanh. i 2 18d).

Let us recall that when Hezekiah sent messengers to Ephraim and Manasse inviting the inhabitants of those parts to celebrate the Passover in Jerusalem, his messengers met at first with derision by the local populace "who laughed them to scorn and mocked them" (ibid v. 10). Now if we keep in mind what has been said about the northern calendar, the mockery and the refusal are well explained. According to Ephraimite time-reckoning Hezekiah had sent word for Passover to be observed one month before the appropriate time. It seems that this was the main issue about which the north and the south were at variance, since in the end "divers of Asher and Manasse and of Zebulun humbled themselves and came to Jerusalem" (ibid. v. 11). But it appears that Hezekiah had to make one important concession in order to persuade the northerners to acclaim Jerusalem as the central place of worship. He actually deferred the Passover to the 14th day of the 2nd month in the Judaean calendar. "For the king had taken counsel, and his princes, and all the congregation in Jerusalem, to keep the passover in the second month" (ibid. v. 2). This had the expected results: "And there assembled at Jerusalem much people to keep the feast of the unleavened bread in the second month, a very great congregation" (ibid. v. 14). The unorthodox date for Passover, the 14th day of the second month, as fixed by Hezekiah, coincided exactly with the 14th day of the first month in Ephraimite reckoning, the appointed time for Passover. And now Hezekiah's summons was accepted by the northern populace.

The Chronicler does not state expressly that this concession to the Samarians was, as we believe it to have been, the historical reason for Hezekiah's decree. The writer had misgivings about this ordinance and pointed out that "the priests and the Levites were ashamed" [1]) because they had "killed the passover on the 14th day of the 2nd month" (ibid. v. 15). But the author of Chr. is obviously favorably inclined towards Hezekiah, whom he pictures as a god-fearing and unfailing man. Hezekiah, according to him, "wrought that which was good and faithful before the Lord his God" (ibid. xxxi 20). He therefore strove to cover up the blemish of this one unorthodox act. This he did by superimposing upon the political reason for the deferment of the Passover, which he apparently did not consider legal, a more acceptable cultic reason. He tells us that "they could not keep it (i.e. the Passover) at that time (i.e. the 14th of the first month) because the priests had not sanctified themselves in sufficient number". And he adds "neither had the people gathered themselves in Jerusalem" (ibid. xxx 3). Thus the fault of undue liberty is removed from Hezekiah's doorstep and his action is justified on objective grounds.

The theory put forward here lends new weight and importance to the Chronicler's account of Hezekiah's celebration of the Passover. This account has often been treated cursorily as a legendary enlargement of Josiah's reform and of the report on the Passover held by that king [2]). But actually we are confronted here with a genuine historical source [3]), accurate even in details. Our author tells us that

[1]) Zimmerman's statement that "that word נכלמו is certainly peculiar" (*JQR* 42, 1951/52, p. 396) is hardly warranted. His suggestion that in translating a supposed original Aramaic text the Chronicler confused two roots here חרף — "do a thing early" and חפר — "be ashamed" is ingenious, but not convincing.

[2]) Cp. e, g. M. Noth, *op. cit.* p. 201.

[3]) Kaufmann, *op. cit.* I. p. 97 f. — "Sefer Biram" p. 19. 1956. — Even scholars who tend to cut down to a bare minimum the amount of original historical material which was at the disposal of the Chronicler will admit that in his account of the Hezekiah and Josiah stories he drew upon sources which the author of Kings had not tapped. (e.g. M. Noth, *op. cit.* pp. 181-82). One should therefore be justified in putting more reliance upon his version of the reform inaugurated by Hezekiah than is usually done.

as a result of Hezekiah's decree "there was great joy in Jerusalem: for since the time of Solomon the son of David King of Israel there was not the like in Jerusalem" (ibid. xxx, 26). This statement exactly fits our reconstruction of developments and is definitely not just a remark taken over from the Josiah story (xxxv 18) as implied by commentators [1]). We will have opportunity to refer again to this point later on. But let attention now be drawn to the clear distinction between 2 Chr. xxxv 18 and its apparent doublet, overlooked by interpreters. In the case of Josiah, we are told that "no such passover was celebrated since the days of Samuel etc." But in the case of Hezekiah the author is careful to remark on the "joy which was in Jerusalem and which had not the like since the days of Solomon". Hezekiah had been successful in again drawing the northern populace to the Temple in Jerusalem, and this caused great rejoicing. If, as argued since the days of DE WETTE, the essence of the Deuteronomic Passover lies in concentrating celebrations in Jerusalem and in changing thus the character of the former family-festival [2]), credit for this innovation should go to Hezekiah and not to Josiah, at least on grounds of the Chronicler's history (2 Chr. xxix-xxx, esp. xxx, 1, 11, 13, 21, 26) [3]). But the celebrations were still impaired by the fact that they were held at the wrong date.

At this stage, at the time of Hezekiah's Passover, the northern calendar prevailed over the southern time-reckoning. But it is probable that this was a solitary occurrence. Hezekiah's plan to unite Ephraim with Judah did not materialize and it seems that eventually he reverted to the Judaean calendar while the northern tribes kept to their own system of time-reckoning.

Josiah followed in Hezekiah's wake. He was able to go one step further. It would appear that by his time the supremacy of Jerusalem was no longer contested. One can say at least, according to Biblical sources, that he did not meet with forceful opposition when he undertook to abolish the high-places in the towns of Samaria, including

[1]) BENZINGER, *loc. cit*; CURTIS, *op. cit.* p. 471.

[2]) A. ALT, "Die Heimat des Deuteronomiums", *Kleine Schriften* II, p. 253. 1953.

[3]) KAUFMANN places the naissance of the Deuteronomistic trend in the times of Hezekiah (*op. cit.* IV, pp. 234; 266; 271 ff; V, p. 485). But, on the other hand, he accepts the view that the celebrations of the Passover in Jerusalem were a complete innovation of Josiah's (IV, p. 270), since originally Passover was kept as a family festival (Ex. xii 6 ff"; xii 20 etc.). He therefore arrives at the conclusion that the old tradition had not been altered by Hezekiah's reform, in spite of the rulings of Deut. xvi and in spite of the Chronicler's report.

Bethel (2 Kings xxiii 15-20; 2 Chr. xxxiv 6-7) [1]). — He could therefore impose the Judaean calendar upon the remnants of Ephraim. In his days Passover was observed on the 14th day of the first month (ibid. xxxv 1) in an unprecedented fashion. The authors of Kings and Chronicles alike emphasize the fact that "Surely there was not such a passover from the days of the judges that judged Israel, nor in all the days of the kings of Israel, nor the kings of Judah; but in the eighteenth year of king Josiah was this passover kept in Jerusalem" (2 Kings xxiii 22-23; cf 2 Chr. xxxv 17-19) [2]).

The novelty here referred to is — on the lines argued — the reenforcement of a calendar common to Judah and to Ephraim and the reestablishment of Jerusalem as the national centre of worship — two features which had never coincided during the period of the divided kingdom.

Josiah's Passover was therefore essentially different from Passover celebrations held by Hezekiah insofar as it was observed on the 14th of the first month according to southern reckoning and in accordance with a "national calendar" assumedly introduced by Solomon. The authors of Kings and Chronicles were justified in stressing this uniqueness. We cannot concur with PEDERSEN's contention that "the narrator (of 1 Chr. xxxv 1-19) evidently did not remember Hezekiah's passover" [3]). Quite to the contrary, the Chronicler's presentation of facts should be taken as further evidence for the substantial accuracy of his sources.

It fell to Josiah to make amends for Jeroboam's wrongs [4]). He picked up where Solomon had left off. Now the whole people, represented by pilgrims ascending to the temple in Jerusalem from all parts of the country, observed the festival of Passover at one time.

[1]) ALT's assumption to the contrary (*ibid.* p. 261) is hardly borne out by Biblical sources.

[2]) The Bible reports the celebration of Passover immediately after the entry of the people of Israel into Canaan (Josh. v 9 ff). — The shorter version in 2 Chr. reads: "And there was no passover like that kept in Israel from the days of Samuel the prophet; neither did any of the Kings of Israel keep such a passover as Josiah kept". — On the whole the Chronicler's report of Josiah's Passover is more elaborate than that in Kings.

[3]) *Ibid.* p. 391.

[4]) The author of Kings links the stories of these two personalities by direct allusions to Jeroboam's deeds in his report on Josiah's acts (2 Kings xxiii 15-18).

IV

If the interpretation here proposed is accepted two further ideas come to mind and these have yet further to be explored.

1) Hezekiah's acceptance under stress of the northern calendar, may point to the historical background of the "Second Passover". The inception of this ordinance which has been ascribed to Moses by later redactors and has been inserted into the book of Numbers (ch. ix) could then be traced back to pre-exilic times, and would thus have emanated from the Deuteronomic school. But, though resulting from Hezekiah's reform, this law cannot be adduced for the explanation of his action, as already stated [1]).

2) The assumed discrepancy in calendar-reckoning between Judah and Ephraim may have contributed in some cases to divergences in chronology apparent in the historical books of the Bible. Since, most probably, northern material was embedded sometimes in the southern groundwork of the Biblical reports conflicting chronological data may be expected.

One example shall be adduced here to illustrate the impact of the phenomenon under review.

Two different synchronisms with the regnal years of Nebudchadrezzar are given in the Bible for the capture of Jerusalem in the reign of Jehoiachin, and for the exilation of the captivity after the destruction of Judah in the days of Zedekiah.

Our main sources place the deportation of Jehoiachin in the eighth year of Nebudchadrezzar's reign (2 Kings xxiv 12), and the downfall of Zedekiah in Nebudchadrezzar's ninteenth year (ibid. xxv 8; Jer. lii 12). But in a short excerpt, appended to the report on the Fall of Judah in Jer. lii, in which the diverse deportations effected by Nebudchadrezzar are summarized, the dates for the events mentioned are given as the seventh, respectively the eighteenth year of the Babylonian king [2]).

These latter dates derive now support from the new Babylonian

[1]) Cp. pp. 11-12 supra.

[2]) For suggestions with regard to the explanation of these discrepancies see now — D. J. Wiseman, *Chronicles of Chaldaean Kings* (626-566 B.C.) *in the British Museum*, p. 34, 1956. — D. N. Freedman, "The Babylonian Chronicle", *BA* XIX, 3 (1956) pp. 56-7. — E. R. Thiele, "New Evidence On the Chronology Of The Last Kings Of Judah", *BASOR* 143 (1956) p. 24. — W. F. Albright, *ibid* pp. 31-32.

chronicles recently published by WISEMAN [1]). Nebudchadrezzar is reported there to have marched to the Hatti-land in his seventh regnal year and to have seized Jerusalem and captured the king (Jehoiachin) on the second day of the month of Adar. This fits in perfectly with 2 Chr. xxxvi 10 where we are told that Jehoiachin was brought to Babylon "at the turn of the year" — לתשובת השנה —, i.e. at the beginning of the new year starting with Nisan [2]). According to Ez. xl 1 the exiles — and most probably Jehoiachin among them — arrived at Babylon "in the beginning of the year, in the tenth day of the month", which the Babylonian chronicle now proves to have been the month of Nisan [3]).

For the period under discussion the Biblical writers employed the Nisan-to-Nisan system when speaking of the regnal years of Babylonian rulers [4]). From here follows that Jehoiachin's exile was dated, in accordance with Judaean reckoning, in Nebudchadrezzar's eighth year, since Nisan had already set in. But to the Ephraimites, whose calendar lagged one month behind, New Year was yet ahead. The event was therefore included in the annals of the outgoing year, the seventh year of Nebudchadrezzar's reign [5]).

Calculating from these different points of departure and bearing in mind that Jerusalem was destroyed in the eleventh year of Zedekiah the Judaean and Ephraimite chronists synchronized this latter event with the nineteenth and the eighteenth year of Nebudchadrezzar respectively.

Vv. 28-29 (30) of Jer. lii should henceforth be considered an extract from an Ephraimite chronicle [6]).

V

The question yet remains to be considered whether Josiah's celebration of a national Passover in Jerusalem remained a solitary

---

[1]) BM 219246 reverse, lines 11-13. — WISEMAN, *op. cit.* p. 73.

[2]) Cp. 2 Sam. xi 1.

[3]) See W. A. IRWIN, *The Problem of Ezekiel*, p. 256 f., 1943. — E. R. THIELE, *The Mysterious Numbers of the Hebrew Kings*, pp. 162-3. 1951.

[4]) THIELE, *ibid.* pp. 157-8.

[5]) The Biblical text is correct. There is no need to introduce emendations proposed by EWALD (*Geschichte des Volkes Israel* III, 1. p. 435, 1847) and accepted by many commentators. For references consult W. RUDOLPH, *Jeremia* (*HAT*) pp. 280-1, 1947. — Neither have we to presuppose "minor captivities, preliminary to the major captivities of the eighth and nineteenth year" (THIELE, *BASOR* 143. p. 25).

[6]) And not, as suggested by FREEDMAN, *loc.cit.* n. 29, excerpts from Babylonian sources.

incident, or whether in its wake the other festivals in the north as well were synchronized with the dates obtaining in the south. — We must furthermore ask ourselves whether the impact of Josiah's reform affected all the remnants of the Ephraimite kingdom, either permanently or temporarily.

The Biblical historiographies do not shed any direct light on these problems. But there are some indications that at least in certain parts of northern Palestine and especially in the region bordering on Judah Josiah's calendar came to stay [1]). Gedaliah ben Ahiqam was assassinated by Ishmael and his men in the seventh month at a ceremonial meal which marked apparently the end of the grape and fruit harvest (Jer. xli 1-3) [2]). On the second day after the murder "there came certain from Shechem, from Shilo and from Samaria . . . with oblations and frankincense in their hands to bring them to the house of their Lord" (ibid. v. 5). These people from the central parts of Palestine, from former Ephramite territories, are described as being "in mourning, having their beards shaven and their clothes rent, and having cut themselves" (ibid.), most probably as a sign of distress over the destruction of the Temple [3]). But it holds to reason that their ascent to Jerusalem in the seventh month was connected with the main feast of the season, the feast of Tabernacles, or else with the Day of Atonement [4]). This would hint at the acceptance of the Judaean calendar by at least some groups of the northern populace.

Little further knowledge is to be gained from our sources. Some explanation for this omission can be derived from the events which followed close upon Josiah's reform. The Biblical historiographers report briefly on reactions which set in shortly after his death (2 Kings xxiii 31ff; 2 Chr. xxxvi 5ff.), though without commenting directly on the point discussed here, viz. the attempted synchronization of the

[1]) A. ALT, "Zur Geschichte der Grenze zwischen Judäa und Samaria", *Kleine Schriften* II. pp. 348-63.

[2]) According to Jewish tradition the meal in question coincided with the New Year Festival. "In the month" without further reference to the day concerned often alludes to the new moon. It is therefore held that the murder of Gedaliah was committed on the 3rd day of the 7th month which is the 2nd day after the New Year Festival (Jalk. Shim. 574) When in a later period the celebrations of this festival were extended to two days, Gedaliah's assassination was commemorated by a fast on the 4th day of the 7th month.

[3]) Bab. Moed Kat. 26a. Jer. ibid. iii 7 (83b).

[4]) We are not concerned here with the origins of this festival and its development. Cp. MORGENSTERN, *JQR* (N.S.) VIII (1917) pp. 40 ff., *HUCA* I (1924) pp. 22 ff.

northern with the southern cultic calendar. There was actually no opportunity to mention again Josiah's calendar reform. Some twenty years after his death, and barely more than thirty years after the reform movement had started, the State of Judah ceased to exist. The reports on those last troubled years consist mainly in the description of external political events and their repercussions on the life of the Judaean nation, events which overshadowed completely the interest in the fate of the northern populace.

The Biblical historiographers being silent on this point, we shall have to probe into post-exilic sources for further information on the problem. There are, on the one hand, the books of Ezra-Nehemia, the leaders of the returning exiles, in which is depicted the life of a Jewish community that embraced without reserve the trends of thought inaugurated by Hezekiah and Josiah.

On the other hand, we may possibly derive enlightenment on the subject treated here from extra-Biblical sources, namely the Elephantine papyri, which mirror to some extent the ideas and habits of a Jewish group cut off from the main body of the nation as a result of political adversities.

Let us first turn to the returning exiles. We may recall that the adjustments in calendar-reckoning mentioned previously pivoted around the two main agricultural festivals, Tabernacles and Passover. These festivals continued to attract the attention of the post-exilic leaders and writers. They had lost nothing of their importance although their cultic features had undergone changes and were to undergo still further changes.

The Bible records a synchronized celebration for Passover in the days of Josiah but for Passover only. Josiah had set a precedent which was continued by later generations of adherents to his precepts. It is quite in line with these considerations that the author of Ezra ch. iii did find no reason to mention the celebration of Passover in the second year after the return, though he reports on the festival of Tabernacles held in the first year (ibid. vv. 1-4) and on further activities of the community starting with the second month of the second year.

A similarly conspicuous omission may be observed in the report on the return of the group led by Ezra. They left from the river Ahawa on the 12th of the 1st month (ibid. viii 31) [1]) and arrived in

[1]) This date was possibly chosen with a view to the Exodus from Egypt.

Jerusalem at the beginning of the 5th month (ibid. vii 8-9). Once again Passover ceremonies are not mentioned. Another occasion appropriate for referring to this festival presents itself in Neh. ii. Here Nehemia's first intervention with the King of Persia on behalf of the community in Jerusalem is placed in the month of Nisan (v. 1). Though no accurate dates are given, Passover must have concurred with some of the events described in chapters i and ii.

Surely Passover was observed by the exiles before and after the return. Hezekiah and Josiah had introduced new forms of celebration, but they had not done away with traditional family ceremonies. The silence of the Biblical books seems therefore to imply that the pattern for Passover and its appropriate time had been fixed definitely by Josiah. His rulings were observed, as far as possible, even by those of the returning exiles who originally came from the Ephraimite territories, such as "the men of Bethel and Ai" (Ezra ii 28; Neh. vii 32) [1]). It is for this reason that the Biblical writers felt no compulsion to enlarge upon events which had become routine matters.

But the same was not the case with those sections of the Hebrew people who had been allowed to remain in Palestine after the destruction of Judah. The population of Palestine at the time of the Return was composed of three elements in unequal proportions. There were remnants of the Ephraimites interspersed amongst the Judaeans who were not sent into exile. There was an additional influx of people of foreign stock — the percentage of whom in the general populace cannot be ascertained — who had come to Palestine in the wake of conquering armies or had been brought there by the conquerors (2 Kings xvii 24ff.). The mode of celebrating Passover among these groups differed from the way which had been accepted by the returning exiles and which was rooted in Josiah's reform, as has already been stated.

An open clash between the two sectors, the returning exiles and the גויי הארץ, in regard to Passover seems to underly the story of the first Passover on record to be celebrated by the repatriates. According to the book of Ezra this Passover was observed in the sixth year of King Darius, after the completion of the altar i.e. in 516 B.C.

[1]) Though it was part of Ephraim, the pottery discovered on the site reveals affinities to Judaean types and seems to indicate that economically Bethel was orientated more towards Judah than towards Ephraim. (*Encyclopaediah Miqraith*, vol. II, col. 62).

(Ezra vi 15). We are told that "The sons of the captivity [1]) kept the passover on the 14th day of the first month" (ibid. v. 19). The author stresses the fact that "they (the priests) killed the passover for all the children of the captivity, and for their brethren the priests, and for themselves" (ibid. v. 20). It is then made clear that in addition to the returned exiles, such of the inhabitants of Palestine were included in the ceremonies "as had separated themselves unto them from the filthiness of the people [2]) of the land" (ibid.). It is far from being established, as is sometimes assumed, that this latter class to whom "filthiness" adhered was permanently excluded from Passover celebrations, being an alien and hostile element. It seems to us that the term "filthiness" must be interpreted here in the technical sense of oppositeness to the status which the participants at the ceremonies had attained as the result of ritual cleansing processes: "For the priests and the Levites had purified themselves together; all of them were pure" (ibid. v. 20). This is proved by the fact that those of the "people of the land" who had joined the new community in their preparations for the festival had thereby "separated themselves from the filthiness". — The wording of this story calls to mind not so much the report on Josiah's reform in 2 Chr. xxxv 1-19 [3]) as Hezekiah's Passover. In both these cases we are confronted with a similar situation [4]). Just as in the days of Hezekiah, so in Ezra's period "there were many in the congregation that had not sanctified themselves" (2 Chr. xxx 17) and these came mainly from former Ephraimite territories (ibid. v. 18). We maintained above that in the days of Hezekiah this state of affairs had resulted from a different timing of Passover which separated one part of the nation from the other. It appears that the same interpretation holds true for the Period of the Return. The גויי הארץ who were mainly northerners, or southerners and foreigners who had become assimilated to their mode of life [5]), were not yet prepared to begin ablution ceremonies for Passover

[1]) The interpretation offered here relieves us of the necessity to alter with Esdr. the text into "sons of Israel", as suggested by Batten (*Ezra-Nehemia*, *ICC*, p. 153. 1913).

[2]) The translation adopted by RV — "heathen of the land" is rather presumptuous.

[3]) Batten, *ibid.*

[4]) The similarity has apparently influenced the Greek translator of Esd. vii 11. — Cf. W. Rudolph, *Esra und Nehemia* (*HAT*) p. 64, 1949.

[5]) But see now Kaufmann, *op. cit.* VIII, pp. 183-186 who identifies גויי הארץ with "foreigners" exclusively.

which according to their reckoning was yet a month ahead. While Hezekiah had bridged the gulf by accepting ad hoc the Ephraimite date for Passover, for reasons stated above, the returning exiles adopted Josiah's attitude and clung to the Judaean calendar. Therefore only such of the גויי הארץ were admitted to their celebrations as were prepared to "separate themselves from the filthiness [1]) etc.", at the time fixed by the repatriates in accord with their own calendar.

A secondary argument in support of this line of reasoning may be adduced. The "people of the land" referred to in Ezra vi are, in a way, the forerunners of the Samaritan community. Now, we know from rabbinic sources [2]) that whenever the Samaritan Passover preceded the Jewish festival by some days, Jews were not permitted to partake of Samaritan bread immediately after Passover, since this bread had been baked during the days of Passover when it was forbidden to keep leaven in the house. The rejection of the Samaritan bread is not based on a difference in principles. The Samaritans are praised for adhering meticulously to rulings they had accepted [3]), including prescriptions for Passover. The rejection of their bread arose therefore necessarily from a difference in calendar reckoning. As is well known, Samaritan calendar calculations were independent from the Jewish timing and have remained so until this very day. The Rabbis' ruling dealt with here would constitute a further case of a social rift stemming from different timing of cultic seasons [4]).

The train of thought pursued here leads to the conclusion that Josiah's synchronization of the northern with the southern calendar was only accepted temporarily by the majority of the Ephraimite population. Soon after the destruction of the Judaean kingdom, or even before that event, the old difference in the cultic time-tables was reintroduced.

[1]) It is the author's opinion that this same filthiness underlies the parable of "the clean and the unclean meat" in Hag. ii 10-14. This passage should be interpreted on the lines indicated by Rothstein (*Juden und Samaritaner*, pp. 31 ff., 1908) in spite of the rejection of his proposal by the majority of scholars. The latest to take a critical view is Kaufmann, *op. cit.* VIII, pp. 220 ff.

[2]) Jer. Orla ii 7 (62 b-c); Tos. Pes. ii 1; Mass. Kuthim ch. ii (ed. Kirchheim, p. 34, 1851).

[3]) Bab. Kid. 76a; Tos. Pes. i 15.

[4]) See S. Talmon, *ibid.* p. 559.

VI

Let us now turn to the other source of information mentioned above, to the Elephantine papyri. We tend to believe that the approach outlined here will help in reconstructing the background on which the famous Passover Edict, contained in letter no. 21, should be seen [1]). This papyrus — written in the year 419 B.C. — is badly mutilated. It tells of a decree issued by King Darius II in which the Jewish soldiers at Elephantine are admonished to keep Passover according to specifications given. The days of the month on which the feast is to be observed — the 15th-21st day — are clearly indicated. But the name of the month has disappeared in lacunae. It is nevertheless the accepted opinion that "Nisan" should be restored twice in line 5.

Two questions arise from this letter.

1) Why should the Persian authorities take trouble about ritual obligations incumbent upon the Jewish colony in Elephantine?

2) Why was it at all necessary to admonish those Jewish soldiers to keep the Passover?

1. It is obvious that as in the case of the proclamations issued by Cyrus I (Ezra i 2-6; vi 3-5) and by Darius I (ibid. vv. 6-13) so in the case of the Passover Edict of Darius II, Jewish agents were at work. The royal consent once given, it was the task of his Jewish advisers to put the king's general intentions into proper legal language and to press for action to be taken.

This was done overtly since Cyrus had conferred upon Ezra, the leader of the returning exiles, the right to "appoint magistrates and judges, which may judge all the people that are beyond the river, all such as know the laws of (thy) God; and teach (ye) him that knoweth them not" (Ezra vii 25). It is therefore easily understood that also the leaders of the Jerusalem community in the times of Darius II invoked the authority of the Persian government in order to enforce the observance of Passover among the Jews of Elephantine.

2. We have yet to ask (a) what necessitated the issue of a special decree to the Jews at Elephantine in regard to Passover, and (b) whether the injunction was served on the Elephantine community exclusively.

---

[1]) A. Cowley, *Aramaic Papyri of the 5th Century*, p. 60 ff., 1923. — Ed. Meyer, *Der Papyrusfund von Elephantine*, p. 96, 1912.

As to the second point, it was Ed. MEYER's conviction that the edict under review illustrates conditions brought about by Ezra. Going counter to the intentions of the Priestly Code, Ezra had allegedly divorced the Mazzoth Festival from Passover, which should be sacrificed in Jerusalem alone in accordance with Deuteronomic prescriptions. The new law was now put into force with the sanction of Persian authorities [1]). From this it follows that the decree affected equally all Jewish communities and that the letter preserved from Elephantine is just one copy out of many which were circulated by the Jewish leaders in Jerusalem.

But the majority of scholars tend to regard the letter under discussion as a document pertaining exclusively to the Elephantine garrison. The present author concurs with this opinion. That community was comprised at least partly of former Ephraimites who had not been affected by Josiah's innovations [2]) either because they had been expelled from Palestine prior to Josiah's great celebration of Passover or else had left there of their own will. In any case these colonists did not know of the synchronization of the Ephraimite calendar with Judaean time-reckoning. From this it follows that their cultic calendar — being a direct continuation of the Ephraimite time system — lagged by one month behind the calendar in force among their Jewish contemporaries in Judaea [3]). The letter sent to them by special envoy from Jerusalem was obviously intended to adjust the Elephantine time-table to the calendar obtaining at Jerusalem.

The accurate date for the month of Nisan — according to Judaean reckoning — was established in the Passover Edict with the aid of

[1]) Ed. MEYER, *ibid.*

[2]) KAUFMANN, *op. cit.* vol. I p. 88; III, p. 680.

[3]) Ed. MEYER contended already that problems of timing may constitute the core of the friction between different groups of the Hebrew people: "Vor allem wird die Festlegung auf ein bestimmtes Kalenderdatum vielfachen Widerspruch gefunden haben . . ." (*ibid*). COWLEY assumed "that the passover in early times was irregularly observed, that Josiah really revived it after a period of neglect, and that its yearly celebration was only established, like so much else, under Ezra." (*op. cit.* p. XXIV). It is therefore understandable "that this colony (in Elephantine) which was probably (already or) soon afterwards (i.e. after 622) established in Egypt, should either know nothing of it, or should regard it as intended only for residents in Palestine, to be celebrated at Jerusalem" (*ibid.* p. 61). But it is hardly plausible that Passover was not observed annually from its inception as it was closely connected with the agricultural cycle. COWLEY has therefore to admit that "no doubt the national festival was founded on primitive practices of some kind", though he dismisses this point with the remark, "but that is a totally different question" (*ibid.*)

synchronization with the independent Egyptian calendar. It would coincide (partially) with the month תיעובי, if COWLEY's reconstruction of line 4 is accepted: בחודש תיעובי יהיה פסח לחיל היהודים.

A further allusion to Passover in an inscription on a potsherd which was found in Elephantine [1]) appears to be of some importance for our question. At the end of a short message dealing with a different matter we read the line: שלח לי אמת תעבדן פסחא. E. L. SUKENIK and J. KUTSCHER, who dated the sherd on grounds of palaeography ca. 500 B.C., explained these words most convincingly as an enquiry concerning the date at which Passover would be celebrated [2]). The writer who apparently dwells outside Elephantine asks Hosh'ajah the addressee: "Send me (note) at what time you will keep Passover". This enquiry is well understood at a time when the Judaean calendar was revived in Jerusalem and when the exiles in Egypt had not yet taken a definite stand on this problem. Although the Passover Edict of Darius II was issued nearly a century later it constitutes in a way the answer to the unknown writer's question.

The review of passages in the Bible and of some extra-Biblical documents, pertaining to the problem treated in this paper leads to the conclusion that the difference of one month between calendar calculations in Ephraim and Juda introduced by Jeroboam I. remained in full force until the destruction of Samaria. At least some of the inhabitants of former Ephraimite territories clung to their specific calendar still after that event. The lingering influence of Jeroboam's calendar decree was observed even in Biblical reports on post-exilic events and had its repercussions on the life of the Jewish community in Elephantine. It is obvious that under the climatic conditions of Egypt and in a community that was not anymore predominantly occupied with agriculture the specific features of the Ephraimite calendar had lost their raison d'être which was anchored in the natural conditions of far-away Ephraim and had become now a petrified cultic relic.

The termination of national indepence of Ephraim, the recurring deportations of the native populace and the progressing alienation from agriculture brought obscuracy upon the initial causes of the

[1]) A. H. SAYCE, "An Aramaic Ostracon from Elephantine", *PSBA*, vol. XXXIII (1911). pp. 183 f.

[2]) *Kedem*. Studies in Jewish Archaeology, vol. I. (1942). pp. 53-56. — An extensive bibliography on the sherd is appended there.

Ephraimite calendar revision. These reasons — i.e. the divorce of that calendar from its proper environment — seem to account for the fact that by and by it fell into oblivion. The process was enforced by the emergence of a new set of questions which caused frictions over calendation between rival groups in Judaism during the Second-Commonwealth and subsequently and which superseded the features over which calendar contentions had arisen between Ephraim and Judah. We are referring to the strife over adherence to either a lunar, a solar or a lunar-solar calendar and — in the orbit of a lunar calendar — to the problem of fixing the new-moon upon direct observation or upon pre-calculation [1]).

Yet a far echo of the calendar struggle between Ephraim and Judah reverberates in the Abib-issue over which Karaites and Rabbanites were divided [2]). Karaite calendation was dependent upon the actual state of Abib (= freshly ripened barley) in the Holy Land. The adherence to this principle, even in Egypt and in Byzantium, was insisted upon to such a measure that the Karaites saw fit to make its observance a binding clause in marriage contracts, especially in cases of mixed Karaite-Rabbanite marriages [3]). Now, whenever the ripening of the new grain in Palestine was delayed by climatic adversities a leap-year would be proclaimed, by aids of intercalating Nisan in Nisan [4]). Resulting from that Passover would be postponed by one month, coinciding now with the Rabbanite month of Iyyar and with the Second Passover. Mutatis mutandum a situation would arise which bear resemblance to the ancient calendar divergency between Judah and Ephraim. Though political and sociological conditions had undergone profound changes the direct dependence of the Karaite calendar upon actual agricultural phenomena as against pre-calculated official calendation in Rabbanite circles gave rise to a calendar feud which was in principle a replica of the strife over the calendar between northern and southern Palestine in Biblical times.

[1]) For relevant material see now A. Jaubert, "Le calendrier des Jubilés et de la secte de Qumrân", *VT* III, (1953), pp. 250-264. — J. Morgenstern, "The Calendar of the Book of Jubilees, its Origin and its Character", *VT* V. (1955) pp. 34-76. — S. Talmon, *op. cit.* —

[2]) My thanks are due to Dr. Z. Ankori of the Hebrew University for having brought this issue to my attention.

[3]) For a concise treatment of the question with extensive bibliography appended consult Z. Ankori, "Some Aspects of Karaite-Rabbanite Relations in Byzantium on the Eve of the First Crusade", *PAAJ* vol. XXV, (1956), esp. pp. 25-38.

[4]) Cp. Pes. 56 b and above p. 49.

BIBLICAL VISIONS OF THE FUTURE IDEAL AGE

Introduction

Biblical man's hope for an ideal future age has been investigated on various levels in innumerable publications. For this reason alone, the issue will not be reviewed here in comprehensive detail, nor is such a review required, since scholarly discussion of the matter is amply documented.[1] Therefore, rather than survey and assess prevailing opinions, I shall restrict myself to the elucidation of some exegetical aspects of texts which are rightly viewed as salient expressions of biblical concepts regarding the perfect age to come, set unvaryingly within the frame of actual history.[2]

In the overall fabric of biblical descriptions of that future aeon, varied strands of thought are interwoven. By applying analysis, these can still be separated and traced back to initially independent traditions, which presumably spring from diverse historical and social settings and conceptual frameworks. In relevant biblical texts, several pairs of ideas can be distinguished which, at first glance, appear to be mutually exclusive, but upon closer scrutiny are found rather to complement each other. This duality, which permeates biblical visions of a perfect future, may be categorized in two different ways:

(a) Particularity vs. Universalism[3] (Ethnocentricity vs. Anthropocentrism),

1. Bibliographical information and surveys of the literature are given by, among others, L. Dürr, *Ursprung und Ausbau der Israelitisch-Jüdischen Heilandserwartung* (1925); H. Gressman, *Der Messias* (1929); M. Buber, *Königtum Gottes* (Berlin, 1932); J. Klausner, *The Messianic Idea in Israel from its Beginnings to the Completion of the Mishnah*, translated from the Hebrew (1955); S. Mowinckel, *He that Cometh, The Messianic Hope in the Old Testament and in the Time of Jesus*, tr. by Anderson (1956); G. Scholem, "Zum Verständnis der messianischen Idee im Judentum", in: *Eranos Jahrbuch* 28 (1960) (Frankfurt a/M, 1969) 193–239 = *Judaica* (1969) 7–74 = "Towards An Understanding of the Messianic Idea in Judaism," in: *The Messianic Idea in Judaism and Other Essays on Jewish Spirituality*, ed. N.N. Glatzer (New York, 1971) 1–36.
2. See S. Talmon, "Eschatologie und Geschichte im biblischen Judentum", in: *Zukunft – Zur Eschatologie bei Juden und Christen*, ed. R. Schnackenburg (Düsseldorf, 1980) 13–50.
3. S. Talmon, Particularity and Universalism – A Jewish View," in: *Jewish–Christian Dialogue, Six Years of Christian–Jewish Consultations* (Geneva, 1975) 36–42; M. Weber, *Das antike Judentum, Gesammelte Aufsätze zur Religionsoziologie*, Bd. 3 (Tübingen, 1921) 418 = *Ancient Judaism*, trans. H.H. Gerth and D. Martindale (Glencoe, IL, 1952).

(b) A משיח (Anointed)-centered Expectation vs. A Diffuse-Redemption Hope.[4]

That is to say, it is helpful to view the Hebrew Bible's statements about a coming age of peace and prosperity through this grid of parallels. We may say that the first of the above two pairs consists of two types of visions of an ideal age. One is centered on the particular national entity of Israel, set in the geographical framework of the Land of Israel. The other pertains to humanity as such.

The second pair consists of two differently accentuated visions of the future: one centered on the expectation of an Anointed (משיח), and another in which no central figure is mentioned and redemption is diffuse.

The two pairs can be cross-combined: there can be the expectation of an Anointed set in a particularistic frame of Israel only, or there can be the expectation of an Anointed in a setting which encompasses the universe. Similarly, there can be a diffuse-redemption hope which is centered on Israel only, or a hope for an ideal future which encompasses the entire universe.

These traditions appear to be rooted in diverse historical and societal settings and conceptual frameworks. It is proposed that both the universalist and particular types of משיח centered expectation reflect the experience of Kingship. As against this, both the universalist and particular types of diffuse-redemption hope do not show any such dependence on the specific experience of the monarchy. They could well be pre-monarchic.

These theses will serve as guidelines in the discussion to follow. However, it should be stressed that in biblical literature as we know it, the diverging concepts have already been harmonized and for the most part are jointly embedded in comprehensive literary units.

The examples I shall adduce are taken mainly from biblical books which tradition connects with two men of the first generation of prophets — Isaiah ben Amoz and Micah of Moreshet, who were active in Judah in the second half of the 8th century B.C.E. The dating of these texts is debated. On the one hand, the view is held that some or all of the passages cited may contain older material which was taken over by the prophets named above and incorporated into their books, either by the authors themselves or by later editors. On the other hand, it is assumed that we have here literary products of a late, even post-exilic, period, which were 'retrojected' into earlier prophetic works.

Dating these visions is a complex issue, which, however, we do not need to discuss here. It is sufficient for our purpose to point out that oracles proclaiming Redemption and the advent of an Anointed occur in the earliest

4. See S. Talmon, "Eschatologie und Geschichte im biblischen Judentum" (n. 2 above) 18 ff.

strata of biblical prophecy and are also found in books which stem from later periods. Thus the hopes expressed in them are shown to be constant and well-defined articles of faith in biblical ideology. We can trace their development from the rise of the monarchy through the period of restoration after the Babylonian exile and into the Hellenistic age.

Particularity and Universalism

Prophetic texts disclose a vision of an ideal future in which universalism and particularity are viewed as complementary values and not as antitheses.[5] The future ideal world is conceived as a *communitas communitatum*,[6] that is to say, a composite structure in which particular-national units become integrated in a general framework by virtue of the fact that each one recognizes in its own way the all-embracing power of one God. The concept is universalist; the expression it takes is particular. It is a structure comprising separate national units who are united in their devotion to God, which, at the same time, is peculiar to each of them. Therefore, the universalistic orientation, which in the Hebrew Bible appears especially, but not exclusively, in prophetic literature, is in no way impaired by the recognition of Israel's particularity, to which both the prophets and other biblical thinkers equally subscribe: Israel is God's chosen people in the community of nations.

The special and separate status of Israel is accepted and defended; indeed, it is unreservedly affirmed as a religious, social and historic right. The centripetal all-embracing universalism which is the hallmark of biblical faith, actually presupposes the particularity of Israel and of other nations, even tolerating the centrifugal tendency which all particularity must necessarily involve. As long as the special features of factual particularity do not go beyond the limits assigned to them, they do not clash with the conceptual proclamation of a universalist faith in God which embraces all mankind.

In the course of history the twin concepts of *particularity* and *universalism* have been differently interpreted not only in Judaism and Christianity, but also by various social and political ideologies. It is inevitable that the understanding of such concepts, which are relevant to spheres beyond that of religion alone, should have been influenced by opinions and attitudes prevailing in the realm of sociology and politics. Hence a dichotomy arose between *universalism* and *particularity*, understood as *particularism*, which is reflected not only in present-day political ideologies, but also historically in the mainstreams of Christian theology. The envisaged equality of all human beings, when viewed in the framework of the Kingdom of God, presupposes, explicitly or implicity,

5. S. Talmon, *op. cit.* (above n. 3).
6. For this concept, see M. Buber, *Paths in Utopia*, trans. R.F.C. Hull (Boston, 1958) 147.

the conversion of all mankind to a single faith: Christianity – the universal creed of humanity, Hegel's "absolute religion". Thus the future world community must *ipso facto* be the (ecumenical) community of the Church. The portrayal of the future that we encounter in biblical ideology is very different: *universalism* and *particularity*, far from being mutually exclusive ideas, were rather conceived as complementary values.

Diffuse-Redemption Hope

This understanding of the future ideal world is exemplified by the prophet Micah's vision of the future aeon (which is also extant in a significantly shorter version in Isaiah 2:2–4):

Micah 4:1–5

In days to come
The mountain of YHWH's house shall be set over the mountains, exalted over the hills.
Peoples shall come streaming to it
and many (or great) nations shall come and say:
Come, let us go up to the mountain of YHWH, to the house of the Jacob's God
That he may teach us his ways and we may walk in his paths;
for out of Zion issues instruction and the word of YHWH from Jerusalem;
He will judge between many (or: great) peoples and adjudicate mighty nations afar.
They shall beat their swords into plowshares and their spears into pruning knives;
Nation shall not lift sword against nation nor will they ever train again for war.
Each one shall dwell under his vine, and under his fig tree, undisturbed.
For YHWH Sabaoth has spoken.
All the peoples will proceed each in the name of his god;
and we will proceed in the name of YHWH our God for ever and ever.

It should be stressed that the unambiguously utopian tone of prophetic visions of the future does not entirely conceal the implied references to past history. The envisaged future reconciliation of all peoples, each in its own way paying homage to the common universal God who reigns in Zion, can be seen as a hyperbolic reflexion of conditions which actually obtained during the era of David and Solomon.

In Solomon's days, the peoples that comprised the Kingdom of Israel are said to have experienced a period of peace, contrasting favourably with the years of David's rule, which had been marked by war and conflict. The picture of Solomon's reign contained in the Book of Kings conveys the clear impression that in those days Jerusalem was indeed an international meeting-place, not only for members of the ethnic and national groups which made up the Israelite Empire, but also for representatives of independent peoples and states which maintained more or less permanent commercial relations with Israel. An atmosphere of peace is shown to have prevailed throughout. The biblical historiographer expressed his enthusiastic appraisal of this epoch in a brief summary: "Judah and Israel dwelt safely, every man under his vine and under his fig tree, from Dan to Beer-Sheba, all the days of Solomon" (1 Kgs 5:5). The reader will not fail to observe that the passage from Micah (4:1–5), adduced above, summarises the vision of the future world-order in almost identical words, applying the picture not to Israel alone, but to the entire human race.[7] Thus, the particular-national experience of Solomon's reign, viewed as an ideal, served the prophets as a *primeval prototype* on which they patterned their "universalistic expectations for the future."[8]

In view of the fact that biblical hope for the future was intimately connected with history, it can easily be understood that such hope is characterized by a trend towards the restoration of past glories. This is based on the expected reconstitution of a situation which has already been experienced but which – it should be emphasized – is idealized and depicted in utopian hues. It expresses the belief that the hoped-for *turning-point in time* (not the "End of Time") will eventuate in a 'new edition' of what has already been, but one infinitely better than the first. This visionary picture reflects the notion that 'hope is the memory of the past transplanted into the future' – a longing to relive past history without the disappointments which marked the former times and without the flaws which disfigure the present.

Martin Buber has summarized the two-layered character of Israel's hope for the future with impressive brevity: "... 'eschatological' hope in Israel, the 'historical nation par excellence' (Tillich), ... is first and foremost always hope in history: it arises only through increasing disappointment in history. During this process faith takes possession of the future as the unconditioned turning-point in history and hence as the unconditioned subjugation of history. This explains how those visions of the past become matters of eschatology, which converts them into myth ... Myth is the spontaneous and legitimate language of the faith that awaits the future as the faith which recalls the past .... But myth is not the substance of faith .... Real eschatological faith is born from real history with the great birth-pangs of historical experience: any other attempt to trace its origin fails to recognise its true nature."[9]

7. See S. Talmon, "Towards World Community: Resources and Responsibilities for Living Together," *Ecumenical Review* 26 (1974) 604 ff.
8. See G. Scholem, *op. cit.* (above n. 1); S. Talmon, "Types of Messianic Expectation at the Turn of the Era," in this volume 209–212.
9. The biblical hope for an ideal aeon in history which was transferred into metahistory as a result of recurring disappointments: the historical hope that was turned into an eschatological vision. See M. Buber, *Königtum Gottes* (Berlin, 1932), Introduction = *Kingship of God*, trans. R. Scheimann (London, 1967), Preface.

משיח – Centered Expectation

There is little doubt that the biblical משיח idea, the basis of all the messianic concepts which grew out of it, has a definitely political character. The historical experience of the monarchy, projected in an idealised form, served as a pattern for the picture of the hoped-for future time which in the messianic visions is always marked by an "anointed king". It is predominantly from the 'primeval' pattern of Israel, united under the rule of David and Solomon, that the picture of the future is developed.[10]

A consequence of the primary unified concept of biblical Israel, which connected society inseparably with faith and the state with religion, was that the 'political' משיח idea had from the very beginning a 'religious dimension.' This ambivalence, too, reflects Israel's historical experience during the epoch of David and Solomon. At that time of unity, Israel experienced unprecedented political and economic advancement. This was also the time when the central Sanctuary dedicated to Israel's God was erected in Jerusalem, the place where biblical monotheism found its clearest cultic expression. This glorious period served as a guiding light in the portrayal of the future.

The Fusion of the Concepts

The assumption that the biblical hope of salvation was originally independent of the expectation of a משיח, but that in most instances the two types have been interlinked in biblical literature as we know it, can be corroborated by relevant scriptural texts.

The passages set out below in tabular form illustrate how hopes of salvation tended to merge with those of a Messiah. At the same time, they enable us to draw conclusions about their suggested original independence. In these passages we can still trace the process whereby distinguishable elements came to be fused, or more precisely strung together. Occasionally the diverse types have been combined in what may be called a "ring-composition." That is to say that within a given passage two different visions have been inter-linked in such a way that one type is ringed by two parts of another type.

In order fully to prove the thesis, one would have to present an exegetical analysis on a scale which cannot be undertaken here. We must therefore content ourselves with a few observations and confine our scrutiny to a small number of examples.

The relevant passages are arranged below in the following manner: In the

10. A concise summary of this issue is provided by W.S. McCullough, "Israel's Eschatology from Amos to Daniel" in *Studies on the Ancient Palestinian World*, Presented to F.V. Winnett, eds. J.M. Severs and D.E. Redford (Toronto, 1972), 86–101.

left hand column are shown texts which may be regarded as typical examples of a biblical diffuse-redemption hope, that is to say, a time in which salvation is promised to many peoples in many places. In the right hand column, passages are adduced which foresee the arrival of a future משיח, *i.e.* the appearance of an "anointed king." The columns are arranged in such a way that one may see at a glance how the texts, thought to have been originally independent, were conjoined in the literary tradition of the biblical canon. Accompanying these columns are some remarks which may shed light on this process of fusion.

Diffuse-Redemption Hope

Isa 9:1–4 (*Eng 2–5*)

The people who walked in darkness
have seen a great light;
dwellers in the land of shadows,
light has dawned upon them.
You have multiplied their joy;
you have increased their gladness.
They rejoice before you
as men rejoice at harvest,
as [men] are glad when they share
out the spoil.
For the yoke of their burden
and the crossbar [on] their shoulders
and the goad of the overseer
you have shattered like the day of
Midian['s defeat].
For all [the boots of] soldiers
that noisily march on,
and the garments fouled with blood
shall become [fuel for] burning,
food for fire.

Expectation of an Anointed

Isa 9:5–6 (*Eng 6–7*)

For to us a child is born,
to us a son is given;
and the government will be upon his
shoulder,
and his name will be called
'Wonderful Counsellor, Mighty (as)
God,
Everlasting Father, Prince of Peace.'
Of the increase of his government
and of peace there will be no end,

Expectation of an Anointed

upon the throne of David, and over his kingdom,
to establish it, and to uphold it
with justice and with righteousness
from this time forth and for evermore,
The zeal of the LORD of Hosts will do this.

The first four verses of Isaiah 9 (left column) describe a future time in which "the people" (Israel) will be delivered from the "darkness" of oppression by their enemy. The enemy's power will be broken (v. 3; cp. Jer 30:8). His soldiers, marching noisily, will be consumed by fire (v. 4; cp. 17:12–14). People are filled with joy and jubilation "as at harvest-time" (cp. *int. al.* Ps 126:5–6; Judg 9:27; 21:19–22) or while "sharing out the spoil (cp. *int. al.* Judg 5:30). Nowhere in this description do we find any mention of a משיח, an "anointed one" or of any other leading figure. The message refers solely to the people as a collective and thus exhibits a profound and indubitable expectation of the *state of redemption* which awaits the nation.

Verses 5–6 (right column), which follow immediately upon this passage, show a completely different emphasis. Thy give us a portrait of the future ideal ruler, on whose "shoulder" the power wrenched from the enemy (v. 3) will lie (v. 5). Although the key-word (my) "Anointed" is not mentioned, the passage leaves us in no doubt that the biblical author had his eye on the "seed of David," who would "sit upon David's throne" (v. 6) and bring peace to the world [from Jerusalem] (cp. Isa 2:4; Mic 4:3 *et al.*). The explicit reference to the House of David is shown in the choice of the titles of honour to be bestowed upon the future king, echoing parallel phrases, the Davidic character of which requires no proof:[11]

Isa 9:5:
A child is born to us, a son is given to us; and the government is upon his shoulder.

This verse calls to mind the proclamation about David in

Mic 5:1–2:

You, Bethlehem-Ephrathah, who are so small among the districts of Judah,
from you shall come forth one who is to be ruler over Israel . . .
The Lord instates him,[12] when she who is in labor gives birth . . .

11. H. Junker, "Die messianische Verkündigung des Buches Jesaja", *RB* 48 (1938) 189–193; 49 (1939) 5–11; 279–285; 338–346; 50 (1940) 5–11.
12. Read יתנו for MT יתנם, assuming that נו was misread ם. Cp. *e.g.*, 2 Kgs 22:4 and 5. Micah

It also calls to mind

Isa 7:14:

The young woman shall become pregnant and give birth to a son,
and she [or people] will name him Immanuel.

This name is an additional epithet which is joined to those mentioned in

Isa 9:5–6:

Prince of Peace . . . of peace there shall be no end . . .
through justice and righteousness from henceforth and forever

(cp. Isa 11:1–5; 42:1–4 *et al.*).

This verse has counterparts in

Mic 5:4:

And he shall be peace . . . ,

and, relating to Solomon, in

Ps 72:2–7:

Give the king your office of judgment, O God;
give your righteous rule to the king's son,
that he may judge your people with righteousness
and your poor with justice.
Let the mountains bring peace for the people
and [may] the hills [bring peace] through righteousness
Righteousness flourishes in his days
and abundant peace until the moon shall be no more.

(cp. also Ezek 37:24–28).

Similar thoughts and images referring to a future king descended from David appear in the Book of Jeremiah. It is particularly impressive to compare a passage which in the Hebrew text occurs twice (Jer 23:5–6; 33:14–16), whereas the LXX has it only once (23:5–6). As in Isaiah 7:14 and 9:5–6, the message in Jeremiah culminates in a "title of honor" by which the future hoped-for [anointed] king will be distinguished.

Jer 23:5–6:

Behold, the days are coming, says God,
when I will cause a righteous shoot to spring up
  for [or from] David.
He will reign as king and will act wisely:

5:2 is thus to be translated: "He [God] will appoint him [the future ruler]" *not* "will give *them* up," as is often done. For the technical connotation of נתן = 'appoint as king,' cp. 1 Sam 8:6; 12:13 with 8:5, 22; 12:12–14. See also R. Weiss, "On Ligatures in the Hebrew Bible," *JBL* 82 (1963) 188–194.

he will perform justice and righteousness
  in the land . . .
he will be given the name, 'God our righteousness.'

The particular and national orientation shows in most of these משיח-utterances through their restriction to the people of Israel, their country, and the future restoration of national sovereignty (cp. Dan 9:24–25).

Diffuse-Redemption Hope

Expectation of An Anointed

Isa 11:1–5
A shoot will sprout from
  the stump of Jesse,
a branch shall grow out of his roots.
And the spirit of the LORD
  shall rest upon him,
The spirit of wisdom and
  understanding,
the spirit of counsel and might,
the spirit of knowledge
  and the fear of the LORD.
He shall not judge by what his eyes see,

or decide by what his ears hear;
but with (the power of) righteousness
  he shall judge the poor,
and decide with equity
  for the meek of the earth;
he shall smite the earth
  with the rod (word) of his mouth,
and with the breath of his lips
  he shall slay the wicked.
(The power of) righteousness
shall be the girdle of his waist,
faithfulness the girdle of his loins.

Isa 11:6–9
Then wolf shall live with sheep,
and leopard lie down with kid;
calf and lion shall grow up together,
and a little child shall lead them.
Lion shall eat straw like cattle;
Infant shall play over the cobra's hole,
and a young child dance over the
  viper's nest.

Diffuse-Redemption Hope	**Expectation of an Anointed**
They shall not hurt or destroy in all my holy mountain; for as waters fill the sea, so shall the land be filled with the knowledge of God.	
	Isa 11:10 On that [future] day [the shoot that] will arise out of the stump of Jesse will be a banner to the nations; peoples will rally around him. Glory will be in his [royal] seat.

A similar phenomenon, a presumed combination of a declaration of hope for the expected משיח with a vision of a time of redemption (actually in reverse order), appears in Isaiah 11. The passage begins with a message directed solely at the person of the future ruler (vv 1–5), after which it leads on to the description of a time of redemption marked by universal peace. The portrayal of this period centres upon te situation currently envisaged and does not mention any figure of a personal "saviour." the future king of the first section is depicted as having power and authority such as we already know from the texts cited in our exposition of the first example: "The divine spirit of wisdom, understanding and counsel shall rest upon him"[13] (vv 2–3, cp. 9:5; 42:1; 52:13; 53:11; 1 Kgs 5:9–14 *et al.*). He will judge with equity" (vv 4–5; cp. 9:6; 32:1; Ps 72:1 ff *et al.*); with "the rod of his mouth" (*i.e.*, his pronouncements; cp. Prov. 14:3). "He breaks (the rod of) those who do violence." This portrait evidently draws upon the vocabulary of the **'redemption-visions'** and applies it to the future king (cp. v. 4 with 9:3).

An opposite tendency seems to show in the use of the 'child' motif. Whereas in the passages hitherto discussed, there is explicit reference to the son of David (Isa 7:14; 9:5; cp. 1 Kgs 13:2; Ps 87:56), in the **'vision of redemption'** in Isaiah 11:6 ff. the concept is expanded to embrace humanity in general (vv 6 and 8). It may even – in a manner unusual for the Hebrew Bible – extend to cover the brute creation (v 7), the only parallel being Job 38:41; 39:3.[14]

13. See *int. al.*: R. Koch, "Der Gottesgeist und der Messias," *Bib* 37 (1946) 376–403; *idem, Geist und Messias – Beitrag zur biblischen Theologie des Alten Testaments* (1950).
14. Of 91 occurrences of ילד in the Hebrew Bible only three refer to animals, of these only four to domestic animals, three of them in the same context (Gen 30:39; 31:8; Lev 22:27).

Although there is no mention of "anointing", the Davidic descent of the future king is confirmed by the reference to Jesse, the father of David (Isa 11:1). It is also supported by the motif of "the shoot (of righteousness)" (Isa 11:1). But the most crucial point is the attribution of צדק to him. The semantic range of the Hebrew word צדק is not confined to the conceptual field of righteousness and justice; it also includes the idea of power justly wielded or of power to dispense justice. This concept of justice, expressed by צדק and cognate words, may well have originated in a title of honour which was current in pre-Israelite Jerusalem. This is suggested by the name Melchisedek, whose meeting with Abraham is recorded in Genesis 14. Melchisedek united in his person the secular authority of the king (מלך) of (Jeru-)Salem with that of the high priest of the Supreme God כהן לאל עליון (Gen 14:18). When Jerusalem was established as the capital of the Israelite and later the Judean kingdom, the dynasty of David took over various local traditions,[15] including the title צדק with all the significance of that term. As in the past, so too in later history and in the hoped-for future time, Jerusalem is the "city of צדק, a stronghold sure (Isa 1:26; cp. Jer 31:23).[16] Therefore, the king of the davidic dynasty who is to rule there also bears the title of Melchisedek.

Ps 110:1–4:

> "Thus speaks God to my lord, 'You sit at my right hand ....'
> The LORD sends out the sceptre of his might from Zion ...
> The LORD has sworn and will not repent:
> 'You are a priest forever after the manner of Melchisedek'."

He will discharge the functions of the צדק-king in Jerusalem.

Isa 16:4-5:

> "The extortioner is undone; the oppressor is no more; those who trampled have disappeared from the land;
> then by [God's] mercy a throne will be established
> on which there will sit in the tent of David
> One who judges, seeks justice and hastens to do צדק (cp. Zech 9:9)

In his authority as the 'justice-dealing ruler on earth', the ideal king has a

15. Thus David built the altar for YHWH at a place which had presumably served as a (royal) santuary for the Jebusites, thereby determining the site on which the Temple at Jerusalem was later to be built. See S. Talmon, "The Biblical Concept of Jerusalem," *Journal of Ecumenical Studies* 8 (1971) 300–316.

16. I surmise that in using the phrase ושלם נות צדקך the author of Job 8:6 intentionally suggested overtones of the Jerusalem epithets נוה צדק (Jer 31:23; 50:7) and של(ו)ם.

share in God's justice (צדק) whereby he rules over the Creation (Isa 45:19; 58:2; 62:1; Jer 11:20; Zeph 9:18; Ps 4:2; 119 *passim*, etc.).[17]

Against this background it is not surprising that both the royal house of David and the priesthood of Jerusalem repeatedly incorporated the element צדק into their personal or family names; the high priestly house, the בית צדוק, traced its ancestry back to Zadok,[18] whom David had appointed (2 Sam 8:17–20:25; 15:24), and whom Solomon confirmed in his office (1 Kgs 2:35; 4:1). One of the post-exilic priests descended from this family bore the name Jehozadak (Hag 1:1, 12, 14 *et al.*; Zech 6:11; 2 Chr 5:40–41). Even more impressive is a report concerning the last king of Judah before the destruction of Jerusalem in 586 B.C.E.:

2 Kgs 24:17:

> Then the king of Babylon made Mattaniah, the uncle of Jehoiachin, king in his stead, and he [Mattaniah] changed his name to Zedekiah.

This is clearly a case in which the king put on the throne by the Babylonians wished to mark his connexion with the dynasty of David and with Jerusalem by adopting a special royal title.[19]

In contrast to the designation צדק, which goes back to a pre-Israelite tradition of Jerusalem, the image of the "Plant" or "Shoot," which we often find in biblical passages dealing with David and the משיח, seems to belong originally to the royal house of David. The famous prophecy about "a shoot

17. Cp. also the use of שלום as a divine and royal title (Judg 6:24; Isa 9:6; Mic 5:4). In view of this, the term עצת שלום (Zech 6:13) should be understood as an indirect reference to Zerubbabel, the scion of David.
18. See H.H. Rowley, "Zadok and Nehushtan," *JBL* 58 (1939) 113–141; *idem*, "Melchisedek and Zadok," *Festschrift Bertholet* (Tübingen, 1950) 461–472; and C.E. Hauer, "Who Was Zakok?," *JBL* 82 (1963) 89–94.
19. The Hebrew text admits the possibility of taking the king of Babylon as subject of the sentence. However, I do not recommend this interpretation. Similarly Solomon (Shelomoh) can be understood as a throne name which David is said to have conferred upon his son Jedidiah (2 Sam 12:24–25) so as to suggest his (future) appointment as king in (Jeru)salem. This tradition should perhaps be regarded as anticipating the change of name which Solomon himself assumed when he succeeded to the throne. It is surely not without significance that of the four sons of David who claimed the succession (Amnon, Absalom, Adonijah, and Solomon), only Solomon was born in Jerusalem (2 Sam 5:14). Also his mother was probably a native of Jerusalem (2 Sam 11–12, esp. 12:24–25), while his rivals were born in Hebron and their mothers were not of Jerusalemite origin (2 Sam 3:2–5). The name *Absalom* may have expressed a similar intention. Since his mother Maachah, the daughter of the king of Geshur in Transjordan, was a foreigner (2 Sam 3:5 *et al.*), it would have been to both their advantage to integrate themselves into the Jerusalem tradition by giving him a 'shalom' name.

from the stock of Jesse" (Isa 11:1) is echoed in various passages, with or without a reference to צדק. Some of these refer to the post-exilic era:

Jer 23:5:

Behold, the days are coming, says the LORD,
when I will raise a צמח צדיק for David;

Jer 33:15:

In those days and at that time I will cause a צמח צדקה to grow up for David.

Similarly phrased is

Ps 132:17:

There I will cause David's power (literally, "horn") to shoot up — שם אצמיח קרן לדוד;[20]
there I will set up a lamp for my anointed.

It is in Isaiah 11 that we have what may be the most complete description of the future davidic anointed who is to rule over the whole world, and the fullest collection of the attributes applied to thim.

Zechariah and Haggai, whose texts can be more readily dated, use language similar to Isaiah and Jeremiah:

Zech 3:8:

Hear now . . . I bring my servant, the Shoot — עבדי צמח

Zech 6:12:

Here is a man; his name is the Shoot — צמח שמו,
for where he stands he will shoot up — ומתחתיו יצמח.

Both here and in comparable passages (*e.g.* Hag 2:23), the context leaves no room for doubt that in these cases the epithets צמח, צד(י)ק and עבד[21] refer to Zerubbabel, the last scion of the house of David to perform the functions of ruler in biblical times (cp. Isa 61:10) and that they must be evaluated in their literary relation to the vision of King David in Isaiah 11:1–5.

In the last-mentioned passage, a vision of the era of redemption (vv 6–9) follows upon the proclamation of the future ruler. Here, as in 9:1–4, we have a description of the ideal situation which extends beyond Israel's national aspirations. The entire creation is included in the picture, in which we can detect no substantive connexion with the preceding 'messianic' text and no epithets like those applied to the descendants of David.[22] On the other hand,

20. The metaphor is applied to the Israelite people in Ezek 29:21. In some respects, God, people and king share a common vocabulary. See S. Talmon, "Kingship etc.," in this volume, p. 21 ff.
21. For such an intertextual approach to interpretation, see S. Talmon, "The Navel of the Earth and the Comparative Method," in: *Scripture in History and Theology, Essays in Honor of J. Coert Rylaarsdam* (1977), 243–268.
22. See S. Talmon, "Types of Messianic Expectation," in this volume, 209–210.

the final verse of the paragraph does not contain any motif taken from the redemption-oracle. What we do find here, again in a context referring to the people and the nation, is the typically davidic image:

Isa 11:10:

On that day [a shoot burst forth from]
the root of Jesse will be a sign for the nations.
Peoples will seek him and his resting place will be glory.

This verse can be regarded as a restatement of the messianic prophecy with which the paragraph began (Isa 11:1–5). Thus the passage is constructed on a cyclic plan in which the centre-piece, the **oracle of redemption** (vv 6–9), is sandwiched in between two **messianic prophecies** (vv 1–5 and 10). Although there is no conclusive proof of this, the inclusio-pattern would suggest that in this literary composition two originally independent elements have been artistically combined.

Diffuse-Redemption Hope	**Expectation of an Anointed**
	Isa 32:1–2 Then a king will reign with just [power], Nobles will rule with integrity. He will be to everyone like a shelter from storm[s] and a refuge from torrent[s]; like waterstreams in the desert, like the shadow of giant rock in a parched land.
Isa 32:3–7 The eyes of those who see will not be blinded, The ears of those who hear will be alert, The heart of the hasty will discern and know, The tongue of stammerers will speak distinctly. A wrongdoer will no more be called noble, Nor a villain be deemed honorable. For the wrongdoer speaks evil, and his heart meditates wickedness to practice godlessness, to speak abusively about God; He leaves the hungry man unfed, and denies a drink to the thirsty.	

Diffuse-Redemption Hope	**Expectation of an Anointed**
The villain's works are evil. He devises wicked plots to ruin the poor with lies; and when the pauper speaks [in court] [he perverts] justice.	
	Isa 32:8 But the noble person thinks nobly, and stands firm for what is noble.
Isa 32:15–20 Again will be poured on us the spirit from above; The desert shall become fertile land and the forest shall become fertile land.[23] In the desert justice will dwell, and integrity in the fertile land. Integrity will bring forth peace and justice produce lasting security. My people will reside in a peaceful habitation, in safe houses and secure dwellings. - - - - - - - - - - - - - - - - - - Happy will you be, sow by every stream, letting ox and donkey roam free.	

Isaiah 32:1 exhibits a comparable structure. The first two verses describe the rule of the future king in standard, characteristic terms – צדקה and משפט – such as we have encountered in the texts already cited. Next comes a series of images drawn from nature, presenting the king – the Anointed – as protector of the realm, similar to the references to Solomon in Psalm 72. This line of thought is resumed in 32:8. Here the key word is נדיב, which is used as a title of honour also in other biblical texts (*e.g.* Isa 13:2; Ps 47:10; 107:40 = Job 34:18; Ps 113:8; 118:9; 146:3; cp. 1 Sam 2:8; Prov 19:6; 25:7), sometimes in parallelism with שׂר, "prince" (Num 21:18) or שופט, "judge/saviour/ruler" (Prov 8:16; cp. Ps 83:12).[24]

23. In biblical imagery, יער parallels מדבר in that both represent uncultivated land. Therefore, in order to preserve the positive note in this verse, a syntactical rearrangement is required. We propose to read ולכרמל יער יחשב, assuming an inversion for which also other examples can be adduced.
24. In this context, נדיב serves as a synonym of the royal epithet נגיד. See W. Richter, "Die *nagid* Formel," *BZ* N.F. 9 (1965) 71–81.

Theese two passages enclose a section which depicts a future state free from disaster, physical defects, blasphemers and rebels, and pervaded by wisdom and understanding (Isa 32:3–7). The description relates to mankind in general and is not limited to Israel. In contrast to the first and last verses, there is no mention of a "king" or "anointed one." After an interpolation of a somewhat different kind (vv 9–14), the portrayal of a time of redemption is resumed and delineated in greater detail at the end of the chapter (vv 15–20), but now with special reference to Israel ("my people"), who is assured of a safe and peaceful future (v 18). The motifs introduced here – safety, prosperity and fertility of the soil – are intrinsic to the biblical hopes for the time of redemption. These motifs occur frequently without any connexion with the expectation of a future משיח. To the texts already cited, one should add Ezekiel's vision of Gog and Magog (39:8–16). There, that future situation is foreshadowed by several different means: (1) images taken from historical experience (cp. Ezek 28:25–26; 34:25–28; Isa 14:30; Jer 32:36ff; Judg 18:7, 27–28; 1 Chr 4:40 and Jer 49:31–32); (2) images from an embellished conception of former times[25] (1 Kgs 5:5; cp. 1 Sam 12:11); and (3) images taken from ideal notions derived from such earlier periods (Deut 12:10; 33:28, etc.). In the present case, Isaiah 32, an internal link between the constituent elements within the whole structure, is forged by transferring motifs and ideas connected with the expectation of a משיח to the depictions of visions of the era of redemption: נדיב (v 5; cp. v 8), משפט, צדק(ה) (vv 16–17; cp. v 1), and the all-embracing term שלום (vv 17–18).

Diffuse-Redemption Hope

Isa 2:2–4
In days to come
The mountain of YHWH's house
Shall be set over the the mountains
  exalted over the hills.
All peoples shall come streaming to it
  and many (or great) nations
  shall come and say:
Come, let us go up to the mountain of YHWH,
  to the house of Jacob's God.
That he may teach us his ways
  and we shall walk in his paths;
four out of Zion issues instruction
  and YHWH's word from Jerusalem.
He will judge between the peoples
  and adjudicate mighty nations.

25. See "Types of Messianic Expectation etc." in this volume, 209–211.

They shall beat their swords into
plowshares
And their spears into pruning knives.
People shall not lift sword against people,
nor will they ever again train for war.

The most distinct and probably the best known picture of the future era of salvation is given in the vision of the "days to come" presented in almost identical words in Isaiah 2:2–4 and Micah 4:1–3. The vision cannot be dated with certainty. We have no reliable clues by which to determine whether Micah quoted from Isaiah or *vice versa*, or whether both prophets used a source available to them but unknown to us. These questions cannot be probed here,[26] but for our purpose two important points must be emphasized:

(1) That vision of the future recorded in two prophetical books can be regarded as perhaps the purest example of the genre **'Redemption-time Oracle,'** if one is inclined to assume the existence of such a genre in biblical literature. We find here the picture of a hoped-for situation in which all peoples and nations are included and pervaded by universal peace. There is no more war, no victory or defeat. The trade of war is learned no more, having become altogether superfluous. Weapons are scrapped and reforged into useful agricultural tools. Micah adds some further touches: political security will result in economic prosperity, which is conceived, interestingly enough, in agricultural terms:

Mic 4:4:

Each man will sit under his vine and under his fig-tree
and none shall make him afraid.

The echo of other biblical representations of the 'Era of Redemption', nearly all culminating in the theme of political and economic security, is clear and unambiguous. It may be presumed that they draw upon a single stock of concepts and motifs which must be regarded as the common conceptual property of ancient Israel: the notion of an ideal future state which is expected to be realised within the bounds of human experience, *i.e.* within the horizon of history.

(2) The centre of the picture is taken up not by a משיח, an anointed king, but by God himself. He will judge the nations from Zion and maintain equity among them. The *King's Peace*, which we have encountered in the messianic visions cited above (*e.g.*, Isa 9:5–6; Ezek 37:24–28) and which, as I have already pointed out, originates in the pattern of the *Pax Solomonica* during the

26. For the recent discussions of the issue see *int. al.* H. Wildberger, *Jesaja 1–12, BKAT* X, 1 (Neukirchen-Vluyn, 1965); 0. Kaiser, *Das Buch des Propheten Jesaja, Kapitel 1–12 ATD* 17 (Göttingen, 1981), *ad loc.*

peaceful period of King Solomon's reign (cp. Ps 72:2–7), is sublimated to become the *Peace of God* and assumes cosmic dimensions. These features are even more strongly defined when we come to consider other descriptions of the future 'Era of Redemption' such as Isaiah 11:6–9 and 65:25. It is tempting to combine all the differently stressed aspects of that hoped-for 'Era of Redemption,' and thus to reconstruct a composite picture from which – it can be assumed – various biblical authors borrowed elements which they then incorporated into their own visions.

Expectation of an Anointed

Mic 5:1–4a
You, Bethlehem Ephrathah, the
smallest among Judah's tribes,
Out of you will come forth for me
one who will be a ruler in Israel
whose origin goes back to ancient times.
He will appoint him [as king]
until the one heavy with child
gives birth;
Then the rest of his brothers
will return to the house of Israel.
He will then stand [firm]
and lead them with divine power
and with the majesty of YHWH's name,
his God.

Jer 23:5–6 (=33:15–16)
'See, the days are coming,' says YHWH
'when I will raise for David
a righteous branch
who will reign as king, wise,
practicing justice and integrity
in the land.
In his days Judah will be saved
and Israel dwell in security'.
And this is the name he will be called:
'YHWH – our righteous power.'

A similar attempt could be made to trace the process by which the expectation of a future "Anointed" or משיח came to be formulated in concrete terms. The passages already mentioned – Jeremiah 23:5–6 (=33:15–16) and Micah 5:1–4a – which are quite definitely directed at the future king of the House of David, when taken together, provide, as it were, a catalogue of the royal titles and attributes by which the expected "Shoot" is distinguished. The view is concentrated exclusively upon his personality. Even though the radiance of his rule over Judah and the whole of Israel is central (Jer 23:6 =

33:16; Mic 5:2b, 3b), the universal or even cosmic extension which characterizes the prophecies of the 'Era of Redemption' cannot be overlooked. A synopsis of these passages, together with the "messianic" texts already mentioned (*e.g.*, Isa 9:5–6; 11:1–5, 10; 32:1–2; Hag 2:23; Zech 3:8; 4:6; 6:12–13), supplies an inventory of the future king's attributes which may have been taken from a common stock of messianic oracles.

It must once more be stressed that the proposed classification of biblical visions for the future into two types (particular and universalistic), *viz*, the hope for a diffuse redemption and the expectation of a משיח, can be substantiated only by a full exegetical analysis of the relevant texts which in their present form are already conflated. The possible existence of originally independent literary units which on the one hand expressed the hope for a future era of redemption and, on the other, the expectation of an anointed king – משיח, can only be assumed but not be definitely proved from biblical texts that have come down to us. In the Hebrew Scriptures these two aspects of our second thesis – **'Redemption'** and **'Anointed'** oracles – are to a very great extend fused and in only a few cases can they be shown to be independent of one another. Nor can the process of fusion be demonstrated in detail. We therefore must be content with hypotheses arrived at by means of literary analysis. This is where the discovery of an "inclusio composition," such as indicated above, can in some cases yield noteworthy results. If we not only apply such an analysis to the smaller text-units presented above, but also go beyond these limits, and especially beyond the chapter-division which has become established in the texts of the Bible since the Middle Ages, the extensive inter-weaving of **'Redemption'** prophecies and **'Anointed'** oracles is even more clearly revealed. Viewed in this light, the **'vision of redemption'** in Micah 4:1–5 and the **'royal oracle'** in 5:1–4a can be comprehended as forming a framework for the intervening (presumably composite) passage 4:9–14. From a still more comprehensive viewpoint, the 'redemption-era' prophecies of Isaiah 2:1–4 and 11.6–9 (with the sequels 11:10 and 11:16) could be understood as framing a comprehensively conceived cyclic composition embracing the first (composite) part of the Book of Isaiah (chapters 2–11), which is marked off from the rest of the book by the free-standing units chapters 1 and 12.

Biblical visions of the future probably originated in the early history ot Israel. There can be no doubt that these visions had their roots deep in the thought of the ancient Hebrews – so deep that one can speak of a biblical determinism in regard to the משיח or to the time of redemptionm̈This determinism reached its full flowering against the background of the destruction of Jerusalem and the conquest of Judah by the Babylonians in 586 B.C.E., which brought to an end, at least for the time being, political sovereignty and the rule of an "anointed king." At that time, especially in the diaspora community in Babylonian, the expectation of a restoration of national independence in the near future received a great stimulus. As in the past, so now, each new generation expected and each political upheaval contained the possibility that the awaited 'Redemption-King' would arise and the era of Divine promise begin. The "ingathering of the dispersed," *i.e.*, the return of the exiles to their homeland, was more than ever regarded as an unmistakable sign that the time of redemption was at hand (cp., *e.g.*, Isa 56:8; Jer 29:14; 30:10–11; 31:18; Ezek 11:17; 20:34, 41; 28:25; 36:24; 37:21; 39:27).[27]

The historical circumscription of the biblical hope for the future, *i.e.* of its realization within some foreseeable time in history, is most distinctly revealed in passages which tell of a משיח. The motif of the "Branch" – צמח –, and especially that of the "birth" and of the "child", is meant to suggest that the contemplated vision of the future awaits imminent realization. As already mentioned, this event is expected to take place during the lifetime of the next generation, or a few generations later, when an anointed King of Davidic lineage will arise, as mentioned, for example, in

Isa 7:14:

> A young woman shall conceive and bear a son,
> and she (or you) will call his name Immanuel.

This insistence on an imminently-awaited fulfilment of future hope shows a characteristic of biblical religious and political thinking which appears less clearly, if at all, in later crystalizations of the messianic concepts.

Some biblical authors interpreted the restoration of the Temple in Jerusalem and the establishment of a social and political autonomy, even though on a limited scale, which had been made possible by the edict of Cyrus (538 B.C.E.), as a historical realization of the expected future salvation. The returning exiles from Babylon considered themselves to be the "holy seed" (cp. Ezra 9:2 with Isa 6:12–13), from which God would once again make his people sprout. It had been vouchsafed to them to see the time of redemption in its historical reality, and to witness the rise of the promised 'Anointed', whom they perceived in the person of Zerubbabel, as can be seen from the oracles of the contemporary prophets:

Zech 3:8:

> Listen . . . I will now bring my servant, the Branch;

27. See S. Talmon, "Exil und Rückkehr in der Ideenwelt des Alten Testaments", in: *Exil-Diaspora-Rückkehr*, ed. R. Mosis (Düsseldorf, 1977) 31–55; and S. Safrai, *Das Jüdische Volk im Zeitalter des Zweiten Tempels* (Neukirchen-Vluyn, 1978) 43 ff.

Zech 6:12:

Here is a man named the Branch;
he will shoot up from the ground where he is

(cp. *int. al.* Isa 11:10);

Hag 2:23:

On that day, says the LORD of hosts,
I will take you, Zerubbabel . . . my servant,
and will wear you as a signet ring;
for you it is that I have chosen.

In his days Israel's fate will change for the better (cp. Hag 2:15, 18):

Hag 2:22:

I will . . . break the power of heathen realms

(cp. 2:7; Zech 1:15; 1:2–4, 12–13), as God once crushed the army of the Egyptians (Exod 15:4 ff.). Peace and salvation will prevail in the land forever (cp. Hag 2:9; Zech 8:12, 19; 6:13; Mal 2:5 with Isa 52:7; 57:2, 19; 60:17; 66:12 *et al.*). Fields and vineyards will yield their fruits to the people resettled in their land (cp. Hag 2:15–19; Zech 3:10; 8:12 with Hos 2:23–25; Joel 4:18; Amos 9:13–14 *et al.*, contrasted with Hag 1:3–6, 9–11).

The returnees' belief that they were living at the 'turning point of time', enables us to understand the absence from post-exilic biblical writings of the historical perspective which permeates especially pre-exilic prophetic literature. For the people of the period of the return the 'future redemption' had become the actual present. Their main concern was to translate the traditional visions of the future into concrete facts of everyday life. Utopian hyperbole and practical realism were mingled in the effort to form the present according to the pattern of the 'proto-typical age' of David and Solomon. The decisive factor is that the down-to-earth character of biblical expectations for the future precluded any escape into Utopia, to the ideal 'Never-never Land'. Their view of the future was closely bound to history. From this resulted that biblical thought was not conditioned by the essentially non-existential or anti-existential trends of later eschatological and messianic faith. Thus, biblical thought escaped having to pay the "price of Messianism"[28] so aptly described by Gershom Scholem:

> The magnitude of the messianic idea corresponds to the endless powerlessness in Jewish history . . . There's something preliminary, something provisional about Jewish history; hence its inability to give of itself entirely. There is something grand about living in hope, but at the same time there is something profoundly unreal about it . . . Thus in Judaism the Messianic idea has compelled a *life lived in deferment*, nothing can be irrevocably

28. G. Scholem, *Debarim Bego* (Tel-Aviv, 1975) 189–190 (Hebrew).

accomplished. One may say, perhaps, the Messianic idea is the real anti-existentialist idea.[29]

Since biblical literature is deeply rooted in the soil of the actual experience of a historical and social entity, it follows that the biblical images of a future world did not become an escape into mere wish-fulfilment. Biblical hope for the future is the memory of the past transplanted into a vision of the future. It is this peculiarity of the ancient Israelites' experience of the world which manifests itself in the Hebrew Bible and which, according to Franz Rosenzweig, distinguishes these writings from those of the New Testament:

> In contrast to the pointed paradoxes (of the New Testament), the Jewish Bible, having grown out of the whole extent of a people's life and the whole extent of a national literature, with its deep and living faith, even amid trenchant and separatist polemical prophecies, offered a firm basis for constructive effort in this world, here and now, not in some visionary, utopian, extra-historical future."[30]

The concrete fabric of the expectation of redemption places upon the People of the Bible a responsibility for forming the future which grows out of their responsibility for forming their present. While the biblical visions of a משיח and of the era of redemption are conditioned by history, they can at the same time open up vistas which go beyond the limits of biblical experience. For this reason the concept of a future era of redemption does not remain exclusively confined within the bounds of history. Although deeply rooted in Israel's experience, it nevertheless contains the seed of a vision which transcends the horizon of experienced history.

The state of living in hope, permeated as it is by the idea of redemption, inspires the principles and decisions which should serve as guidelines for living in history. Each person is called upon to help bring about the realization of the 'time of redemption' in history. Human obedience to divine commands is expected to lead to a transformation of the world, not to bring about a world revolution.

Conclusion

Thus, biblical hope for the future becomes a call for education – and for self-education. The biblical view of the future imposes upon every moral person the task of shaping day-to-day life-style and re-shaping society in such a manner that each 'now' can become a step towards the realization of the ideal 'then' perceived as a vision. The ground must be thoroughly prepared. Personal commitment to the re-forming of one's ego and the social structure grew out of

29. G. Scholem, "Toward An Understanding of the Messianic Idea," *op. cit.* (above n. 1), 35.
30. F. Rosenzweig, "Weltgeschichtliche Bedeutung der Bibel" in: *Kleine Schriften* (Berlin, 1937), 125.

a hope for the future,[31] which pointed the way to and formed the basis of what Martin Buber called "Hebrew" or "Biblical Humanism."[32]

The instability and variability of past experience which served as a backdrop of biblical hope for the future, and with it the 'educational imperative', account for the fact that the picture of the **'Redemption-Era'** cannot be painted in detail, nor can the way which leads the individual and the community towards it be programmed in advance in all its particulars. Biblical authors were content to depict the structure of the future world-order in a few bold strokes. This sparsity of detail stands in fundamental contrast with the colourful and often over-richly embroidered portrayals that we encounter in later messianic and eschatological passages as *e.g.* in apocalyptic, Qumran, rabbinic-midrashic, Christian and Islamic literature. The essential features of the expected **'Redemption-Era'** can be ascertained from a collation of diverse passages in the books of the Bible, such as those I have quoted. The result is a composite affair, pieced together from parts taken from various strands of biblical literature. It is impossible to construct from these variegated materials a systematic description of the process of internal development to which biblical Visions of Redemption were subjected. The picture must remain incomplete, as the biblical thinkers probably intended it should.

The expected future epoch, considered as a whole, consists of two stages. It begins with a historically conditioned and at the same time utopian portrayal of a "Day of Reckoning." God wages war against the nations that have been Israel's enemies in the past. He judges the sinners in Israel and among humanity at large. This is the יום ה' – "the Day of the Lord," the time of Divine Judgment. This portrayal is closely modeled on God's deeds in history already experienced. The collective memory preserves the thought of critical moments in the past when God intervened in human affairs and waged war against oppressors, generally represented as Israel's enemies. The stage of purgation is the pre-condition for the dawn of redemption which will then break for the righteous remnant of Israel and of all nations. The flawed world of history will be succeeded by the hoped-for perfect world, just as the antediluvian (=prehistoric) world which had gone astray was replaced by the world of history.

This two-tier picture of the future may also be understood as a transfigured image of historical experience in the reigns of David and Solomon. Some

31. S. Talmon, "Utopie und Wirklichkeit im Denken Martin Bubers," in: *Toleranz heute – 250 Jahre nach Mendelssohn und Lessing* (Berlin, 1979), 129 ff.; *Idem*, "Towards World Community etc." *op. cit.* (above n. 7).

32. See S. Talmon, "The Bible in Contemporary Israeli Humanism," *Judaism* 21:1 (Winter, 1972) 69–73.

features of the times of war under David show perhaps in the picture of the future cosmic conflict, while the *Pax Solomonica* shines through the blueprint for the era of redemption. Even the prophets, who generally took a negative attitude toward the history of their times and subjected the nation and its kings to severe criticism, did not offer for the future any social or political structures other than those experienced in history: the existing diversity of societies, peoples and states was envisaged also for the future, without any signs of revolutionary change. The actual pluralism of ethnic identities and differences of creed is to be maintained in a *communitas communitatum* which will achieve peace and reconciliation, like that foretold by the prophet Micah in the verses quoted above:

Mic 4:4–5:

> Each one shall dwell under his vine and under his fig tree
> and no one frightens them . . .
> For all the peoples proceed, each in the name of its god;
> and we proceed in the name of YHWH our God for ever (and ever).

Every believer and every society is called upon to strive towards this common goal. The touchstone of morality, for the individual as for society, is not so much the attainment of that goal as the intensity of the effort and vision with which men seek the future ideal age.

THE EMERGENCE OF JEWISH SECTARIANISM IN THE EARLY SECOND TEMPLE PERIOD

I

The biblical scholar who purports to review Max Weber's seminal sociological analysis of ancient Judaism, perforce vascillates betwen praise and criticism in his appreciation of the work.

He cannot escape being impressed by the audacious attempt to portray the societal life and the Ideenwelt of Ancient Israel on an immensely wide and colourful canvas which reveals a powerful faculty for integrating the diverse components into a highly suggestive meaningful picture; to trace the reverberations of the mores and modalities of that ancient civilization in later stages of the development of Judaism; and, beyond these limits, to tie them in with phenomena which come into the fore in other religions and civilizations, predominantly, but not exclusively in Protestant ethics.

Weber was not concerned with particularized historical investigations, but rather with the revealment of overall processes which he believed to discern in often quite disparate historical societies and situations. Therefore, says Talcott Parsons: "the total result of Weber's comparative study, becomes much more reliable than the judgement of one particular case can be from its own data, taken alone."[1]

In a similar vein, R. Lennert observed: "Max Webers Grösse wird immer in der Kraft liegen mit der er tatsächlich das *Ganze* der noch erkennbaren Geschichte zu umfassen versucht hat . . . und in dem rücksichtslosen Mute, mit dem er Konsequenzen gezogen hat, die auch uns zu ziehen bleiben."[2]

It is precisely this comprehensiveness of the endeavor which constitutes the most conspicuous innovation in Weber's presentation of Ancient Judaism, as was pointed out by Julius Guttman in a review of *Das antike Judentum* a few

1. Talcott Parsons, *The Structure of Social Action* (New York 1937), 542. Although concurring with Weber's procedure on the whole since it is based on a "well-recognized methodological principle" (*ib.*), Parsons seems to have entertained some doubts about Weber's detailed studies.
2. M. Lennert, *Die Religionstheorie MaxWebers* (Stuttgart 1935), 3–4.

years after its publication:[3] "Die interne Arbeit der Jüdischen Wissenschaft hat diese Fragen, so sehr sie ihnen im einzelnen überall auf ihrem Wege begegnet, systematisch nicht behandelt. Was wir an Versuchen zu soziologischer Erkenntnis des Judentums besitzen, rührt in der Hauptsache von Vertretern anderer Disziplinen her, die durch Fragen ihres eigenen Faches zur Untersuchung jüdischer Probleme veranlasst wurden. Naturgemäss beschänken sie sich am meisten auf bestimmte für ihre besonderen Zwecke wichtige Einzelfragen. Das gilt auch für den bedeutensten älteren Versuch soziologischer Erfassung des Judentums, für Sombarths viel unstrittenes Buch *Die Juden und das Wirtschaftsleben.* Ganz abgesehen von seinen standpunktlichen Vorurteilen, behandelt es das Judentum nur als eine der Entstehungsursachen des modernen Kapitalismus und analysiert es nur so weit, wie diese Fragestellung es verlangt. Weber beabsichtigte demgegenüber eine allseitige soziologische Untersuchung des Judentums zu geben." Guttman's judgement has lost nothing of its poignancy, as a survey of later appraisals of Weber's study proves. It may suffice to quote as an example David L. Petersen's recent succinct statement: "Even though Weber wrote a creative study analysing the social system of Ancient Israel few scholars have moved beyond that work".[4]

The very title *Das antike Judentum* given to a study which is planned to present an analytical survey of ancient Israel from its very beginnings to early Christian times, appears to evidence Weber's grasp of the historical and religious continuity of Judaism throughout the ages. In this, Weber showed a comprehension which is commensurate with the Jewish self-understanding, and compares to advantage with the bi-section into 'pre-exilic Israel' and 'post-exilic Judaism' which in his time denoted, and to a large extent yet denotes the work of old Testament theologians and historians.

True, the praise which Weber drew from specialists in diverse branches of Jüdische Wissenschaft, not alone from Bible scholars, always was accompanied by more than a grain of criticism. A caveat was sounded against Weber's 'typological' approach which, in the eyes of his critics, sometimes

3. J. Guttman, Max Webers Soziologie des antiken Judentums, in: *Monatsschrift für die Geschichte und Wissenschaft des Judentums*, Bd. 69 (1925), 196–197.

4. D.L. Petersen, Max Weber and the Sociological Study of Ancient Israel, in: *Religious Change and Continuity*, ed. H.M. Johnson, *Sociological Inquiry* 49, 2–3 (1979), 137; cp. int. al. F. Raphaël, Max Weber et le judaisme antique, in: *Archives Européennes de Sociologie* (=*AES*), Vol. 11 (1970), 334 ff; N.K. Gottwald, *The Tribes of Yahweh – A Sociology of Liberated Israel.* 1250–1050 B.C. (New York 1979), XXV.

played havoc with or at least clouded historical realities, as far as they could be extracted from the transmitted sources. A case in point is I. Schiper's objection raised in a paper published in 1924: "Weber used the so-called 'typological methodology' which consists, in the first place, of bringing forth out of the multitude of historical particulars those elements which are considered 'typical' and putting into the background all those which have atypical and individual features. The whole dynamics of historical development is derived from typical traits. At first sight such a methodology appears to be an excellent means of discovering 'objective truth'. But it is only an illusion. As a matter of fact the typological methodology has only a relative value, not greater than other methodologies which put individual and specific features in the forefront.[5] One cannot deny that in the typological methodology the subjective approach of the investigator plays a prominent part and it is his own fancy which decides what factors are to be classified as 'typical' and what 'specific' or 'individual'. Only one truth remains: The subjective 'truth' of the author and his own standard of values."[6] Schiper's strictures on Weber's method appear to bear the imprint of Benedetto Croce's dictum that a historian – let alone a sociologist – always views history from the vantage point of his own existential situation and in the light of it, and therefore is prone to colour and even distort historical 'realities'.[7] In a somewhat similar vein, A. Causse took Weber to task for having retrojected a medieval social phenomenon into (Jewish) antiquity, by introducing the concept of 'pariah-people' into his sociological analysis of biblical Israel.[8]

5. For some limitations of the 'type-approach' in reference to biblical literature, Israelite history and sociology, see: S. Talmon, The 'Comparative Method' in Biblical Interpretation – Principles and Problems, in: *Congress Volume – Göttingen* 1977, ed. by J.A. Emerton. *Suppl. to Vetus Testamentum* (=*VT*), Vol. 29 (Leiden 1978), 320–356.
6. I. Schiper, Max Weber on the Sociological Basis of the Jewish Religion (translated from the Russian by P. Glikson), in: *Journal of Jewish Studies* 1959, 1. 258. In contrast, Talcott Parsons (op. cit., 539) evaluates Weber's type-approach positively, at least in reference to Confucianism and Hinduism. Cp. further: J. Neusner, Max Weber Revisited: *Religion and Society in Ancient Judaism with Special Reference to the Late First and Second Centuries* (Oxford 1981), 1.
7. Weber was conscious of this danger: "Der Sinologe, Indologe, Semitist, Aegyptologe wird in ihnen (diesen Darstellungen, S.T.) natürlich nichts ihm sachlich Neues finden. Wünschenswert ware nur: dass er nichts zur Sache wesentliches findet, was er als sachlich falsch beurteilen muss", *Gesammelte Aufsätze zur Religionssoziologie* (=*GARS*) Bd. I (1920), 13–14.
8. A. Causse, *Du groupe ethnique à la communauté religieuse* (Paris 1937), 9; see further: F. Crüsemann, Israel in der Perserzeit. Eine Skizze – Thesen zur Auseinandersetzung mit Max Weber, in: E. Schluchter, ed., Max Webers Sicht des antiken Christentums:

Even harsher is the judgement which Jay A. Holstein passed more recently on Max Weber's *Ancient Judaism*: "An analysis of Weber's thought leads one to doubt its theoretical and practical value in biblical studies. His insistence that all thought can be reduced to cultural considerations is sustained by a premise which claims to be free of such considerations. And the practical application of his method caused him to misunderstand, reinterpret, alter, or simply to ignore the biblical text itself."[9]

Weber realized the 'dangers' which inhere in his method generally, but he was quite ready to live with the onus of 'subjectivity', as the following quotation, which could be amplified by others, reveals: "Die *objektive* Gültigkeit alles Erfahrungswissens beruht darauf, und nur darauf, dass die gegebene Wirklichkeit nach Kategorien geordnet wird, welche *in einem spezifischen Sinne subjektiv*, nämlich die Voraussetzungen unserer Erkenntnis darstellend, und an die Voraussetzung des Wertes derjenigen Wahrheit gebunden ist, die das Erfahrungswissen allein uns zu geben vermag."[10]

The strictures raised against Weber's methodology caused that *Ancient Judaism* had an only marginal impact on the 'professional' study of Israel's history, the biblical cult, and even biblical prophecy[11] which is at the very centre of his interest. He did, though, influence some Old Testament scholars who, like him, incline toward conceptual generalization[12] and could readily

Interpretation und Kritik (Frankfurt a/M 1985), 205–232. It stands to reason that such 'Rückprojizierungen' resulted from Weber's own 'rücklaufige Betrachtung' of ancient Israel: "Er sieht das Judentum weitgehend aus der Perspektive des asketischen Protestantismus", W. Schuchter, Altisraelitische Ethik und okzidentaler Rationalismus, in: *Wax Weber's Studie über das antike Judentum etc. = MWSJ* (Frankfurt a/M 1978), 14.

9. J.A. Holstein, Max Weber and Biblical Scholarship, in: *Hebrew Union College Annual*, vol. 46 (1975), 179. Cp. his more comprehensive criticism, *ib.*, 163: "Weber's attempt to interpret the Hebrew Bible is an epitome of his methodological stance toward the study of the past. To create order from the chaotic biblical material he always sought to place a text within its societal context in order to determine that text's Zeitgeist. To accomplish this he constructed ideal types. To justify his ideal types he appealed to extrabiblical analogies. Only then did he seek corroborative data from the Hebrew Bible". Gottwald gives a more balanced assessment: "I shall not . . . conceal my commitment to the larger need for large-scale social theory of the sort associated with Marx, Durkheim, and Weber and their successors, while emphasizing that all the theory in the world is only as good as the empirical observations on which it is based" (*op. cit.*, 13, cf 627–631).
10. *Gesammelte Aufsätze zur Wissenschaftslehre = GAW* (Tübingen 1922), 213.
11. My appreciation of the situation differs considerably from Crüsemann's, see *op. cit.* (n. 8).
12. To mention just a few names and titles: W.F. Albright, *From the Stone Age to Christianity* (Baltimore² 1957); M. Buber, *Königtum Gottes* (Berlin 1933); G. Mendenhall, *The Tenth*

subscribe to his dictum: "Begriffe sind nicht Abbilder der Wirklichkeit, sondern gedankliche Mittel zum Zwecke ihrer Beherrschung."[13] It would appear that the lack of attention given to Weber's work may be related to the waning of the 'Pattern of Culture' school and the concomitant increase of an anti-type orientation in Old Testament studies which tends to stress the particular and the a-typical in biblical society and its conceptual universe.

Even more weighty is the following consideration: Weber's types of correlation and interaction between religious and economic – in the case of ancient Israel more decidedly between religious and societal – processes, are deduced predominantly from his inquiries into historical situations in which these phenomena are adequately documented and therefore sufficiently discernible, as is the case in reference to Protestantism and Capitalism. In his endeavor to evince a similar interdependence in biblical society, he encountered the difficulty, of which he indeed took notice, that the biblical literature "rarely provides socio-economic data... that it is characterized not by scientific exactitude but by fabulous imagination,"[14] and certainly does not provide systematic descriptions of any facet of the social and intellectual world-view of the ancient Israelites. Thus he was forced to distil his categories from raw, disconnected materials which at times are not altogether intelligible or are open to divergent interpretations. While being aware of flaws and errors in Weber's presentation and synthesis of biblical Judaism, in the last count, I would yet side with the praisers of his study rather than with its detractors.[15]

II

Time and again it has been stressed that Weber did not live to complete his work on ancient Judaism. All that we have are three studies which deal with three socio-religious phenomena – the covenant between Israel and Yhwh; the

Generation (Baltimore and London 1973); N.K. Gottwald, *op. cit.* – In this context it is noteworthy that in some 'sociologically' oriented works by Old Testament scholars, Weber's *Ancient Judaism* and his other studies are most sparingly, if at all, referred to. Examples are: R. de Vaux, *Les institutions de l'Ancien Testament* (Paris 1958–60), tr. into English: *Ancient Israel – its Life and Institutions* (London and New York 1961); Y. Kaufmann. *The Religion of Israel*, tr. from the Hebrew and abridged by M. Greenberg (Chicago 1960, London 1961); M. Smith, *Palestinian Parties and Politics that Shaped the Old Testament* (New York and London 1971).

13. *GAW*, 208.
14. As quoted by Holstein, *op. cit.*, 163.
15. See my review of R. de Vaux, *Ancient Israel – its Life and Institutions*, in: *Christian News from Israel*, vol. 13, 3–4 (1962), 40–44; cp. Gottwald, *op. cit.*, 223–224.

emergence of the Jews as a 'pariah-people'; the ideology and the historical significance of the Pharisees – which were incorporated in the third volume of his *Gesmmelte Aufsäze zur Religionssoziologie*,[16] Of these three essays, only the first is more or less fully worked out, comparatively speaking, while the one dealing with the Pharisees, does not amount to more than a mere sketch.[17]

Weber's Nachlass proves, as Johannes Winkelmann assures us,[18] that he had intended to fill in the lacunae and, in fact, had worked out a program for doing so, intending to deal with the following topics:

a. Zunächst sollte die religionssoziologische Analyse des Psalter (vrgl. den Schluss auf Seite 400 in GAZRS III), des Buches Hiob sowie der Spruchweisheit folgen.

b. Sodann beabsichtigte Max Weber die Fortführung der Analyse der nachexilischen Entwicklung bis zur Makkabäerzeit.

c. Speziell sollten ... die Ergebnisse der religionssoziologischen Üntersuchungen zu Israel und Judäa einer Darstellung der entsprechenden ägyptischen, phönizischen, babylonischen und persischen Verhältnisse gegenübergestellt werden ...

d. Danach war eine Darstellung des *talmudischen* Judentums vorgesehen. Das aber hatte nicht nur den Beginn mit der jüdischen Sektenbildung zu Zeiten des Jochanan und Jesus von Nazareth – wie das erhaltene Fragment über das Pharisäertum dartut erfordert, sondern auch das Eingehen auf die allmähliche Entwicklung der Mischna-Aufzeichnungen von Hillel und Schammai (z.Z. Jesu) bis zu Jehuda hannasi[19] zu Ende des 2. Jahrhunderts, sowie die Behandlung der Rabbinatserziehung an den Akademien von Sura und Pumpedita ...

e. Schliesslich ist eindeutig ersichtlich, dass auch die Erörterung des zeitgenössischen Anliegens des Jesus von Nazareth im Rahmen der judäischen Verhältnisse weder in der Darstellung des Antiken Judentums (Sektenwesen und Reformbestrebungen um die Zeitwende) noch am Ende der 'Religionssoziologie' in Wirtschaft und Gesellschaft (vrgl. dort den Schluss von §12) in dem jetzigen fragmentarischen Zustand verblieben ware".

16. Tübingen 1920–21.
17. As was already pointed out by Schiper, *op. cit.*, 250 and Guttmann, *op. cit.*, 197. See further: H. Liebeschütz, Max Weber's Historical Interpretation of Judaism, in: *Yearbook of the Leo Baeck Institute*, Bd 9 (1964), 45.
18. Exkurs zur werkgeschichtlichen Stellung des "Antiken Judentums", in: *MWSJ*, 221; see also Schluchter's incisive analysis of Weber's work, *op. cit.* (n. 8), 11–77.
19. Not, as in the original publication – *hannabī*.

It may be said that in the three studies a diminishing reliability manifests itself, the nadir being reached in the last, viz. the literary torso which deals with the Pharisees. This progressive decline reflects the unsatisfactory Stand der Forschung in the history of the Second Temple period in Weber's days, especially with reference to the last two centuries B.C.E. and the first century C.E.[20] The weakness of the analysis, and the questionability of the models and types which Weber applied to that period, are commensurate to the fallacies and misconceptions of the informants on whom he perforce relied.[21]

It follows that while, to quote Liebeschütz[22] "the work of the Heidelberg sociologist can still serve us as starting point for further inquiries", at the present day, Max Weber's study must be subjected anew to scrutiny.

Some of the questions to be asked with regard to the, to all intent and purpose, fully worked out presentation, of "The Covenant etc."[23] are:

20. Research carried out since Weber's days has decisively changed the scholarly appreciation of the history and sociology of Judaism in the pre-Pharisaic, Pharisaic and Rabbinic periods. In the framework of this study, even a most restricted selective listing of pertinent publications in this area of inquiry cannot be attempted. It must suffice to draw attention to only a few titles which reflect the impressive results achieved by scholars in Israel, the U.S.A. and Europe: J. Klausner, *Jesus of Nazareth – His Life, Time and Teaching*, tr. from the Hebrew (London 1947); A.C. Schalit, *König Herodes: der Mann und sein Werk*, tr. from the Hebrew and enlarged (Berlin 1969); A. Ben-David, *Talmudische Ökonomie* (Hildesheim 1974); D. Sperber, *Roman Palestine, Money and Prices* (Ramat-Gan 1974); idem, *Roman Palestine 200–400, The Land* (Ramat-Gan 1974); M. Stern–S. Safrai, *The Jewish People in the First Century* (Assen 1974–76); E.E. Urbach, *The Sages, their Concepts and Beliefs*, tr. from the Hebrew (Jerusalem 1975); G. Alon, *Jews, Judaism and the Classical World*, tr. from the Hebrew (Jerusalem 1977); idem, *The Jews in their Land in the Talmudic Age* (70–640 C.E.), tr. from the Hebrew (Jerusalem 1980); S. Safrai, *Das jüdische Volk im Zeitalter des Zweiten Tempels*, übers. aus dem Hebr. (Neukirchen–Vluyn 1978); idem, *Die Wallfahrt im Zeitalter des Zweiten Tempels*, übers. aus dem Hebr. (Neukirchen–Vluyn 1982); S. Lieberman, *Greek in Jewish Palestine* (New York 1942); idem, *Hellenism in Jewish Palestine* (New York 1950); J. Neusner, *Early Rabbinic Judaism: Historical Studies in Religion, Literature and Art* (Leiden 1975); idem, *First Century Judaism in Crisis* (Nashville 1975); G. Stemberger, *Das Klassische Judentum – Kultur und Geschichte der rabbinischen Zeit* (München 1979); *idem, Das rabbinische Judentum in der Darstellung Max Webers*, in: *MWSJ*, 185–200.
21. However, one cannot fully ward off the suspicion that in his dealing with that period, some of the professionalists' anti-Jewish bias shows in his own thinking. See: E. Fleischmann, Max Weber, die Juden und das Ressentiment, in: *MWSJ*, 263 ff.
22. *Op. cit.* (n. 17), 68.
23. The 'Covenant' (ברית) concept has come under intensive scholarly scrutiny during the last decades, primarily in comparison with covenant forms and terminology in the Ancient Near East. For a comprehensive survey, see: M. Weinfeld, *Theologisches Wörterbuch zum Alten*

a. Has Weber sucessfully coped with the material available to him when he wrote das *Das Antike Judentum?* Does his analysis show adequate knowledgê of, and is his synthesis based on the then available pertinent data? Was he sufficiently equipped for an independent philological and historical evaluation of those data? Did he have the prerequisite knowledge to judge them critically, as well as their interpretation by divergent trends in Old Testament scholarship of his own time?[24]

b. Satisfied on the above points – is the 'grouping of data' which he proposed yet tenable by standards of biblical research accepted today?

More important: we have to go beyond Max Weber, and to integrate into the picture, new evidence which had not been available, when *Das Antike Judentum* was written. In this respect, issues and problems pertaining to "Jewish Sectarianism" constitute a most promising field of inquiry. A host of recent discoveries, such as the Gnostic materials from Nag Hammadi[25] and foremost the Scrolls from Qumran,[26] throw welcome light on dissenting religious groups and trends in the Second Temple period. They help in illuminating, even though only partially, the otherwise undocumented age in the Geistesgeschichte of the late biblical and the early post-biblical era, which from a Christian point of view has been termed the 'inter-testamental' period. The decisively richer information on the socio-religious profile of Judaism in the Second Temple Period which the new documents provide, calls for a reassessment of Weber's typology and his presentation of some phenomena

Testament, hrsg. von G.J. Botterweck–H. Ringgren, Bd I, 781–808, s.v. ברית (Stuttgart 1972).

24. See his own thoughts on this question (above n. 7). He allayed his apparent qualms by stating somewhat defiantly: "Fast alle Wissenschaften verdanken Dilettanten irgend etwas, oft sehr wertvolle Gesichtspunkte. Aber der Dilettant als Prinzip der Wissenschaft wäre das Ende", *GAR*, vol. I, 14. Compare also his letter to von Below, as quoted by G. Roth, in his Introduction to Weber's *Economy and Sociology* (1968), lvii: "I am dealing with the structure of the political organizations in a comparative and systematic manner, at the risk of falling under the anathema: 'dilletantes compare'."
25. The new insights have been fully assimilated by K. Rudolph, in: *Die Gnosis – Wesen und Geschichte einer spätantiken Religion* (Göttingen² 1980), which goes beyond the classical study of H. Jonas, *Gnosis und spätantiker Geist* (Göttingen 1934). See further: H.G. Kippenberg, Intellektualismus und die antike Gnosis, in: *MWSJ*, 201–218. Rudolph and Kippenberg provide an up-to-date bibliography. See also: G. Stroumsa, Gnosis und die christliche Entzauberung der Welt, in: W. Schluchter, ed., op. cit. (n. 8) 486–508.
26. A concise description and evaluation of these discoveries may be found in F.M. Cross. *The Ancient Library of Qumran and Biblical Studies* (New York 1958, 1961); G. Vermes, *The Dead Sea Scrolls: Qumran in Perspective* (Oxford 1978, London 1982).

pertaining to post-exilic Israel and its socio-religious structure. A case in point is his treatment of the Samaritans to whom he refers only en passant, though conceding that "they are ... quite interesting in that one may study their fate in comparison with that of the Jews in order to establish negatively what the exclusively Torah oriented religion of the Israelite priests lacked for becoming a 'world religion'."[27] The diametrical opposition Jews vs. Samaritans (as a prefiguration of the dichotomy Pharisaism vs. heterodoxies), now must be viewed in the light of the Qumran finds which add a new dimension to the phenomenon of Jewish sectarianism.[28] In deliberating on this issue more novel information can be brought into play than, probably, with respect to any other topic which comes under scrutiny in the present framework.

An investigation of the new materials, and especially of the Qumran writings, may throw light on processes which Weber traced in *Das Antike Judentum* and on concepts which constitute the warp and the woof of his typology. Let me mention just a few to which reference will be made in the ensuing discussion:

a. Weber's crucial assumption that post-exilic Israel experienced a decisive transition from peoplehood and nationhood to a (mere) confessional Glaubensgemeinschaft must be put to the test by its application to the self-understanding of the Samaritans and the Qumranians.

b. In this connection, also his contention that then Israel developed to an increasing measure traits of a pariah-community will come up for review. An analysis of the Qumran (and Samaritan) Ideenwelt provides tools for a reconsideration of the in-group – out-group morality which, in Weber's view, is rooted in the early biblical ethos, grew stronger in the setting of the Babylonian exile, and since Pharisaic times has shaped the attitude of Jews toward the non-Jewish world. Concurrently some attention must be given to the question whether, and if so to what degree, the presumed dual-morality indeed was conducive to or precipitated the crystallization of a stringent behavior-pattern which consolidated Judaism from within and at the same time cut it off from the surrounding society.

c. The constitution of the Qumran community may serve as a teststone for Weber's proposition that in the last centuries before the rise of Christianity, a

27. *Ancient Judaism*, (transl. by H.H. Gerth and D. Martindale (Glencoe, III. 1952)' *AnJu*, 360 ff, 415f. See Further: S. Talmon, The Samaritans, in: *Scientific American*, 236 (1977), 100–108.

28. See: S. Talmon, Types of Messianic Expectation at the Turn of the Era, in this volume, 215–224.

rigid cultic code, the rabbinic halakhah, prevented Jews from engaging in agricultural occupations which by their very nature engender infringements of ritual proscriptions,[29] and that resultingly Judaism became urbanized and developed an intrinsically städtische Ethik.

d. As already mentioned, the study of the dissenters' Commune of Qumran may bear on the more general question of how the socio-religious phenomenon 'sect' should be defined in distinction from other socio-religious structures.[30] The results of this enquiry may prompt a reevaluation of Weber's describing the Pharisees' religious stance as Sektenreligiosität.

e. The presentation of the Righteous Teacher, the dominant figure of leadership in the Qumran writings, invites a reconsideration of Weber's typology of religious leaders.

f. These writings also reflect the progressive dénouement of the Rationalisierungsprozess which plays such an important role in Weber's thinking, as well as the increasing Demokratisierung of one-time esoteric religious learning. However, because of its many ramifications, this process requires a rather involved exposition which cannot be attempted in the present framework.

At this stage of our inquiry, a characteristic of the sources on which all observations concerning ancient (biblical) Judaism are founded, must be brought under consideration: Any attempt to retrace the social and religious development of Israel in the pre-exilic period is perforce based almost entirely on inferences drawn from the interpretation of literary materials which already in the biblical age itself had been handed down over centuries and now are before us in the forms and formulations which the latest tradents or redactors gave to them. While the extent of the time-lag between the occurrence of a particular event and its recording remains a matter of scholarly debate, that fundamental characteristic of the biblical traditions is generally recognized in modern biblical scholarship. Weber was cognizant of these facts. He knew e.g. fully well that the patriarchal stories reflect, to a degree, concepts and conditions of the early monarchy and that they "were influenced by the social

29. *An Ju*, 363f.

30. See int. al. T.F. O'Dea, Mormonism and the Avoidance of Sectarian Stagnation: A Study of Church, Sect and Incipient Nationality, in: *American Journal of Sociology*, vol. 60 (1954/55), 285–293; P.L. Berger, The Sociological Study of Sectarianism, in: *Social Research* (=*SR*) vol 21 (1954), 467–485; B.R. Wilson, *Sects and Society* (London 1961); idem, Patterns of Sectarianism, in: *CSSH* III (1963); E. Benz, ed., *Messianische Kirchen, Sekten und Bewegungen im heutigen Afrika* (Leiden/Köln 1965); G. Stroumsa, op. cit. (n. 25).

problems produced by kingship."[31] It follows that in the endeavour to recover the mainstays of the Israelites' socio-religious organization and world of ideas in the pre-exilic age, scholars by necessity have recourse to the extrapolation of sources which are a mélange of historical facts and historographical fantasy. This is an unremediable predicament which Weber shares with all students of the early biblical society and, for that matter, also of other ancient civilizations.

At times one suspects that, although aware of the inherent pitfalls, Weber did not sufficiently take into account that crucial gulf between the historical actualities and their recordings which are coloured by the recorder's existential situation. Notwithstanding his critical acumen, he tends to take the biblical traditions at face value whenever it suits his purpose, as has been pointed out by critical reviewers of his work.[32] His, at times unqualified, reliance on the biblical sources attenuates especially the reliability of the presentation of Die Enstehung des Jüdischen Pariavolkes for which the analysis of the historico-social and religious phenomena pertaining to the Israelitische Eidgenossenschaft and Prophetie serves as a launching pad.[33]

No such chronological gap between the historical circumstances and their reporting, manifests itself in the biblical account of the early post-exilic times. The books which relate the details of the Return from the Exile – foremost, Ezra, Nehemiah, Haggai and Zechariah – are contemporaneous with or were composed shortly after the actual occurrence of the events which they record. While the contemporaneity does not yet allay the scholar's concern over the 'objectivity' of these presumed eye-witness-reports, for once the biblical records are practically synchronous with the historical situation and reflect, *grosso modo*, the ideonic stance of that age.

Viewed from this same angle, the Qumran Scrolls have quite a special significance. They are the only extensive contemporary documentation which relates to a Jewish group from the last centuries before the turn of the era. Being first-hand records, penned by scribes of the New Covenant-Commune for the benefit of its members, and having come to us in their pristine form,[34] these

31. *An Ju*, 208, cp. 49 ff, 231 f. et al. It has been recurrently suggested that the Pentateuchal traditions about the Patriarchs, especially those concerning Abraham, in part are modelled after prototypes provided by the (Davidic) monarchy. See, e.g.: B. Mazar, The Historical Background of the Book of Genesis in: *Journal of Near Eastern Studies*, vol 28 (1969), 73–83 and pertinent publications cited there.
32. Such as Schiper, *op. cit.* (n. 6), Holstein, *op. cit.* (n. 9) and others.
33. *An Ju*, 61–148; 267–335.
34. See: S. Talmon, The New Covenanters of Qumran, in: *Scientific American*, vol 225, 5 (November 1971), 73–81.

socuments are of unsurpassed value for a sociological case study of an ancient religious group or sect.

The Qumran Scrolls have been investigated almost exclusively by students of 'Die Wissenschaft des Judentums', foremost by Old and New Testament scholars who extricated from them illuminating information on a variety of Einzelfragen concerning Jewry and Judaism in the last two pre-Christian centuries. But, to the best of my knowledge, no trained sociologist as yet has submitted the Covenanters' literature to a comprehensive socio-historical and socio-religious analysis, comparable to Weber's "allseitige Untersuchung"[35]) of the Bible and biblical Israel. This is to be regretted, since the information on this until recently unknown heterodox trend in Second Temple Judaism could contribute significantly to the study of 'sect'[36] as a phenomenon.[37]

The task obviously cannot be adequately carried out in the framework of this discussion. But the Bible scholar can at least try to wet the sociologists' appetite by presenting some basic information on the Covenanters. In doing so, I shall restrict my remarks to aspects of their communal life, societal structure and theology which bear directly on issues treated by Weber in the essays: The Establishment of the Jewish Pariah People and The Pharisees.[38]

III

Before embarking on this task, I wish to stress that I am concerned with the beginnings of Jewish Sectarianism between the late fourth and the early second century B.C.E., and not with the sects which made their appearance at the turn of the era and for a long time have been a matter for scholarly investigation.

I propose, in fact, that the emergence of Jewish Sectarianism must be viewed in conjunction with Judaism of the sixth and fifth century B.C.E., which presents itself to the scholar in the post-exilic biblical literature. The internal diversification of Judaism which ultimately found one of its structural expressions in the formation of sects, can be fully appreciated only against the backdrop of the experience of the Babylonian Exile and the Return From the Exile.

Viewed from this angle, the very phenomenon of Jewish Sectarianism, links

35. Guttman, *op. cit.* (n. 3), 197.
36. See, int. al.: P.L. Berger, The Sociological Study of Sectarianism, in: *SR*, vol 21 (1954), 467–485; B.K. Wilson, *Sects and Society* (London 1961); idem, Patterns of Sectarianism, *CSSH III* (1963).
37. Petersen, *op. cit.* (n. 4), 141.
38. *An Ju*, 267–424, 455–461.

up directly with the history and the Geistesgeschichte of early post-exilic Judaism.[39]

My comments will be directed to two pivotal aspects of the socio-religious transformation to which the biblical body politic was exposed in the wake of the cataclysmic events of 586 B.C.E., *viz.* the destruction of the Temple, the capture of Jerusalem, and the concomitant loss of political sovereignty:

a. Changes in the internal structure of the Israelite society and in the interaction of the main societal agents of leadership: king – priest – prophet.

b. The transformation from the pre-exilic monocentric nation, defined by the geopolitical borders of the Land of Israel, to the post-exilic people characterized by a multicentricity which resulted from deportations and voluntary or semi-voluntary emigration.[40]

a. The social structure of Israel in the monarchical period hinged upon the interaction of three pivotal socio-religious institutions: kingship, priesthood and prophecy, which gave expression to a basic cohesiveness and unity, notwithstanding social and economic differentiation and the political division into two realms.

The priests embodied the guardianship over established norms which found their tangible expression in the temple – whether in Jerusalem or in Bethel – and the sacrificial service. By their very call and nature, the priesthood and the cult signified permanence and stability in the public and personal domain. The kings, motivated by the realism which the mundane affairs of the realm dictated, on the whole shared with the priests the overriding interest in constancy and continuity. As against this, the prophets would not acquiesce in the pragmatism which guided kings and to a degree also priests in their decisions. Never doubting the legitimacy of these institutions,[41] they aimed at

39. See: F. Crüsemann, *op. cit.* (n. 8).

40. See: S. Talmon, Exil und Rückkehr in der Ideenwelt des Alten Testaments, in: R. Mosis, Hrsg., *Exil-Diaspora-Rückkehr* (Düsseldorf 1978), esp. 40–51); S.N. Eisenstadt, Max Webers antikes Judentum und der Charakter der jüdischen Zivilisation, in: *MWSJ*, 162 ff.

41. A more detailed discussion of this aspect may be found in S. Talmon, Kingship and the Ideology of the State (in the Biblical Period), in this vol. 18, 34–38. The matter has been sometimes differently assessed in OT scholarship. It must suffice to mention here some works on biblical royalty which also provide ample bibliographical information: J.A. Soggin, *Das Königtum in Israel*, in: *BZAW* 104 (Berlin 1967); T.N.D. Mettinger, *King and Messiah. The Civil and Sacral Legitimation of the Israelite Kings*, in: *Coniectanea Biblica, Old Testament Monograph Series 8* (Lund 1976); T. Ishida, *The Royal Dynasties in Ancient Israel*, in: *BZAW* 142 (Berlin–New York 1977); F. Crüsemann, *Der Widerstand gegen das Königtum. Die anti-königlichen Texte des Alten Testaments und der Kampf um den frühen israelitischen Staat* (Neukirchen 1978); B. Halpern, *The Constitution of the Monarchy in Israel*, in: *Harvard Semitic Monographs* 25 (Ann Arbor, Michigan 1981).

elevating their status by impressing upon them the demand to emulate in historical reality the ideal standards of personal and public conduct which informed their own utopian visions.[42]

The societal integrity of Israel in the monarchical period rested upon the equilibrium maintained between the forces of 'constancy' – kings and priests – and the generators of 'creative movement' – the prophets. An undue gravitation toward institutional realism could impair Israel's uniqueness shaped by the precepts of biblical monotheism. An overemphasis put on utopian idealism could intensify eschatological speculations and messianic dreams to a degree which would undermine the will to live in actual history. Neither of these extremes appears to have materialized before the end of the First Temple Period.

b. In the days of the monarchy, and essentially also in the preceding stages of the Hebrew tribes' implantation in the Land of Canaan, the life of the people of Israel was marked by a fundamental geographical circumscription which furthered social, religious and political cohesion. Shared traditions of a common ethnic extraction and a common historical past caused that the division into two rival kingdoms – since approximately 900 B.C.E. – was generally considered a temporary breach which would be healed at some future time in history. It did not sap the Ephraimites' and Judeans' consciousness of being one nation, in the last count. Although constituted in historical actuality of two political entities, (all-) Israel thus retained a basic unity, safeguarded by the geographical compactness which encompassed all those who considered themselves of Abraham's stock. The external pressure of the surrounding 'foreign nations', and ongoing contacts between Judah and Ephraim – of war and intermittent alliances, commerce and the two-way migration of groups and individuals among whom prophets, such as Amos, stand out – helped in preserving the pathos of an intrinsic oneness, symbolized in the tradition of the 'Twelve Tribes'. Even when no 'one place' was recognized by all Israel as the nation's religious and political pivot, the very boundaries of the Land sufficed to circumscribe Israel's 'monocentricity'. No constituted group or groups of Israelites existed outside the space of the divinely promised and sanctified 'Land'. Also the recurrent deportation of Ephraimites in the wake of the conquest of Samaria by the Assyrians in 722 did not materially affect this 'monocentricity'. There is no tangible evidence which suggests that the relocations effected an emergence of 'Ephraimite centers' in Mesopotamia or

42. See: S. Talmon, The Biblical Concept of Jerusalem, in: *Journal of Ecumenical Studies*, vol 8 (1971), 300–316.

elsewhere. Even if this should have been the case, as is sometimes surmised, those presumed Ephraimite exilic communities disappeared within a comparatively short span of time. In any case, there is nothing to show that a new lasting understanding of 'Judaism' which differed significantly from that of pre-destruction Samaria ever was conceived by Ephraimites in exile.

One readily acknowledges the existence of differences in the social structure of the Southern kingdom on the one hand, and the Northern on the other. In both one observes a diversity of interpretations of Israelite monotheism, entertained by various strata of society. However, it appears that the latitude of deviation remained sufficiently restricted to prevent the complete estrangement of any segment of Israelite society from the fundamental tenets and patterns of life which distinguished Israel as a whole from neighboring societies and cultures. The cohesion indeed was at times strained, due to economic-social, political-religious, and even ethnic differences which prevailed in the citizenry of the two realms. But at no stage in the history of the monarchies did the stratification into poor and rich, oppressors and oppressed, pure monotheists and syncretists, effect a fundamentally different development in the existing societal structures, either in Judah or in Ephraim.

In sum: throughout the First Temple Period, 'homogeneity' prevailed in Israel over 'heterogeneity', 'uniformity' over 'multiformity', thanks to internal cohesion and geographical compactness.

IV

All this changed abruptly after the debacle of 586 B.C.E. when Judah and her capital city fell prey to the Babylonians. With the political framework in shambles, the monarchy in actual history lost its raison d'être. However, the idea and the ideal of 'royalty', in the configuration of the 'anointed shoot of the house of David' (cp. Is. 42:1–3 with 11:1–5),[43] gained in strength and became the embodiment of a restoration-hope and ideology. With the Temple sacked, the cultic paraphernalia looted and carried away by the conqueror, the priests were in effect deprived of their sphere of function and influence. This did not result though in a religious reorientation leading to a search for new means and forms of worship, but rather in the emergence of an intensified dream of a

43. The Anointed King-Messiah-concept has been abundantly discussed in scholarly publications which are too numerous to be listed here. For an overview and selected bibliography, see: S. Talmon, Kingship etc. (n. 41), 16 ff; idem, Types etc. (n. 28), 578 ff; idem, Biblical Visions of the Future Ideal Age in this volume 140–164. K. Baltzer, Das Ende des Staates Judah und die Messias-Frage, in: *Studien zur Theologie der alttestamentlichen Überlieferungen*, hrsg. von R. Rendtorff and K. Koch (Neukirchen 1961), 33–44.

future restitution of the age-honored holy place and the sacrificial cult.[44] In short, the 'institutionalized' political and religious agencies, and their representatives who had been imbued with office-charisma, survived the historical setback by a temporary transfer from the plane of factuality to that of conceptuality. Their reactivation in historical reality was considered a certainty, depending on Israel's conduct which would lead to a reconciliation with God and the restitution of her fortunes.

Most severely affected was the prophetic leadership and the very phenomenon of prophecy. The prophet's personal charisma lacked the staying power which the institution-character conferred upon monarchy and priesthood. Thus, the fall of Judah and Jerusalem signaled the wane of prophecy. Although there will be a short-lived reemergence of prophecy in the Period of the Return (Haggai, Zechariah and Malachi), the need for a replacement of personal inspiration as a principle of public guidance, by more rational and controllable forms of instruction had become acute. Ultimately, the transformation will crystallize in new classes of spiritual leaders – the Scribes, and then the Sages. Their authority rested on the expert extrapolation of the hallowed traditions by techniques whose reliability can be objectively ascertained, rather than on personal inspiration which cannot be subjected to any generally acknowledged checks and controls.

Concomitant with the developments which affected the leadership, the original geographical compactness of Israel was shattered. An era of multicentricity set in; multiformity replaced uniformity; heterogeneity supplanted the former homogeneity. It is to these features that we must now turn our attention.

After the fall of Jerusalem, the Babylonians, emulating a strategy introduced by the Assyrians, deported segments of the Judean population to other parts of their empire, and settled them in various places in Mesopotamia. The biblical records imply that the exilation affected mainly the upper strata of the society. The figures of deportees adduced in the biblical sources may not be altogether accurate, or may not give the correct total of all Judeans abducted. Allowing for some latitude, a total of 30,000–40,000 may be considered a conservative estimate. But more important for the subsequent historical development than the sheer numbers, is the circumstance that the expatriates were either forcibly settled by the conquerors on specific sites, or elected out of their free will to

44. See: S. Talmon, The Emergence of Institutionalized Prayer in Israel in the Light of Qumran Literature, in: *Qumran, Sa piété, sa théologie et son milieu*, ed. by M. Delcor, *Bibliotheca Ephemeridum Theologicarum Lovaniensium*, vol 44 (Paris 1978), 265 ff.

cluster in compact localities. Some of these are mentioned by name in the biblical sources, e.g. Tel-Abib (Ezek 1:3; 3:15) and Casiphiah (Ezra 8:15–20). Also the Ephraimites deported after the fall of Samaria in 722 B.C.E. had been settled by the Assyrians in specific locales (2 Kgs 17:6; 18:11; 1 Chr 5:26). But it appears that in contrast to them, the transplaced Judeans turned their ghetto-like settlements into an advantage. The concentration enabled them to maintain their identity, and in effect to further their tradition in ways and manners which were not shared by the 'remnant' left by the conquerors in Judah which subsequently was to become the Persian province of Jehud. Thus, there emerged in Babylonia a new 'center' of Judaism in which a particular understanding of the biblical monotheism was cultivated. The Babylonian community entertained a fervent messianic hope for an imminent return to the homeland which restrained them from sinking roots in the foreign soil (Jer. 29:4–7). Therefore it could provide eschelons of Returnees when the liberating edict of Cyrus the Great in 538 B.C.E. made a return achievable. However, not all exiles returned. It is quite possible that those who stayed back even constituted the majority. In any case, they were to become the matrix of a flourishing community which in later days will compete with, and at times surpass the Palestinian in literary achievements and social weight.

Another centre emerged in Egypt. Information on the presence of Jewish communities comes from two disparate sources which are some 150 years apart. The more detailed evidence can be gleaned from the archives of a Jewish garrison stationed in Elephantine and Syene (Assuan) in Upper Egypt.[45] The documents pertain to a period of approximately 40 years, between 420–380. However, references to earlier historical events indicate that the settlement preceded the conquest of Egypt by the Persian King Cambyses in 525. Of special importance for our purpose is the knowledge gained from the Elephantine papyri on the internal structure of the garrison and its religious outlook,[46] as well as its relations to their homeland. We learn that already before 525, that is, merely some decades after the destruction of the Jerusalem Temple, the Jewish garrison had built a local temple. The construction of a permanent sanctuary outside Jerusalem, in a foreign land, constitutes a significant departure from biblical concepts. Its very existence flaunts the

45. See: A.E. Sayce–A.E. Cowley, *Aramaic Papyri Discovered at Assuan* (London 1906); A.E. Cowley, *Aramaic Papyri of the Fifth Century B.C.* (Oxford 1923); E.G. Kraeling, *The Brooklyn Museum Aramaic Papyri: New Documents of the Fifth Century B.C. from the Jewish Colony in Elephantine* (New Haven/London 1953).

46. For a comprehensive analysis of the material, see: B. Porten, *Archives from Elephantine* (Los Angeles 1968).

uniqueness of the Jerusalem Temple and its exclusive legitimacy. We must conclude that Egyptian Jewry had adjusted to their 'Diaspora' conditions. They had accepted life outside the 'Land' as final, and did not entertain any hope for a restoration, or at least did not believe in the possible realization of such a hope in historical times.

The other set of evidence derives from the book of Jeremiah 43–44. There it is reported that an unspecified number of Judeans fled to lower Egypt a short while after the fall of Jerusalem, fearing Babylonian reprisals for the murder of Gedaliah, the governor whom the conqueror had appointed over the province (*ib.* 41). They interpreted the calamity which had befallen them as proving the inefficacy of Yhwh, rather than as a punishment for their sins and disregard of his commands. It may be presumed that this attitude ultimately led to a complete separation between them and their former compatriots and coreligionists in the Land of Israel and in the Babylonian diaspora. In consequence, Egyptian Jewry will have no share in the founding of the new community in the 'Land' after the Return from the Exile in the wake of Cyrus' declaration (538 B.C.E.).

A synoptic view of the constitution of the Jewish people after the fall of the Kingdom of Judah in 586 reveals a situation which is fundamentally different from the one which obtained in the First Temple Period. Not only has multicentricity replaced the former monocentricity, but what is more, the different Jewish communities present to the viewer diverse sociological and spiritual, in short, existential profiles: Those who had been permitted by the Babylonians to remain in the 'Land', in essence did not change their life-style, economic structure, and religious-cultic customs, notwithstanding the loss of political sovereignty and cultic institutions, and the incurrence of economic hardship. They were the conservatives who clung to their established system of values, despite the changed circumstances.

In Egypt there emerged an emigrants-community of Jews who had elected to leave their homeland, even though under pressure. The severance of ties with the 'Land' and with biblical monotheism, severely undermined their staying-power and their will to resist the inroads of the surrounding society and its conceptual universe. Hated and persecuted by their Egyptian neighbors, as some Elephantine papyri evidence, they nevertheless could not preserve their identity and social cohesion. They embraced an accomodating syncretistic stance which ultimately caused their community to dry up.

In contrast, the exiles-community in Babylonia-Persia, at least in part,[47]

47. The Book of Esther appears to reflect an 'adjusted' exiles-community in the Persian Period. It may, though, be presumed that this diaspora-stance had already developed when this

persisted in its particularity. The exiles indeed 're-formed' and reinterpreted traditional values so as to be able to cope with the situation of a stubborn minority into which they had been hurled. Their unmitigated sense of being-in-exile, reinforced their insistence on the strict adherence to their spiritual heritage and furthered the formation of societal structures adjusted to exilic conditions, e.g. by concentrating in specific locales. More than that, the consciousness of being expatriates intensified the hope for a repatriation in an appreciable historical future, and for a reconstitution of their political sovereignty under an anointed king of the Davidic line. It stimulated an intrinsically activist stance.

Before proceeding to the next stage of our inquiry, some salient characteristics of Israel in the exilic times should be highlighted, which seem to have a special bearing on Weber's conceptual framework.

a. Post-destruction Palestinian Jewry did not come to be divorced from agriculture nor did it become urbanized. Quite the opposite appears to have been the case, as the biblical sources intimate and archaeological research bears out.[48] The cities became the pivots and mainstays of the imperial civic and military administration with the concomitant influx of foreign bureaucrats, army personnel and population groups which first the Assyrian and then the Babylonian suzerain transplanted into the conquered territories of Samaria (see: 2 Kgs 17:24–41) and most probably also of Judah (see Ezra 4:7–6:5; Neh 3:33–4:2; 6:1–7; 13:16). It may be postulated, in fact, that then and there, the Jewish population of the 'Land' became increasingly deurbanized, being forced out of the cities and pushed into the rural periphery.

The continued attachment of considerable parts of the Jewish populace to agricultural pursuits persisted into or was renewed in the Period of the Return from Exile and beyond it into Rabbinic times.[49] This fact clearly emerges from the accounts preserved in the post-exilic biblical literature which prove that the "Landbevölkerung" played an important role in the reconstituted body politic

community was yet under Babylonian rule. See: S. Talmon, Wisdom in the Book of Esther, *VT*, vol 13 (1963), 419–455; W.L. Humphreys, A Life-style for Diaspora: A Study of the Tales of Esther and Daniel, *JBL*, vol 92 (1973), 211–213; S.A. Meinhold, *Die Diasporanovelle – eine alttestamentliche Gattung*, Diss. Greifswald 1969; idem, Die Gattung der Josephsgeschichte und des Estherbuches: Diasporanovelle, I, II, *ZAW* 87 (1975), 306–324.

48. Some of the legal documents found at Elephantine demonstrate that also in Egypt Jews owned land and presumably engaged in agriculture.
49. This has been abundantly documented in post-Weberian research. See the literature cited in n. 20.

of the Returnees. Recurrent references to cattle, vineyards, fields and crops and the failure of crops (Hag 1:6, 10, 11; 2:15–19; Zach 8:10–12; Ezra 3:7; Neh 5:1–15, 18 *et al.*) point to the existence of a substantial rural class with agricultural interests and not to a landless urbanized Bürgertum, as Weber surmised. Biblical reports have it that Nehemiah was forced to have recourse to the conscription of every tenth member of the Returnees' families for settlement in Jerusalem, so as to ensure that former exiles would predominate in the citizenry of the capital (Neh 7:4–5; 11:1–2). Equally revealing is the 'roster of returning exiles' which has been preserved in two, slightly diverging versions (Ezra 2:1–70 and Neh 7:6–72).[50] It served Nehemiah as basis for the just referred to repopulation of Jerusalem with trustworthy men. In part, this list is arranged according to localities in the Land of Israel (Ezra 2:21–35), mostly villages and rural townships. This arrangement reflects the Returnees' intention to take root in domiciles in which their forebears had been settled before their exilation. The concluding line of that roster: "the (returning) priests . . . Levites . . . and all Israel (settled) in their villages" (Ezra 2:70 = Neh 7:72), is echoed in the 'conscription notation' which directs that nine out of ten members of each family should remain in their "locations", whereas one should transfer to Jerusalem (Neh 11:1).

b. The enforced status of 'konfessionelle Glaubensgemeinschaft' had been regarded by the Babylonian exiles as a mere temporary adjustment to prevailing adverse circumstances. However, as yet will be explicated, once this new form of communal life had come into existence, it will not be discarded even when the conditions which had brought it about, seemingly were reversed or attenuated by the Return to the Land which, though, did not put an end to the existence of an exilic community. The structure of the 'konfessionelle Glaubensgemeinschaft' will be absorbed into the future societal framework of Jewry, in transformations which are concordant with its changing religio-societal configuration. When the returning exiles reconstituted the political framework of Judah in the early Persian period, there evolved a symbiosis of Glaubensgemeinschaft with Nation. After that time, Jewish peoplehood will enfold communities which differently accentuate their national-religious heritage. Rather then replacing one the other, the, according to Weber, mutually exclusive types of socio-political and religious organization – 'konfessionelle Glaubensgemeinschaft' and 'nationhood' – will coalesce.

c. The continuing adherence to pre-exilic socio-religious structures finds its

50. Weber's contention that "These sib registers have been fabricated" (*An Ju*, 350) and therefore can be disregarded, is unwarranted.

expression also in the circumstance that immediately upon their return to the 'Land', the former exiles began rebuilding the Temple (Ezra 3:2 ff.; 4:1 ff, cf. Hag pass; Zach 3:1 ff; 6:9 ff et al.) and reinstituted the sacrificial service (Ezra 3:2–6; 6:16 ff; 7:17 ff., Neh 10:35 ff; 12:43 ff; 13:30–31; cp. Mal 1:6 ff; 2:12 ff et al.). Like in the past, the Temple was not considered an institution exclusively dedicated to 'religious' concerns, but also a symbol of nationhood and political sovereignty, as was well understood by the local Persian officials (see Ezra 5:6–8 and 4:12–22, 24). In this respect, the Temple differs from the Synagogue which will replace it at a later stage in the Second Temple Period, as Weber correctly recognized, but which has no discernable roots either in the exilic setting[51] or in the days of the Return.

d. Weber's contention that since access to the 'religiöse Glaubensgemeinschaft's was regulated primatily by 'ritual law', proselytism became a constitutive phenomenon of post-exilic Judaism,[52] certainly does not apply to the Returnees' community. The above mentioned roster of returning paternal houses, obviously is intended to help preserve the ethnich-national circumscription of its membership, and to block altogether or at least to brake the infiltration of outsiders. The restrictive effect of the thus achieved self-identification becomes exceedingly visible in the ensuing campaign of Ezra, Nehemiah and their followers against the intrusion of "foreign women" into the Judean society.[53] The traditional endogamy principle which precludes the intermarriage with ethnic foreigners, now is expanded to apply also to non-Judean Israelites whose version of the biblical faith was at variance with the Returnees' understanding of biblical monotheism. Again one encounters the concentric structure of 'Glaubensgemeinschaft' within 'Nation': the religious-credal factor causes connubium to become operative exclusively within the society of the former exiles. Only Returnees can be counted among the "(righteous) remnant", the "holy seed" whose preordained restoration the pre-exilic prophet Isaiah had announced, so that it should become the stock out of which the People (nation) of Israel will rise again (cp. Ezra 9:2 and Neh 9:2 with Isa 6:13). There emerged a triad of relationships which was not recognized by Weber nor, for that matter, by other students of the period:

(credal-national) inner-group
(national) in-group
(religious-ethnic-foreign) out-group

51. As is often maintained, without any tangible evidence. See: S. Talmon, The Emergence of Institutionalized Prayer etc (n. 44).

52. *An Ju*, 362 f; 417 ff.

53. As rightly stressed also by Crüsemann, *op. cit.* (n. 8), 208–210.

This pattern will prevail in later Second Temple Judaism. It will determine, to a large degree, the very character of Jewish sectarianism and the interrelation of the diverse factions that are but structured-societal manifestations of diverging interpretations of the common tradition shared by all. This analysis and the suggested three-tier model lend additional force to J. Taubes' observation that in contrasting Volk und Religion in reference to Judaism, Weber created "eine falsche Polarität".[54]

IV

The multicentricity and heterogeneity of Judaism effected by the dispersion which followed upon the dissolution of the Kingdom of Judah, and the above stressed socio-religious characteristics, constitute the backdrop against which the overall population in the 'Land' after the Return of contingents of Babylonian exiles must be viewed, its internal diversification and the conflicts and clashes which resulted from it, appreciated. Against this background one can attempt to identify the most prominent factors which separated the Returnees from "the People(s) of the Land", and caused some factions of these 'Palestinians' to become prototypical dissenters. I submit that the issue should be regarded initially as a confrontation of two factions in the People (or Nation) of Israel pitted against each other, with the controversy being triggered by motives of a historical-political, economic and religious-cultic nature. This multifariousness of aspects puts the ensuing 'Samaritan schism' in a category by itself, within the wider compass of 'Conformity and Dissent' or 'Mainstream versus Sectarian Judaism' in the Second Temple Period. This schism appears to offer the earliest tangible evidence of a shift in the substance of the problems which confronted Judaism, and foremost the Returnees' 'Torah-Community'.

The 'in-group – out-group' ethos which had characterized Israel's relations with its pagan neighbors in the 'Land' in the pre-destruction period, and in the Diaspora during the Exile, now manifested itself in new configurations. The need for a close circumscription of Jewish identity which had been especially pressing in the setting of a surrounding pagan-foreign majority in Babylonia-Persia, was turned inward, so to speak. The insistence on the observance of religious-ritual norms – foremost Sabbath, Festivals and Circumcision – in the Diaspora had acted as a defence mechanism in the quest for self-preservation vis à vis ethnically 'others'. After the Return, the question-at-issue

54. See: J. Taubes, Die Enstehung des jüdischen Pariavolkes, in: *Max Weber Gedächtnisschrift*, hrsg. von Englisch und anderen (Berlin 1966), 185–194.

progressively became 'internalized'. Compliance with the specific-particular execution of these rites, now became a criterion which set apart constituents of one Jewish 'inner-group' from others. Weber seemingly did not take note of this transmutation, nor did he take it into account in his analysis of 'in-group – out-group' behavior patterns.[55]

The biblical sources indicate that the Israelites (and Judeans) in the 'Land', at first expressed a readiness to join with the Returnees in the efforts of rebuilding the Temple and their community, and probably also to subscribe to their religious norms and values. The Book of Ezra reports that in distinction from "the People(s) of the Land" who sought to prevent the restoration of the Temple (3:3), some inhabitants proposed to actively participate in the building operations. These petitioners are designated "adversaries of Judah and Benjamin" (*ib.* 4:1). This designation implies that they were considered opponents of the Returnees whose community was predominantly, if not exclusively, constituted of exiled Judeans and Benjaminites (see: *ib.* 1:5; 2:11 = Neh 7:6; Ezra 10:9; 2 Chr 34:9 et al.), citizen of the former Kingdom of Judah. The precise specification of the petitioners' identity suggests that the report revolves on an internal Israelite matter, namely the question of whether the Returnees should completely separate themselves from the 'Palestinian' Ephraimites (and Judeans) who had not undergone the Exile experience or whether they should agree to integrate them in their midst. At that time, i.e. around 520 B.C.E., Zerubbabel and his followers rejected them (Ezra 4:1–3), obviously acting under prophetic pressure (see: Hag 2:10–14).[56] The refusal caused bad blood between the two factions. But this apparently did not prevent the 'locals' from trying again in the days of Ezra and Nehemiah (in the second half of the fifth century B.C.E.) to win acceptance into the Judean res publica,[57] once more to no avail. The finality of the rift between the two strata of Israelites in the 'Land' comes to the fore in the pronouncements of the last biblical prophet Malachi who assumedly then was active. At the end of his book which signals the closure of the collection of prophetic writings and altogether the termination of biblical prophecy, the author records a

55. *An Ju*, 336 ff.

56. See: S. Talmon, Polemics and Apology in Biblical Historiography – 2 Kgs 17:24–41, in: R.E. Friedman ed., *The Creation of Sacred Literature – Composition and Redaction of the Biblical Text* (Berkeley–Los Angeles–London 1981), 57–68, esp. 66–68.

57. For the national-political nature of the Returnees' socio-religious community see: F. Crüsemann, *op. cit.* (n.8) 208–211; S. Talmon, Ezra–Nehemiah, in: Interpreter's Dictionary of the Bible, Suppl. Vol. (Nashville 1976), 317–328; N. Avigad, *Bullae and Seals from a Post-Exilic Judean Archive*, in: *Qedem*, vol. 4 (Jerusalem 1976).

controversy between two (certainly 'Jewish') factions: "those who fear God and serve him" and "those who do not fear God nor serve him" (Mal 3:11–21). The first are promised good fortunes and salvation, the other misery and damnation at the "(appointed) day",[58] when God will sit in judgment over his people.[59] It goes without saying that the author sides with those whom he considers to be obedient to God. They may be regarded as akin to those "tho revere (or abide by) the word of God" (Isa 66:5, contrast Isa 65:11) and to the ענוים – 'humble' or צדיקים – 'righteous' of the Psalms, and as forerunners of the later ḥasidim – 'pious' of early Maccabean times.[60]

Having been repeatedly spurned by the Returned Judeans, the Samarians[61] or Ephraimites – subsequently also known as Shechemites – abstained from further overtures. Approximately a century later, they strike out on their own. Renouncing any adherence to the Jerusalem Temple, they reportedly built a rival sanctuary on Mount Garizim near the city of Shechem. Josephus relates that Menachem, a member of the highpriestly family whom Nehemiah had ousted from Jerusalem (Neh 13:28), then married the daughter of Sanballat, whom the Samaritans consider to have been the leader of their community at that time. The priest had taken with him from the Temple in Jerusalem[62] a Torah Scroll which he placed in the sanctuary on Mount Garizim. Josephus' story is not without difficulties. He appears to have telescoped historical events. He linked the priest whom Nehemiah drove out of Jerusalem in approximately 430–425, and who may have been the son-in-law of the Sanballat of Nehemiah's days, with another Sanballat, probably the third,[63] who flourished a hundred years later, in the time of Alexander.

58. The "day" does not necessarily have an eschatological connotation, viz. 'the end of days', but rather connotes a future-historical preordained point in time. See: S. Talmon, Eschatologie und Geschichte im biblischen Judentum, in: R. Schackenburg, Hrsg., *Zukunft – Zur Eschatologie bei Juden und Christen* (Düsseldorf 1980), 13 ff, and bibliography adduced there.
59. Several centuries later, the Sages will condemn anyone "who elicits wrong meanings or falsifies the Torah etc.", and will deny him future salvation (*b. Tal. Sanh.* 99a; *Shev.* 13a).
60. *An Ju*, 382 ff.
61. Nota bene: not 'Samaritans'. This latter designation applies to the Shechemites only after their final separation from the Jews in or after Alexander's days.
62. *Antiq.* (ed. Loeb), XI 306–347.
63. See: F.M. Cross, The Discovery of the Samaria Papyri, *Biblical Archaeologist*, vol 26 (1963), 110–121; idem, Papyri of the Fourth Century B.C. from Daliyeh: A Preliminary Report on their Discovery and Significance, in: *New Directions in Biblical Archaeology*, ed. D.N. Freedman and J.C. Greenfield (New York 1969), 41–62; idem, Aspects of Samaritan and Jewish History in Late Persian and Hellenistic Times, in: *Harvard Theological Review*, vol 59 (1966), 202–211; idem, A Reconstruction of the Judean Restoration, in: *JBL*, vol 94 (1975), 4–18.

But these inaccuracies and inconsistencies do not invalidate Josephus' statement on two points:

a. By the end of the fourth century, the erstwhile 'Samarians' who now will become known as the Samaritans, had entirely severed their links with the Jerusalem community. The foundation of a 'holy place' on Mount Garizim, whatever form it took, gave finality to the break.

b. The secessionists adopted the Torah as the fundament on which they built their communal life.[64] Thus, both major derivates of pre-exilic Israel – the Returnees from Babylon and the Palestinian Israelites – proclaimed the Torah the mainstay of their beliefs and practices.[65] Each one conceived of itself as 'the Torah Community', and strove to outdo the other in professing and exhibiting faithfulness to Torah-laws. Paganism had been totally overcome.[66] On this common platform of basic consent, each faction emphasized particular aspects in the execution of the shared tradition. 'Dissent' expressed itself in differences of interpretation resulting in deviating norms. Technicalities in the execution of circumcision, precision in the observance of the Sabbath and the festivals,[67] matters concerning the Temple and the cult, now will achieve exceeding prominence. The opposition to דרך התורה – 'the (proper) way of the Torah', will be the דרך אחרת – 'another (heterodox) way'.[68] The internal boundary lines between one faction and the other proved to be no less rigid than those which had separated and continued to separate all Israelites from the 'other nations'.

Attention should be drawn also to some, at first sight, less conspicuous but not less weighty discords which show in the Jewish-Samaritan controversy. In discussing the formative impulse which the destruction of Jerusalem and the ensuing exilation gave to the emergence of the post-exilic community, I singled out the transformance of the former monocentricity into a multicentricity and the unhinging of the previously balanced social structure of pre-exilic Judah. It is in these two spheres that the divergent developments of mainstream Judaism and the Samaritan community become eminently manifest.

By claiming to be descended from the tribe of Joseph, the Samaritans also

64. This was correctly pointed out by Weber who specifies that they accepted the Torah "in the revision of the Exilic priests" (*An Ju*, 360).
65. One is inclined to find an expression of this intense Torah-consciousness in Ps 119.
66. See: Urbach, *op. cit.* (n. 20), p. 286–314; Safrai, *Das jüdische Volk* etc. (n. 20), 10, 39–40.
67. See *Bab. Tal. Sanh.* 99a; Shev. 13a. Weber saw these issues entirely within the framework of the relations of Jews and foreigners, i.e. in the compass of his 'in-group – out-group' model (*An Ju*, 354).
68. See: S. Lieberman, Light on the Cave Scrolls from Rabbinic Sources, in: *Proceedings of the American Academy for Jewish Research*, vol 20 (1951), 395–404.

claim a share in the history of the Northern Kingdom in which the Joseph clans predominated. They know and tell of the destruction of Samaria, and of the deportation of contingents of Samarians to Mesopotamia. However, in contrast to Judah, the geographical compactness of the Ephraimite population in the monarchical period was not transformed into a plurality of centers after the fall of their kingdom. As already stated, we have no information on any Ephraimite collectivity which was constituted outside Palestine, and developed a life stance which differed from the one by which the Palestinian center adhered. The original monocentricity of the ten tribes, whom the Samaritans purport to represent, became utterly fragmented. Only the population that had been allowed to remain in the territory of the former Northern Kingdom, preserved vestiges of an Israelite identity. The Ephraimite diaspora appears to have fallen prey to a process of internal dissolution, leading to its eclipse within a comparatively short time – a century or two – after the fall of Samaria. Resultingly, at first the Samarians, and later the Samaritans, never were exposed to the fructifying impact of the 'Diaspora and Restoration Experience' which etched the contours of the post-exilic Judean community. The Samarians first and then the Samaritans persisted in their severely curtailed monocentric uniformity into Hellenistic times. Then, under the impact of various internal and external factors, dissent became rife also in the Samaritan community and generated sectarian secession in its ranks.

The non-acceptance of the prophetic and historiographical literature into the Samaritan biblical canon, and the concomitant accordance of authoritative sanctity to the Pentateuch alone, accounts for some additional conceptual divergences from Judaism. The rigorous exclusive Torah – *viz*. Pentateuch – steadfastness precipitated in Samaritanism the emergence of an utterly ritualistic religiosity which lacks the inner tension which prophecy bestowed upon Judaism.[69] In the Samaritan religious stance, the exact adherence to behavioral norms takes on paramount importance. There is little spiritual movement in Samaritanism, as if religious development had come to a halt already in the early stages of its genesis. Since then, Samaritan men of learning and letters have produced few new thoughts or literary innovations, certainly nothing comparable to the intellectual fecundity of Second-Temple and Post-Second-Temple Judaism.

It may well be that this spiritual immobility was bolstered up by the non-existence in the Samaritan world of ideas of the utopian ferment which the messianic hope imparted to mainstream Judaism, to the Qumran Community

69. For a similar, but in details different analysis, see F. Raphaël, in *MWSJ*, 323.

(as yet will be shown), and then to Christianity. Their opposition to the Davidic dynasty concomitant with the rejection of the biblical prophetic books and the historiographies, impeded the articulation of a messianic vision in the Samaritans' conceptual universe. Although they do foresee a future time of divine mercy in which they expect to be translated from their adverse historical situation into a shining perfect eon, the depiction of that era remains rather vague, with no 'royal anointed' showing on the horizon. The indistinct references to a central figure that will arise in that ideal future age, seem to pertain to a New Moses (Moses redivivus) who is designated תהב. This latter term may be translated 'restorer'. The future eon is conceived as a replica of the Mosaic era in which the restorative thrust is fully dominant and which lacks altogether the utopian cosmic superstructure which prophetic inspiration had envisaged.

Thus, Samaritanism emerges as an offshoot of biblical Israel that embraced only one of the two principles which became the mainstays of mainstream Judaism. Concentrating on the regulation of life in actual history by the normative Torah code, they lost the spiritual tension with which messianism and the idealistic vision of the future had imbued Judaism. While the adherence to the factuality of normative practice may well have been a major factor in the preservation of a structured Samaritan community over two millennia, it also generated a rigidity which prevented this community from creatively dealing with history by absorbing changes through an ongoing process of interpreting and, to a degree, re-formulating tradition.

The above observed 'inner-group – in-group' relationship (in the framework of the proposed three-tier model) which determined the attitude of the Judean Returnees towards the non-exiled Israelites, obtains also in respect to the Samaritans. Also in this case, their self-identification as Volk und Religion defined their posture vis à vis the contemporary Jewish nation and state. By establishing a separate central sanctuary on Mount Garizim as the religious pivot of their 'national entity', the Samaritans in fact reactivated a political-religious pattern which arose out of the secession of the northern from the southern tribes after the death of King Solomon (ca. 900 B.C.E.) and culminated in the establishment of the Kingdom of Samaria and its schismatic Reichsheiligtum Beth-El which was meant to serve as a counterpoint to the (Reichs) Tempel in Jerusalem (1 Kgs 12:25–33).[70]

Before proceeding with our investigation, it is appropriate to make reference to an aspect of the issue under consideration which Weber did not sufficiently

70. See: S. Talmon, The Cult and Calendar Reform of Jeroboam in this volume, 113–139.

take into account in his analysis of ancient Judaism, and which is of special importance in the Second Temple Period, namely the diversity of impacts which the civilizations of successive empires that in their turn subjugated Israel had on the cultural, religious and societal outlook of Judaism. The issue is much too multifaceted and involved to be discussed here in detail. A mere delineation of its contours and its relevancy for the diversity of configurations in which Jewish schismanticism expressed itself at the time, must suffice.

It cannot go unnoticed that the concept of Sectarianism as it figures in our present discussion, does not apply to cases of internal cultic-political dissent in periods in which Israel was in the sphere the political and cultural influence of Semitic (Assyria and Babylonia) or Oriental (Persia) overlords, i.e. before ca. 300 B.C.E. After Alexander's conquest of the Ancient Near East, Judaism in the 'Land' and to a large degree also in the Diaspora, became enfolded in a political framework whose cultural profile was shaped by influences which flowed from the Occident, from Greece-Hellas. At that juncture in history, the Samaritan schism crystallized. The situation changed radically when in 163 B.C.E., the Hasmoneans re-established Jewish political sovereignty for one hundred years, after which time, Rome subjugated the Jewish state. It is precisely in that 'Hasmonean Century' that the Commune of the Qumran Covenanters flourished. Its inception, though, may have preceded the Hasmoneans' success by a decade or two. No definite correlation between the status of political independence and the specific mode of Qumran secession can be readily established. But it must be noted that at this stage, Jewish dissent presents itself to the viewer in a make-up which differs considerably from that of the Samaritan schism, and will reflect in the features of Jewish heterodoxies which emerged in the late Second Temple Period.

We can now turn to reviewing the Qumran Covenanters' Community. The results of this case-study, an exercise in microsociology, must be examined for their bearing on Weber's findings concerning Second Temple Judaism, in his macrosociological approach.

The above underlined chronological coalescence of events in the post-exilic period and their recordings, is even more pronounced in reference to the Commune of the Covenanters of the Judean Desert that became an object of scholarly inquiry in 1947. At that time, some of their writings were discovered in a cave in the Desert of Judah, in the immediate vicinity of a site which now is known under the Arabic name Qumran and is situated approximately 15 km to the south of Jericho, close to the shores of the Dead Sea. In the wake of the initial discovery, a plethora of additional scrolls and fragments were retrieved from another ten caves in that same area. While not all the finds as yet have been published, the material which is already at the disposal of scholars, allows for the painting of a most detailed and fairly complete picture of a Jewish dissident group which appears to have sprung up at the beginning of the second century B.C.E. and existed for some three hundred years. It was probably wiped out by the Roman armies in the wake of their conquest of Palestine and the seizure of Jerusalem, in 70 C.E., or shortly after.

No other pre-Christian Jewish group or community has left for us such a rich literary legacy, authored by some and intended for all its members, which enlightens the reader on its history, societal structure and conceptual universe. In toto, the details gleaned from these literary remains can be fitted into a mosaic which is a true-to-reality mock-up of a secessionist faction in Second-Temple Judaism, nonethelike students of that period or, for that matter, of the entire biblical era had ever encountered before. Being contemporaneous with the events described in them, the Qumran writings constitute the best conceivable basis for the study of any ancient social entity, in this instance of an early Jewish dissident movement or inter-local sect.

In addition, these materials afford the viewer a back-window-view, so to speak, of the 'normative'[71] Jewish society from which the Covenanters had separated and with which they were engaged in an ideonic struggle over the exclusive right to legitimately represent 'true Israel'. Thus, the Qumran-Covenanters may be considered in Weber's terminology, an 'historical object' of interest in itself but even more so a 'heuristic instrument'[72] for testing by it theoretical concepts appropriate to the study of Judaism in the Second Temple Period, and possibly also of 'sect' as a socio-religious phenomenon.

Scholars have attempted to identify the Covenanters' Commune with practically any Jewish sect or religious Strömung of the Second Temple Period which had been known from the ancient sources before the discovery of the new material. The most widely accepted theory identifies them with the Essenes. In comparing these two groups, one highlights affinities which by no means can be disregarded,[73] but does not pay sufficient attention to telling differences.[74] For reasons of method and not only because of historical

71. The term "normative type of Judaism" was introduced into the discussion by G.F. Moore who designated by it 'mainstream' in contrast to 'secessionist' movements at the end of the Second Temple Period. See: *Judaism in the First Century of the Christian Era. The Age of the Tannaim*, vol 1 (Oxford 1927), 3.

72. See: M. Weber, *The Methodology of the Social Sciences*, tr. by E. Shils and H. Finch (Glencoe, Ill. 1959), 156.

73. See: S. Lieberman, The Discipline in the So-Called Dead Sea Manual of Discipline, *JBL*, vol 71 (1952), 206, n. 77.

74. See: S. Talmon, The Calendar Reckoning of the Sect from the Judean Desert. in: *Scripta Hierosolymitana*, vol 4 (Jerusalem 1958), 162–199.

considerations,[75] I prefer to view the Covenanters for the present as a phenomenon *sui generis* the examination of which is bound to add a new dimension to the study of early Jewish sectarianism.

The founding members of that community can be best defined as a group of millenarian-messianic Jews who had figured out the advent of the 'Kingdom to Come' by attaching a real-historical interpretation to a biblical prophecy. The utopian messianists seem to have read a message of hope into the prophet Ezekiel's symbolic act which he performed in the faith of the imminent Babylonian siege on Jerusalem, and which originally was meant to announce a period of punishment which for Israel (Ephraim) would last 390 and for Judah 40 years (Ezek 4:4–6). The Qumranians interpreted this to mean that 390 years after the destruction of the First Temple in 586 B.C.E., Israel's fortunes would be restored. In anticipation of this great event, they segregated from their fellow-Jews and repaired to the desert to prepare themselves there soul and body for the imminent salvation. The date at which they arrived by taking the prophet's visionary figures at face value, astonishingly dovetails with the dating of the emergence of the Qumran-community to the beginning of the second century B.C.E., which is *communis opinio* among scholars. In the resulting high-tension situation the traditional forms of normal social life lost their meaning. Standing on the threshhold of a new age which they expected to be governed by an ideal code of religious, social and political values, those millennarians saw no reason for abiding by accepted notions and maintaining established societal institutions.[76]

The millenarian spirit, thus generated in the first Covenanters an anarchistic anti-establishment stance, such as can be observed also in other millenarian movements.[77] Qumran anarchism, though, was not a deep-seated principle, but

75. As does Lieberman, *ib.*: "Jewish Palestine of the first century (the historical horizon must be widened to include the last two centuries B.C.E., S.T.) swarmed with different sects. Every sect probably had its divisions and subdivisions. Even the Pharisees themselves were reported to have been divided into seven (a round number of course; see *Abot de R. Nathan* 37, ed. Schechter, 109 and parallels) categories. It is therefore precarious to ascribe our documents definitely to any known of the three major (I would include also 'minor', S.T.) sects."
76. A concise presentation of these aspects may be found in S. Talmon, The New Covenanters etc. (n 34).
77. See int. al.: N. Cohn, *The Pursuit of the Millennium* (London 1957); P. Worsley, *The Trumpet Shall Sound* (London 1957); J. Inglis, Cargo Cults, in: *Oceania*, vol 27 (1956/57), 249–263; A.J.F. Kobben, Prophetic Movements as an Expression of Social Protest, in: *International Archives of Ethnography*, vol 49 (1960), 17–64; Y. Talmon, Pursuits of the Millennium. The Relation Between Religious and Social Change, in: *AES*, vol 3 (1962),

rather an *ad hoc* reaction to existing circumstances, a necessary step to be taken for paving the way that would lead into the messianic age. In the Qumranians' vision of the 'Age to Come', the politico-social and cultic institutions will be reinstated in accordance with their concepts, customs and codified law. This vision is patterned upon the basically this-worldly conceptions of the Hebrew Bible, or at least of some major strata of that literature, which put a premium on a good life, on family and kinship, and on an orderly social structure.[78]

Qumran theology and the structure of the Qumran-Commune, illustrate the issue of Change and Continuity. They oscillate between a highly idealized concept of the historical biblical Israel and a utopian vision of a future historical world which is conceived as a glorified restoration of the biblical past.[79] There can be no doubt that the Qumranians viewed their own community as the only legitimate remnant and representative of the biblical people of Israel. They had been chosen to experience in an appreciably near future a restitution of Israel's fortunes, culminating in the re-establishment of the Temple in Jerusalem.

Although one finds at Qumran some mystical inclinations, these play only a minor role in that spiritual framework. The type of millennialism which flourished in that Community does not dovetail with the mystical chiliasm on which Weber based his typology: "Anders da, wo, beim Mystiker, sich der psychologisch stets mögliche Umschlag vom Gottesbesitz zur Gottesbesessenheit vollzieht. Dies ist sinnvoll dann möglich wenn eschatologische Erwartungen eines unmittelbarren Anbruches des Weltalters der akkomistischen Brüderlichkeit aufflammen, wenn also der Glaube an die Ewigkeit der Spannung zwischen der Welt und dem irrationalen hinterweltlichen Reich der Erlösung ausfällt. Der Mystiker wird dann zum Heiland und Propheten. Aber die Gebote, die er verkündet, haben keinen rationalen Charakter. Sie sind als Produkt seines Charisma Offenbarungen konkreter Art und die radikale Weltablehnung schlägt leicht in radikalen Anomismum um. Die Gebote der Welt gelten nicht für den seiner Gottbessenheit Versicherten: πάντα μοι ἔξεστιν. Alle Chilistik bis zu der

125–148; S. Thrupp, ed., Millennial Dreams in Action, *CSSH*, vol 2 (The Hague 1962, New York 1970); B.A. Wilson, Millenialism in Comparative Perspective, in: *CSSH*, vol 6 (The Hague 1963), 93–114; Y. Talmon, Millenarian Movements, in: *European Journal of Sociology*, vol. 7 (1966), 159–200.

78. See: L. Dürr, *Die Wertung des Lebens im Alten Testament und im Alten Orient* (1926); S. Talmon, Die Wertung von 'Leben' in der hebräischen Bibel (in press).

79. See: S. Talmon, *op. cit.* (n. 34).

Täufferrevolution ruht irgendwie auf diesem Untergrund. Die Art seines Handelns ist für den kraft seines 'Gott-Habens' Erlösten ohne Heilsbedeutung".[80] Qumran exhibits a quite different development: the initial temporary anarchistic posture which never seems to have been antinomistic, will be supplanted by a hyper-nomistic stance which exceeded the nomism of most if not of all other religious trends in Judaism of the time, including that of Pharisaism.

The conviction that the exact details of the unfolding latter-days drama had been revealed to them, appears to have induced in the Qumran-membership an elite consciousness which their Jewish contemporaries undoubtedly interpreted as a sign of unwarranted arrogance. They viewed themselves as the divinely appointed elect. They were the Sons of Light who had been authoritatively commanded to part company with the Sons of Darkness, their fellow-Jews, so that in their community could be finally realized the divine promise, as it is spelled out in some biblical prophecies. In their communal life they perceived a revitalisation[81] of biblical Israel before the conquest of Jerusalem by the Babylonians. They believed that the New Covenant which they established was the realization of the prophet Jeremiah's vision of the covenant which the God of Israel would renew with his liberated people (Jer 31:30).

The elite-consciousness which appears to have put its stamp on the self-understanding of the Qumran Covenanters, is utterly discordant with their apparent pariah-status. The Qumran-Commune displays all or most of the qualities by which Weber sought to define the pariah-character[82] of the post-exilic Jewish 'religiöse Glaubensgemeinschaft' – foremost ritualistic segregation, enmity towards non-members and in-group morality, "ökonomische Sondergebarung" and lack of political autonomy.[83] The obvious

80. *GARS*, vol I, 553.
81. See: A.F.C. Wallace, Revitalization Movements, in: *American Anthropologist*, vol 58, 264–281.
82. Weber's use of the term *pariah* has been interpreted in some quarters as an anti-Jewish value judgement rather than as an objective sociological categorization (see: E. Fleischmann, in: *MWSJ*, 263–286; F. Raphaël, *ib.*, 224–262). Without taking sides in this discussion, I would like to put on record that prior to Weber the term was applied to modern Jewry by an author who certainly cannot be suspected of any anti-Jewish sentiments –Moses Hess: "Das Jahr 1789 war die erste Staffel auf eurer Rehabilitation, wenn überhaupt von Rehabilitation gesprochen werden kann, wo nur Ehrlosigkeit, wo nur Unglück war. – In seiner Befreiungsmission suchte Frankreichs Auge alle verfolgten *Rassen*, alle *Weltparias* auf, und fand *Euch in Euren Ghettos* (my italics, S.T.) und sprengte deren Tore" in: *Rom und Jerusalem. Die letzte Nationalitätenfrage* (1862, Neudruck Tel-Aviv 1935), 119–120.
83. *An Ju*, 336 ff.

contradiction between subjective self-understanding and objective classification which jumps to the eye in the Qumran setting, altogether escaped Weber's attention and thus was not taken into account in his treatment of ancient Judaism. It would seem that the omission should be remedied and that this phenomenon should find an expression in an adjusted typology.

Like the Returnees from Babylon and the Samaritans, also the Qumranians viewed themselves as both a Nation and a Glaubensgemeinschaft, and thus present one more case of a mediating type (or: Mischtypus) which resists being subsumed under Weber's dichotomized typology. Since the antithesis nation vs. religious community is founded upon and derived from the analysis of ancient Judaism, and since also later configurations of Jewry, from Pharisaism to modern times, cannot be adequately characterized by it, also in this instance, Weber's antithetical typology should come up for review.

Similarly, the Qumran-Commune defies Weber's contrapositioning of 'church' into which one is born and which has a "compulsory-associational" and "ascriptive" character, and 'sect' which is a "voluntary association" and therefore of an "elective" nature.[84] In the New Covenant, these, according to Weber, "polarized" principles, become inseparably fused: Only Israelites by "ascription" can achieve membership in this "elective" association.

The description of their life-style which the Qumranians provide in their writings, and the preservation and augmentation of legislation pertaining to agriculture in Qumran law-literature, furnish additional proof that agricultural pursuits persisted in practically all divisions and subdivisions of Second Temple Judaism. Arguing *a fortiori* from the intensely nomistic Samaritans and Qumranians whom their rigid ritualistic law-code did not prevent from engaging in agriculture, the comparatively speaking more 'liberal' Pharisees certainly cannot be presented as having been estranged from such occupations. The same holds true for Rabbinic Judaism: "The Mishnah knows all sorts of economic activities. But for the Mishnah the center and fҫcus of interest lie in the village . . . The Mishnah's class perspective described merely from its topics is that of the undercapitalized and overextended upper class farmer . . . The Mishnah therefore is the voice of the Israelite landholding proprietary class. All Israel had was villages".[85]

84. See: The Protestant Sects and the Spirit of Capitalism, in: *Essays in Sociology*, tr. and ed. by H.H. Gerth and C. Wright Mills (London 1947), 305 ff; M. Weber, *The Protestant Ethic and the Spirit of Capitalism*, tr. by T. Parsons (New York 1958), 145 and n 173, 152 f.

85. J. Neusner, *op. cit.* (n. 6), 9, cp. 19–21. Further: G. Stemberger, in: *MWSJ*, 185; S. Safrai, *Das jüdische Volk* etc. (n. 20), 2, 4, 21, 25–26, and authorities quoted there.

According to Weber, the waning of agriculture and village orientation was contiguous with the waxing of a preponderant "städtische Ethik". Nothing in the Qumran conceptual universe gives evidence of this transformation. Since the presumed precondition – the abandonment of agriculture – was, in fact, missing, the posited development towards 'urban ethics' did not materialize, neither at Qumran nor in other groupings of Second Temple Judaism. One suspects that, as already mentioned, Weber at times retrojected his own experience of a de-nationalized and non-agrarian urbanized Jewish (petite) Bourgeoisie and its ethos into earlier stages of Jewish social history.

When the foreseen date of the onset of the 'Kingdom to Come' passed uneventfully, the Covenanters seemed to be losing their bearings. Then and there, a Moses-like figure arose out of their midst, the Teacher of Righteousness. His origins and his biographical data are not explicated. However, he obviously was born out of the existential stress generated by the non-realization of the community's millenarian expectations.[86]

In Weber's conceptual framework, the Teacher would rate as a leader whose charisma resulted from "soziale Zuschreibung".[87] Unlike Jesus whom Weber considers to be representative of the religious 'founder-type', the Teacher did not create, but rather did he solidify a pre-existing "neue soziale Gemeinschaft"[88] which, though, also was in conflict with family and clan. But – like the biblical prophets (see *e.g.* Isa 3–4) – his main aim was not to undo, but rather to re-form the established society and its institutions, so that ultimately it would embrace and act out the traditional values which he and his followers were determined to preserve in their purity.

At the same time, in his figure are welded together characteristics which *pace* Weber should be ascribed separately to two different types of religious virtuosi. While the Teacher never is reported to have executed cultic functions (either as a priest or a prophet), he is presented as a priestly preceptor invested with the spirit of prophecy. Thus, in his personality Amtscharisma coalesces with persönliche Berufung. It follows that he cannot be placed securely and adequately in any one category of Weber's neat schema of four main types of religious leaders: Kultpriester and Kultprophet, Lehrpriester und

86. Since the nucleus-community existed before he came onto the scene, he cannot be classified as an "archegetes" (*An Ju*, 331), i.e. as a "founding prophet" (*GARS*, vol I, 540–541), and is correctly designated *Teacher* in the Qumran Scrolls. See: F.A. Isambert, Fondateurs, Papes et Messies (XIX siècle), in: *Archives de Sociologie et Religion*, vol 3, 5 (1958), 96–98.

87. See: W. Schluchter, *MWSJ*, 65; further: T. Parsons, Introduction to E. Fischoff, tr., (M. Weber,) *The Sociology of Religion* (Boston 1964), XXXIII ff.

88. *GARS*, vol I, 542.

Lehrprophet.[89] While the typology in essence may be upheld in theory, more attention should be given to Mischtypen which in actual reality constitute the majority of cases.[90]

The Teacher seemingly did not innovate any religious concepts and maxims, but rather was an inspired interpreter of the traditional lore. He was instrumental in hammering the group's anarchistic utopian messianism into the basis of a new social and religious structure. During his term of office and through him, the amorphous cluster of men who had figured out the dawn of the 'World to Come' by millenarian speculations, developed its own religious and societal structures. The erstwhile dissenters-community hardened into an institutionalized socio-religious establishment which soon was to surpass in its social rigidity and legalistic exactitude the old order from which they had seceded. *Mutatis mutandis*, the process can be fitted into Weber's model: "Der Prophet und der Heiland legitimierten sich in aller Regel durch den Besitz eines magischen (does not apply, S.T.) Charisma. Nur dass dies bei ihnen lediglich Mittel war, der exemplarischen Bedeutung oder der Sendung der Heilandsqualität ihrer Persönlichkeit Anerkennung und Nachahmung zu verschaffen. Denn der Inhalt der Prophetie oder des Heilandsgebotes war: Orientierung der Lebensführung an dem Streben nach einem Heilsgut. In diesem Sinne also, mindestens relativ: rationale Systematisierung der Lebensführung ... Enstand nun im Gefolge der Prophetie oder Heilandspropaganda eine religiöse Gemeinschaft, so fiel die Pflege der Lebensreglementierung zuerst in die Hände der charismatisch (does not apply, S.T.) dazu qualifizierten Nachfolger, Schüler, Jünger des Propheten oder Heilandes. Weiterhin geriet sie unter bestimmten sehr regelmässig wiederkehrenden Bedingungen, in die Hände einer priesterlichen, erblichen oder amtlichen Hierokratie (does not apply, S.T.) – während der Prophet oder Heiland selbst in aller Regel gerade im Gegensatz zu den überkommenen hierokratischen Mächten: Zauberern oder Priestern stand, deren tranditionsgeweihte Würde er ja sein persönliches Charisma entgegenstellte um ihre Macht zu brechen oder in seinen Dienst zu zwingen".[91]

The above sketched transformation generated at Qumran a gradual increase in specific Covenant precepts which culminated in their codification. Before

89. See: W. Schluchter, *MWSJ*, 23; D. Emmet, Prophets and their Societies, in: *JARS*, vol 86 (1956), 18 ff.

90. In other instances, as in respect to 'Magic and Religion', Weber displayed interest not alone in pure manifestations of the suggested types, but also in "Mischverhältnisse". See: W. Schluchter, *MWSJ*, 23 ff.

91. *GARS*, vol I, 540–541.

long, the particular tenets of the Covenanters solidified in, what may be termed, a written appendix to the traditional law. Some parts of Qumran legislation are preserved in the legal portions of the Zadokite Documents,[92] others in the Manual of Discipline[93] and still others in the Temple Scroll.[94] With all due caution and reservations, this particular Body of Laws may be viewed as a sectarian parallel to the rabbinic law codified in the Mishnah. But in difference from the Rabbinic, the Qumran Code is not formulated in the 'question and answer' pattern without a specific 'address'[95], but rather is expressly aimed at a specific audience, the 'members of the Commune'.

The rapid transmutation of the Qumran-Covenanters, within the time-span of one generation, from the status of a secessionist, anarchistic, millenarianian, inspired fellowship into a structured religious establishment again makes this phenomenon an unwilling object for inclusion in Weber's clear-cut typology of religio-societal bodies, The dichotomy: "Kult gegen Wort, Gesetz gegen Geist, Kirche gegen Sekte, diese Gegensätze markieren schlagwortartig Spannungslinien, die die antike israelitisch-jüdisch-christliche Religionsentwicklung beherrschen",[96] simply does not apply to the Qumran-Community.

The exclusive regulations, at one and the same time had a centripetal and a centrifugal impact on the Covenanters. On the one hand, they effected a marked cohesion between the individual members, and bestowed upon their community a distinctive uniformity; on the other hand, they clearly set it apart from the surrounding Jewish society.

In this context, the issue of "in-group vs. out-group morality" does not apply to the separation of Jews from non-Jews, but rather pertains to the internal diversification which had manifested itself distinctly already in Judaism of the days of the Return, intensified at the height of the Second Temple Period and reached its apex in the first century of the Christian era.

The nature of the Qumran 'ethical dualism' thus is intrinsically different from Weber's understanding of this feature in relation to Pharisaic Judaism.

92. *The Zadokite Documents*, ed. C. Rabin (Oxford 1954); E. Lohse, Hrsg., *Die Texte aus Qumran* (Darmstadt 1971), 63–108.
93. *The Manual of Discipline*, ed. M. Burrows (New Haven 1951); Lohse, *op. cit.*, 1–44 (52).
94. *The Temple Scroll*, ed. Y. Yadin, vol I–III (Jerusalem 1977; Hebrew); J. Maier, Hrsg., *Die Tempelrolle vom Toten Meer* (München–Basel 1978).
95. See: J. Neusner, *op. cit.* (n. 6), 3.
96. *GARS*, Bd. III, 220 f., quoted approvingly by W. Schluchter, *MWSJ*, p. 16; further: E. Troeltsch, *Die Soziallehren der christilichen Kirchen und Gruppen*, 3. Neudruck der Ausgabe Tübingen 1922 (Aalen 1977), 189.

The difference shows in respect to his treatment of 'inner-wordly-asceticism' which he believed to be incompatible with in-group – out-group morality: "... this all-pervasive ethical dualism meant that the specific puritan idea of 'proving' one's self religiously through 'inner-wordly-asceticism' was unavailable (for Second Temple Judaism, S.T.)."[97] This assertion has become untenable in the face of the Covenanters' theology and practice. As a matter of fact, the discoveries at Qumran have irrefutably shown that 'inner-wordly-asceticism' was not first practiced by Protestantism, nor was it innovated by nascent Christianity, but rather is a religious stance which has its roots in a (or possibly some) trend(s) which can be traced in the Judaism of the second century B.C.E. It went together with (possibly only temporary)[98] celibacy and monasticism and with 'vocational' life, like that of ascetic Protestantism, which, according to Weber, "was absent (from Judaism, S.T.) from the outset".[99] While the circumstances pertaining to the genesis at Qumran of these religious facets which go counter to the familistic orientation which predominates in the Old Testament world yet escape our knowledge, the facts in themselves are indisputable.

It follows that once again, some of Weber's types are found to be in need of reinvestigation and possibly of reformulation so as to comprise also the new phenomena which he could not have taken into account.

97. *An Ju*, 343.
98. See: S. Talmon, *op. cit.* (n. 34).
99. Loc. cit.

TYPES OF MESSIANIC EXPECTATION AT THE TURN OF THE ERA

A new consideration of the phenomenon of messianism at the turn of the era, could be viewed with some justification, as carrying coals to Newcastle. The issue has been extensively and intensively dealt with in our own times.[1] There are, however, good reasons for reopening the discussion on this problem. Of decisive importance in this respect are the Scrolls from the Caves of Qumran [often designated 'Dead Sea Scrolls']. They have supplied us with information on yet another, hitherto unknown configuration of the messianic idea in the late Second Temple Period, and with new insights regarding the socio-historical setting and the background of Jewish and Christian messianism.

THE 'NEW COVENANT'

That 'ancient library', as it has been aptly designated by F.M. Cross,[2] sheds light on the history and the conceptual world of a community which emanated from proto-Pharisaic Judaism at the beginning of the 2nd ctry. B.C.E., gradually diverged and ultimately completely separated from it. The existence of the group most probably came to an end in the first half of the 2nd ctry. C.E. Thus, the Qumran community existed altogether for some three centuries.[3]

1. It suffices to mention only a few basic studies, such as: J. Klausner, *The Messianic Idea in Israel from its Beginning to the Completion of the Mishnah* (New York, 1955), tr. from the German ed. (Cracow, 1903); L. Dürr, *Ursprung und Ausbau der israelitisch jüdischen Heilandserwartung* (Berlin, 1925); H. Gressmann, *Der Messias, FRLANT* 43 (Göttingen, 1929); M. Buber, Kingship of God (New York, 1967), tr. from the German ed. (Berlin, 1932); S. Mowinckel, *He That Cometh – the Messianic Concept in the Old Testament and Later Judaism* (Oxford, 1956), ft. from the partly rev. Norwegian ed. (Copenhagen, 1951); H. Ringgren, *The Messiah in the Old Testament, SBT* 18 (London, 1956); G. Scholem, *The Messianic Idea in Judaism* (New York, 1967), tr. from the German ed. (Zürich, 1960).
2. F.M. Cross, *The Ancient Library of Qumran and Biblical Studies* (New York, 1958, 1961).
3. An up-to-date appreciation of the Qumran discoveries is provided *int. al.* by G. Vermes, *The Dead Sea Scrolls: Qumran in Perspective* (Oxford, 1978; London, 1982); D. Dimant, "Qumran Sectarian Literature", *Compendia Rerum Iudaicarum ad Novum Testamentum* Section 2, ed. M.E. Stone (Assen/Philadelphia, 1984) 483–550.

The new discoveries provide first-hand evidence on trends of religious development which affected Judaism towards the end of the Second Temple Period, that is to say, in the last phase of Jewish political sovereignty, which in part preceded the emergence of Christianity and in part coincided with it. The Scrolls reflect the credal concepts of a group of dissenters who propounded an extreme messianism. They indeed parted company with proto-Pharisaic Judaism but never amalgamated with Christianity. A probe into its socio-religious history, thus could provide new, albeit indirect information on the contemporary messianic concepts of rabbinic Judaism and of nascent Christianity whether by pointing up similarities which the Qumran Community shared with either, or else by highlighting contrasting views which set it off against one or the other, or against both.

The great value of these fairly recently discovered writings lies in the fact that they are contemporaneous with the historical events, and with the emergence of the [religious] ideas reflected in them.[4] Therefore, the modern historian will regard them as witnesses of the first order. They offer a welcome addition to our previous knowledge of Judaism in the last centuries B.C.E. and the first centuries C.E. which is derived, almost in its entirety, from later Rabbinic literature and from Hellenistic writings. With some qualification the same may be said of the presentation of nascent Christianity in the NT and the works of the Church Fathers.

The Qumranian have not left us any statements about the name or the names by which they were known in their own days. It would seem best to designate them 'Commune of the New [or: Renewed] Covenant'. The term הברית החדשה looms largely in their writings and clearly encapsules a most prominent concept of their theology. For the sake of brevity, I shall refer to them here as *Yaḥad.* This Hebrew noun is a characteristic of Qumran literature. It serves there as a *terminus technicus* in diverse designations by which the authors refer to their own group, such as יחד בני צדוק – 'Commune of the Sons of Zadok' or 'Community of the Righteous'; יחד בני־אל – 'Commune of the Sons of God' or 'of the Divine ones'.

MESSIANIC IDEAS AT THE TURN OF THE ERA

This paper discusses the variations in the messianic idea which became operative in post-biblical Judaism in the last centuries of the pre-Christian era. It aims at comparing the most articulate formulations of this idea which can be gauged with some accuracy, from the literature which pertains to that period. It

4. See: "The Emergence of Jewish Sectarianism etc.", in this vol., 193.

leaves aside all minor variations on the theme which indeed are discernible in the sources at our disposal, but did not reach that grade of crystallization which is a *sine qua non* for any typological analysis. Type-analysis in the world of ideas can be applied only to phenomena which, on the one hand, spring from a common root and, on the other, develop in diverse, clearly distinguishable directions. Intermediate nuances which arise from the contact between contemporaneous ideas and from cross fertilization, can enrich the picture, but they also blur the well defined traits which must remain the basis of a typology.

I shall, moreover, confine myself to the discussion of those types of messianic expectation which were entertained by structured communities. This means that I shall not take in account substreams which have left their traces in writings of that time, especially in the Apocrypha and Hellenistic literature, but cannot be connected in any tangible way with a structured socio-religious entity.

These considerations turn attention to one other socio-religious unit which existed in Palestine at the end of the Second Temple Period – in addition to Pharisaic Judaism, the *Yaḥad* and Christianity – namely the Samaritans. It will be suggested that the Samaritans presented, as it were, the nadir of messianic expectation in the orbit of Judaism. Therefore, it is especially important to bring this 'negative' pole into the discussion when one attempts a typological analysis of the then current expressions of the messianic idea.

The configurations of messianism at the turn of the era will be reviewed here in reference to the following criteria:

1. Bearing in mind the Bible-oriented ways of thought and the intensive preoccupation with the Hebrew Scriptures, shared by all communities brought under scrutiny, I shall endeavour to trace the roots of the diverse types of post-biblical messianism to distinct strata of Hebrew biblical literature and to characteristic concepts and motifs which inhere in them. This is not meant to imply that post-biblical messianism derived exclusively and in its entirety from the Hebrew Scriptures. Other factors certainly played a role in the forms which it took on in the Second Temple Period. However, all these configurations are bound by their umbilical cord to the world of ideas which is reflected in the Hebrew Scriptures. Therefore, it is of paramount importance to delineate in each case, as precisely as possible, the specific stratum whose impact most clearly shows in this or the other manifestation of post-biblical messianism.

In thus stating the case, additional justification accrues for the exclusion from our survey of messianic strands which may be discerned in the Apocrypha. It can be said that in respect to the messianic idea, the Apocrypha altogether show a far lesser dependence on the Hebrew Scriptures than do the literatures of the above mentioned structured socio-religious entities.

2. Applying Scholem's distinction between 'restorative' and 'utopian' messianism,[5] I shall endeavor to gauge the relative influence of these characteristics on the diverse manifestations of the messianic idea in Second Temple Judaism, without losing sight of the fact that both the restorative and the utopian factor feature in each of them, although to different degrees of formative influence.

3. A further criterion is of a socio-religious nature. It pertains to the difference between conceiving of the messianic redemption as affecting a natural social entity of a national or an ethnic-cultic character, as against presenting its actualization becoming operative in a community of inspired individuals. In the first case, the basis of communality is ascriptive, *i.e.* it arises out of preexisting social factors. In the second it is charismatic-elective, *i.e.* it emanates from the very belief in a redeemer in which all are joined who have chosen to follow him, without being necessarily bound together by previously existing ascriptive bonds.

4. This leads to the consideration of yet another facet of typological differentiation. The realization of the 'Age to Come' can be depicted as an event which will express itself in concrete socio-national institutions, or it can be presented as becoming effective in individuals, on the personal level.

5. This latter difference is connected with the conception of the future aeon as a diffuse ideal state of affairs without any special accentuation of the redeeming figure of a Messiah as against focussing the time of redemption on a pivotal messianic figure.[6]

II.

It may be considered self-evident that the diverse directions which the messianic idea took in post-biblical times derive, one way or another, from the Hebrew Scriptures. However, while the 'eschatological' framework appears to be the indispensable setting of all brands of post-biblical messianism, this does not apply to the concept of 'the [future] anointed king' which predominates in the Hebrew Bible. In this literature, or at least in some of its strata, the expectation of a future 'ideal age' and 'messianism' have not yet been fully blended.[7]

The term and concept of *māšîaḥ* or *māšûaḥ* – "anointed", originated in the world of ideas of the Israelite monarchy. As far as can be ascertained, it has no roots in the socio-religious structure of the pre-monarchic era or in the

5. See *art. cit.* (above n. 1).
6. "Biblical Visions of the Future Age", in this vol., 143–145.
7. See *ib.*, 161–164.

conceptual framework of that age.[8] At first, it was applied to the actual person of the ruling king, predominantly to kings of the Davidic dynasty. With the gradual growing of a critical, nay negative attitude towards kings in actual history especially on the part of the prophets, the concept of *māšîaḥ* increasingly became attached to the idealized figure of a 'King to Come' who was expected to rise in an appreciably near future. In this process, the concept indeed lost some of its initial concreteness. At the same time, it became invested with a measure of non-reality. But for the biblical historiographers and practically all prophets, the term *māšîaḥ* umistakably retained its tangible realistic connotation. The expectation of an 'Anointed to Come' who would remedy the wrongs and sins perpetrated by the ruling king, is set within the frame of actual history and does not reach beyond its boundaries. Also in this matter, the historical horizon of the biblical writers, including the prophets appears to span no more than three to four generations, prospectively and retrospectively, in the past and in the future.[9]

TWO MĀŠĪAḤ CONCEPTS

We discern in biblical literature, foremost in the prophetic writings, two discreet aspects in the *māšîaḥ* concept as the expression of an idea: 'utopian messianism' and 'restorative messianism'. They are differently accentuated at diverse times by one or the other prophet. In the post-biblical age, the relative stress placed on one or the other aspect results in the emergence of diverse configurations of the messianic expectation. This can be illustrated by a comparison of the Pharisaic concept of *Messianism* with that of Christianity and of the Qumran *Yaḥad*.

It may be said that in the, comparatively speaking, subdued messianic hope which obtained in Pharisaic Judaism, the 'restorative' orientation prevailed. For Christianity, the 'utopian' element, seemingly freed from the fetters of actual history, became the most prominent trait of its *Messianism*. In the *Yaḥad* concept of the messianic age, one perceives a distinct fusion of those two divergent trends. Utopia and reality have been blended to the almost total obliteration of any demarcation lines between them. In this, as in many other aspects, the *Yaḥad* concept shows strong affiliations with the Hebrew Bible and biblical Israel, possibly more than any other Jewish community of the Second Temple period.[10]

8. See: "The Idea of Statehood etc.", in this vol. 35–36.
9. See: S. Talmon, "Eschatologie und Geschichte", *Zukunft – Zur Eschatologie bei Juden und Christen*, ed. R. Schnackenburg (Düsseldorf, 1980), 21–30.
10. See: S. Talmon, "Waiting for the Messiah – The Conceptual Universe of the Qumran

The different stress laid on the utopian or the restorative outlook in post-biblical manifestations of the messianic expectation, appears to derive from their respective dependence on different strata of the biblical literature. Any vision of the future which is marked by a restorative thrust, will model its portrayal of the '*Age to Come*' on a historical prototype, on an idealized *Urzeit*.[11] The identification of the specific prototype and of the literary stratum in which this prefiguration of the hoped for future age is anchored, are of decisive importance for the understanding of the particular developments of the messianic idea in the post-biblical era.

For the elucidation of this dependence, it is instructive to turn our attention first to the ideas concerning the future ideal aeon which inform the Samaritans' conceptual universe.

III.

The Samaritans recognize only the Five Books of the Torah as Holy Writ, as is well known. Though it may be assumed that also this community always has been aware of the existence of the other two components of the tripartite Jewish Hebrew Scriptures – the Prophets and the Writings – the Samaritans never acknowledged their binding sancity. As a consequence, the spiritual and social-political factors which affected the development of ancient Judaism and find their expression in these two parts of the Hebrew Scriptures, never made a noticeable impact on the Samaritan creed. It hardly needs stressing that the very concept of *māšîaḥ*, of an 'anointed', is deeply rooted in the biblical monarchy and in the literary strata which pertain to the monarchical period and reflect it.[12] Having rejected those strata of biblical literature and in view of their opposition to the Davidic dynasty, it cannot cause wonder that the Samaritans did not develop a true messianic idea.

However, they do differentiate between two great 'epochs' in their own history and in history generally, which reflect, to a degree, the concepts of a prototypical *Urzeit* and a 'future age' modelled upon it. The initial basic era of *rāḥûtâ*, the Samaritan-Aramaic term for the era of God's mercy, is considered the basic phase of their history, when God watched over them with compassion. That period was succeeded by the negative era of *fānûtâ*, when

Covenanters" (forthcoming); *id.*, "The New Covenanters of Qumran", Scientific American 225,5 (New York, 1971), 72–81.

11. See Scholem, art. *cit.* (above n. 1); H. Gunkel, *Schöpfung und Chaos in Urzeit und Endzeit. Eine religionsgeschichtliche Untersuchung über Gen I und Ap. Joh* 12 (Göttingen², 1922).

12. See: "Messianic Expectations etc." (above n. 6) 140–164; "The Idea of Statehood etc." (n. 7), 38.

God turned his face from them. This latter phase comprises the entire Samaritan history, from the days of Eli the biblical priest, to the present time. Samaritan tradition relates that Eli had snatched the Ark of the Covenant from Mount Garizim – which God had appointed to serve as Israel's 'Holy Place' – and then transferred it to Shiloh. This deed triggered the foundation of the illegitimate sanctuary in Shiloh and caused the concomitant decline of Holy Mount Garizim, originally singled out to become the center of God's worship.

Therefore, the historical period which preceded this lamentable event – from the days of the Patriarchs to the time of the Desert Trek – is the one which the Samaritans have in common with the Jews. It is for them the classical *Urzeit*, the era of *rāḥûtâ*. The ideal future aeon is conceived as the restored image of that positive phase in their history. The renewed era of *rāḥûtâ* will again be a time of divine mercy. Then the Samaritans will be transported from their pitiful condition in actual history onto a shining divinely inspired plane. The depiction of that era remains rather vague. But it is somehow connected with the memory of the Desert Wanderings of premonarchic Israel. Since that stage in its history preceded the *Landnahme* in Canaan, Israel then had as yet lacked the territorial and political circumscription which is a *sine qua non* for the very genesis of the *māšîaḥ* idea. Thus, the concept of a 'royal anointed' could not take root in Samaritan theology.

As far as vestiges of a central figure in the Samaritan portrayal of the ideal future age can be discerned, they appear to pertain to the figure of *Moses redivivus*, designated *tāḥēb.*[13] This title is best translated 'Restorer'. It points up the dominant restorative character of the Samaritans' vision of a future ideal age. The picture is significantly lacking the utopian cosmic superstructure which the biblical prophets had fashioned and which had a formative influence on the other three types of messianic expectation in the Second Temple period, although to varying degrees.

The idea of an "anointed" – a *māšîaḥ* is insolubly connected with the biblical experience of monarchy in which the Samaritans did not share. Therefore, it cannot cause wonder that they did not extrapolate a royalist-messianic concept from the famous verse in the Bileam pericope "a star will arise from Jacob" (Num 24:17) which rabbinic exegesis construed as a foreshadowing of the future institution of an anointed king. The absence of a messianic tension in the Samaritans' world of thought, brought about that no

13. For a concise presentation of the matter see: J.D. Purvis, "The Fourth Gospel and the Samaritans", *NT* 17 (1975) 182 ff.; J. Macdonald, *The Theology of the Samaritans* (Philadelphia/London, 1964), esp. chs. XVI–XXII and index *s.v. taheb.*

such interpretation of this or any other biblical reference could find acceptance with them.

Summing up this part of our discussion, it may be said that the limitation of the Samaritan Holy Writ to the Five Books of the Torah exclusively, and the concomitant rejection of the biblical historiographical, prophetic and psalmodic literature, from the very outset, stifled the emergence of a messianic hope in this community.

IV.

THE RABBINIC MESSIAH CONCEPT

The focus of Jewish (rabbinic) messianism derives from the historical and prophetic literature of the Bible, *i.e.* from the Books of the Former and Latter Prophets which are marked by a pronounced royal ideology. To these complexes the Book of Psalms should be added. The prominent orientation toward royalty and Zion which permeates the Psalms, indicates that their authors were deeply inspired by the Davidic dynasty. It further evokes the surmise that the composition of many a Psalm had possibly been commissioned by Davidic kings.[14]

In a somewhat schematic fashion, it could be said that the restorative stratum in the rabbinic concept of the Messiah derives from the biblical historiographies, whereas its utopian coloring stems from the prophetic books. However, the restorative element appears to carry much more weight than the utopian overtones. The majority of references in biblical literature to a future 'anointed', show that his office and the aeon in which he was expected to reign, were conceived as a surprisingly realistic restitution of the early Israelite monarchy in the days of David and Solomon. *Mutatis mutandis* this pertains also to many, if not most crystallizations of messianism in the literature of mainstream Judaism in the Second Temple period.

King David's successful military exploits had freed Israel from the immediate danger of further wars. His son Solomon who succeeded him on the throne, inherited from his father a comparatively secure realm. In his days, Israel experienced a state of peace and economic prosperity, which resulted from the farflung commercial enterprises which Solomon had inaugurated, and from which presumably many strata of the Israelite society benefited. All this brought about a state of power and splendor, such as Israel never had experienced before. Moreover, the combined periods of the reign of David and

14. See: "The Idea of Statehood etc." (above n. 7), 13–14, 37–38.

Solomon, constitute the one phase in biblical history in which Israel had been a united nation. The enthusiastic appreciation of this epoch by the biblical historiographers finds its salient expression in the succinct saying in which the author of the Book of Kings summarizes that age: "Judah and Israel lived in safety, from Dan to Beersheba, everyman under his vine and his fig tree, all the days of Solomon" (1 Kgs 5:5). That period was idealized and made the prototype which inspired Israel's hopes for a future restitution of its onetime fortunes.

In an utopian-romantic fashion, prophetic vision extended that realistic portrayal of Israel's future peaceful life to make it embrace all mankind. Some depictions of that blissful aeon assume cosmic dimensions. In his vision of the "Latter Days", Isaiah sees them as an era of cosmic peace, when Zion will become the focal point of an ordered ecumene over which God will reign supreme, of a world freed from political and religious conflict: "[This is] what Isaiah the son of Amos saw concerning Judah and Jerusalem. It shall come to pass in the latter days that the mount of the house of the Lord shall be established as the highest mountain, and shall be raised above the hills; all nations shall flow to it, and many peoples shall come and say: 'Let us go up to the mountain of the Lord, to the house of the God of Jacob, that he may teach us his ways and that we may walk in his paths'. For out of Zion shall go forth Torah, and the word of the Lord from Jerusalem. He shall judge between the nations, and shall make decisions over many peoples; they shall beat their swords into ploughshares, and their spears into pruning knives; nation shall not lift up sword against nation, neither shall they learn war any more" (Isa 2:1–4). The book of Isaiah's contemporary Micah contains an almost word for word parallel to this vision (Mic 4:1–5). The question of their relationship, the possible dependence of one upon the other, is yet a matter of debate among scholars. I am inclined to assume that both are derived from a common source.[15]

The variational additions in the Micah reading most probably should be understood as an endeavor to modulate the utopian overtones in the Isaiah version, and to bring into the fore the restorative element in the vision. In place of the verse which concludes the Isaiah version of the vision: "O house of Jacob, let us walk in the light of Yhwh" (Jes 2:5), the Micah text reads: "They shall live every man under his vine and under his fig tree, and no one

15. H. Wildberger, *Jesajah* 1–12, *BK AT* 1 (Neukirchen-Vluyn, 1965) 76–77 and O. Kaiser, *Das Buch des Propheten Jesaja*, Kap. 1–12, *ATD* 17 (Göttingen[5], 1984) 61–64, provide a concise overview of the state of the art in this matter.

shall make them afraid; for the Lord of hosts has spoken" (Mic 4:4). The historical-restorative thrust of these words is easily recognized. They may be viewed as a paraphrase of the above mentioned verse by which the author of the Book of Kings characterizes and evaluates Solomon's reign: "Judah and Israel lived in safety, from Dan to Beersheba, every man under his vine and under his fig tree, all the days of Solomon" (1 Kgs 5:5). Thus the very realistic-political tendency in the Micah vision becomes apparent. It is further accentuated by an added line, lacking in the Isaiah parallel: "For all peoples walk each in the name of its god, but we will walk in the name of Yhwh our God for ever" (Mic 4:5).

It would appear that modern exegetes have not paid sufficient attention to the presumed influence of the phraseology and concepts which inhere in biblical historiography on the wording and contents of the above quoted Micah vision. As a result, the import of the textual variation which points it up vis à vis the Isaiah parallel, has not been accorded the weight which it should be accorded. It may well be a piece of inner-biblical exegesis aimed at providing the restorative emphasis which is required for the balancing of the otherwise exclusively utopian thrust of that vision.

Modern exegetes tend to stress, even overstress, the universalistic, non-national orientation in the biblical visions of the 'Latter Days' and the messianic times. That this orientation is indeed present in those visions cannot be denied. Concomitantly, however, the restorative overtones which cannot be overlooked either, are deemed a primitive remnant of a not yet fully developed monotheism. Theodore Robinson's statement in his commentary on the Book of Micah may serve as an illustration of this trend: "Sein Verfasser hat offenbar die Stufe des Monotheismus noch nicht erreicht, so sehr er dem Gott seines Volkes getreu anhängt. Die Wirklichkeit der anderen Götter erkennt er an und gesteht sogar zu, dass es das Ideal jedes Volkes ist, seinen Gott zu verehren. Er selbst und Israel aber haben sich Jahweh erwählt".[16] While conceding that it would be difficult "ein auch nur ungefähr zutreffendes Datum für das Stück anzugeben," Robinson, like other scholars, dates it rather late. It possibly reflects the hopes and ideals of a Jew living in the Babylonian Exile and could be taken to voice a protest "gegen die Einbeziehung untergeordneter Gottheiten in das hebräische Pantheon. Dass die israelitische Volksreligion solche gekannt hatte man langst vermutet; die Elephantine Papyri haben uns dann mit ihnen näher bekannt gemacht."[17] This conclusion is hardly

16. Th.H. Robinson und F. Horst, *Die Zwölf Kleinen Propheten, HAT* (Tübingen², 1954), 141.
17. *Ib.*

warranted. Taking into account the restorative outlook of early biblical visions of the "Age to Come" and of the messianic times, the dating of the Micah text in the post-exilic period lacks proper foundation. Quite to the contrary, the suggestion could be put forward that the wording of the prophecy gives expression to the separatist religious trend which shows quite prominently in early biblical historiography.

In rabbinic discourses, the 'Age to Come' is portrayed as an all embracive ideal state of national and world affairs. The figure of an 'Anointed' – a *māšîaḥ* – does not necessarily occupy the center of stage. The expectations revolve on the people of Israel, and are expected to be realized, first and foremost, within the boundaries of the Land of Israel.

The portrayal of the 'World to Come' does not exhibit any revolutionary changes in comparison with the actual world experienced in history. A rabbinic saying states that the difference between them is marked by "the delivery of Israel from the yoke of other nations" (*b. Ber.* 34b). This saying quite certainly cannot be construed to give expression to the one and only view regarding the future ideal age entertained by the Sages. But it does reveal sentiments and attitudes which had found widespread acceptance in rabbinic Judaism. The portrayal of the 'Days to Come' is conceived as a reflection of conditions which obtained in the age of David and Solomon. The hoped for restitution of the Davidic empire, in the form it had taken under Solomon, seems to have inspired also the prophetic utterances preserved in variant wordings in the Book of Jeremiah: "For if you will indeed obey this word, there shall enter the gates of this house [palace] kings who sit [rule] on the throne of David, riding in chariots and on horses, they and their servants and their people" (Jer 22:4, cp. 1 Sam 8:11–12; 1 Kgs 9:22; 10:26–28 *et al.*).[18]

CHRISTIAN MESSIANISM

Viewed from the same angle, that is say, in respect to the dependence on specific strata of biblical literature, it may be said that Christian Messianism and eschatological visions derive their inspiration, first and foremost, from the prophetic books of the Hebrew Bible. The dependence on this literary complex, may help in explaining the preponderance of two characteristic features in which Christian expectations of the ideal future age differ from the prevalent Jewish concepts. The restorative political-national orientation which permeates Jewish expectations, has left only faint traces, if at all, in Christian

18. This evidently positive appreciation of "horses and chariots" is in striking contrast to the negative view of them which finds a salient expression in *The King's Statute* (Deut 17:16).

Heilserwartungen. The central figure of the Messiah, without any doubt, is rooted in the Davidic dynasty. This genetic derivation indeed shows the Messiah as being anchored in the historical traditions of the 'royal anointed' of biblical historiographies, the distinctly particular overtones of the *māšîaḥ* idea an idealized replica of the age of David and Solomon. Since the conception of the Messiah is derived almost exclusively from the Books of the Prophets and the Psalms which are much less determined by 'historical realism' than are the biblical historiographies, the distinctly particular overtones of the *māšîaḥ* idea in the Hebrew Bible become muted. Ultimately, the portrayal of the eschaton assumes all-embracive cosmic dimensions. This makes the Christian Messiah-centered eschatology the very opposite pole of the Samaritans' concept of the 'Age to Come'.

The conscious abandonment of the expectation of a realization of the national-political hopes in a future era, conceived in the image of the Davidic *Urzeit*, was accompanied by a concomitant concentration of the eschatological vision on the individual and his personal experience of the Messiah who had risen and will rise again. At the "End of Days", the individual and the community of the elect, will be granted self-realization in the 'Savior'. Salvation will come to a 'community of inspired individuals', rather than to an ascriptive ethnic-political-national entity, the 'People of Israel'. The turning away from the conception of the *Endzeit* in historical and national terms, paved the way for the prophetic utopian outlook to prevail in Christian Messianism.

The beginnings of this orientation can be traced, as stated, to biblical prophecy which, to a degree, had already veered away from the predominantly realistic-political *māšîaḥ*-idea, found in the biblical historiographies. Prophetic criticism of kings who had failed in actual history, furthered the appearance of a utopian-romantic vision of the aspired future age which strained against the limitations imposed upon it by being conceived as a mere replica of actual past experience. At first, the *Endzeit* was still expected to come about within the orbit of history. However, as a result of ever recurring failures and disappointments, the 'Ideal Age' was postponed into an undetermined and undeterminable future, beyond the horizon of history. It cannot be established at what stage in the development of Israel and its conceptual universe, the 'Age to Come' was finally tranposed into metahistory. But we cannot be far of the mark in positing that this transfer and transformation occurred in the phase of transition from the era of biblical to that of apocryphal literature.

Also the ever-growing concentration of Christian eschatology on the figure of the 'Anointed', has its foundations in the Hebrew Scriptures, especially in the exilic and post-exilic prophetic books. An important factor in this shift of emphasis, was the exegetical infusion into Christian messianism of the

'Suffering Servant' motif – a pivotal element in the visions of Deutero-Isaiah, and of the 'Son of Man' – a major motif in the Books of Ezekiel and Daniel. The application of these two biblical terms to the fervently awaited Savior, resulted in a most intense concentration of Christian eschatological expectation on the Messiah-figure, nonethelike can be observed in 'normative Judaism'[19] of the Second Temple Period. This Savior-centrism intensified the development of an individual-personal relation to the figure of the Messiah, no longer perceived within the boundaries of a politically and geographically defined 'Latter Kingdom', but rather in a setting of cosmic dimensions, unfettered by ethnic and national considerations.

THE YAḤAD VISION OF THE 'AGE TO COME'

The vision of a future ideal era that finds its expression in the literature of the 'New Covenanters' of Qumran, is marked by especially pronounced biblical overtones. A comparison with this configuration of Messianism in the Period of the Second Temple, may help in putting into sharper focus some characteristic features of Pharisaic or Jewish-rabbinic messianic expectations. A close reading of the distinctive *Yaḥad* literature puts into relief the linguistic and stylistic affinities of these writings with post-exilic biblical books. This circumstance cannot cause any surprise. After all, these two literary collections are separated by merely a century or two, as far as language and style are concerned. In some instances they were practically penned concurrently. However, at times it would seem that the similarity respective to idioms, style and language patterns did not solely arise from chronological proximity. An additional factor needs to be taken into account. Some prominent facets common to these two sets of writings, seem to disclose more than mere linguistic and stylistic affinities and call for another explanation. This applies especially to the Qumran writers' predilection for using in the description of their own community – its structure, history and future hopes – motifs, idioms and technical terms which are manifestly drawn from the biblical writings of the post-exilic period.

The striking phenomenon prompts the suggestion that the *Yaḥad* viewed itself as the original 'Returners from the Babylonian Exile'. They totally disregarded the 'Return' which according to biblical evidence, had already occurred in the sixth and fifth centuries B.C.E. (three centuries earlier), in the

19. The term was introduced into the discussion by G.F. Moore to designate by it early mainstream (rabbinic) Judaism. See: *Judaism in the First Centuries of the Christian Era – The Age of the Tannaim* I (Cambridge, 1927) 3.

days of Zerubbabel, Ezra and Nehemiah. Or else they conceived of themselves as a belated wave of that preceding 'Return'.[20] The *Yaḥad* considered the days of the 'Restoration' as the prototypical *Urzeit*, on which they modelled their vision of the future ideal aeon for whose realization they yearned. Their commune was the chosen 'remnant' that had been purged of Israel's iniquities in history by the purifying experience of exile. They were the first generation of the 'New Israel', reconstituted by divine grace after the destruction of the Temple and the dissolution of Judah by the Babylonian armies in 586 B.C.E.

A MILLENARIAN MESSIANISM

The biblical real-historical vision of the future aeon, was adopted by the *Yaḥad* in almost its original purity. Initially they expected the onset of that age to occur at a tangibly near juncture in history. The members of the 'New Covenant', believed that they were standing on the threshold of the 'Kingdom to Come', the good tidings already ringing in their ears. Only at a later stage of development was the expectance of that great event shifted to a not anymore datable juncture in history, as will yet be shown.

The *Yaḥad* presents to the viewer a most extreme expression of 'Millenarian Messianism'. At first, the advent of the 'New Age' was not viewed as a cataclysmic upheaval which will disrupt the normal progress of history, but rather as a smooth transition from one stage to the next, from historical actuality to the 'Heavenly Kingdom'. What is more, the onset of that next stage can be determined in advance by extrapolating its date from biblical sources. More precisely, the Covenanters 'decoded' a paradigmatic action of the prophet Ezekiel, originally meant to predict a period of 390+40 years of disaster and exile for Israel and Judah (Ezek 4:4ff), as implying that it will be followed by the ultimate 'redemptive restoration'.

With this reliable information at their disposal, they could prepare soul and body, for the fervently expected restoration and are exhorted to do so. The stage of preparation which separates the imperfect present from the imminently expected ideal future is conceived in the image of Israel's Desert Trek which had been divinely decreed as the rite de passage between Slavery in Egypt and the *Landnahme* in Canaan.[21] Israel had experienced one other such transition

20. See: "Waiting for the Messiah etc." (above n. 10).
21. See: S. Talmon, "The 'Desert Motif' in the Bible and in Qumran Literature", *Biblical Motifs, Origins and Transformations*, ed. A. Altmann. *Studies and Texts of the Philip L. Lown Institute of Advanced Judaic Studies*, vol. III (Cambridge, Mass., 1966) 31–66; *id.*, מדבר *midbār*, ערבה *ʿarābâh*", *ThWAT* IV (Stuttgart, 1983) 660–695.

period after the Babylonian Exile. But it appears that in their credal history the Covenanters underplayed this event or eliminated it altogether, presenting themselves as the genuine 'redeemed remnant' after the exile (CD I, 1 ff).[22] The *Yaḥad* members are destined to undergo another such purification period before being transported into the 'New Aeon'. The interim phase is seen as a time of repentance and purification, and inevitable prerequisite for the attainment of the sublime goal. By retreating into the desert, the Covenanters' reenact that rite de passage by which in the days of old, Israel had readied itself for gaining entry into the 'Promised Land'. To the Qumranians it is a stage on the way leading to ultimate salvation.

As said, the Covananters extrapolated the date of the onset of the new era from exilic or postexilic biblical texts taken as cyphers. They share this characteristic with the exiles whom biblical literature reports to have returned from Babylonia, led by Zerubbabel and Joshua the High Priest (Ezra 2:1 ff). Those generations had viewed their homecoming as a realization of Jeremiah's prophecy in which he had predicted a restitution of Israel's fortunes after seventy years of subjugation to Babylonian overlordship (Jer 25:11, 12; 29:10, cp. Dan 9:4). The Book of Ezra presents the edict proclaimed by the Persian King Cyrus in 538 B.C.E. as the implementation of that oracle (Ezra 1:1, cp. 2 Chron 36:22). Also the prophet Zechariah, himself a former exile, links the Return directly with it (Zech 1:2; 7:5). The biblical sources report that at that time, the repatriation had encompassed several waves of returners. While no definite dates can be established, it appears safe to assume that the process continued into the fourth ctry., beyond the days of Ezra and Nehemiah.[23] However, only some of the Exiles returned. Not all Judeans whom the Babylonians had deported in 586 B.C.E., and presumably also many Ephraimites who had experienced the same fate at the hands of the Assyrians after the conquest of Samaria in 722 B.C.E., availed themselves of the opportunity to return to the Land of Israel. Many, possibly a majority, preferred to stay back in Persia where they had taken root. This is illustrated, *i.e.*, by the Book of Esther. We may assume that the hope for a 'Return' at some future time, remained alive in the midst of that Diaspora community (cp. Isa 56:8). It is possible that the founding fathers of the Qumran Commune who established the "(Re)new(ed) Covenant in Damascus" (CD IV,16; VII,2) either issued from that Diaspora community or else were connected with it, one way or another. Thus, the *Yaḥad* can be viewed as a "belated wave of Returners to

22. See: "The New Covenanters of Qumran etc." (above n. 10), 80.

23. See: S. Talmon, *IDB* Suppl. Vol., *s.v.* Ezra and Nehemiah (1976) 317–328.

Zion". They 'had missed the boat' when Zerubbabel, Joshua, Ezra, Nehemiah and some of their contemporaries had grasped the chance offered to them by Cyrus the Great. This supposition would go a long way in explaining the Covenanters' predilection for using postexilic biblical phraseology. They apply to their own community designations, borrowed from the particular stock of epithets which postexilic authors employ to define the community of the returnees, and to thus distinguish it from the 'People of the Land' who had not experienced the formative impact of the Exile on the returnees' understanding of their religious heritage and vocation.[24]

The Covenanters had had no share in the 'Return' in the early days of the Persian Empire, in which the biblical writers perceived the realization of Jeremiah's prophecy. For them, the termination of the period of 'seventy years' had passed uneventful. Or else, they did not consider that Return as the true realization of the restitution foreseen by Jeremiah. However, since they themselves could not anymore utilize Jeremiah's prophecy as a cypher from which to extrapolate the prefixed date of their own Return and Restitution, they searched for another peg in Scriptures on which to hang the calculation of that date. They found it, as said, in Ezekiel's divinely commanded symbolic act by which he was to exemplify a period of doom of three hundred and ninety years for Israel (Samaria) which would follow upon the destruction of the Temple, as a further extension of the punishment for the wrongs which the people had perpetrated: 'Ly upon your left side and lay the iniquity of the House of Israel upon it; according to the number of days that you shall ly upon it, you shall bear their iniquity. For I have laid upon you the years of their iniquity, according to the number of days, three hundred and ninety days: so shall you bear [the punishment for] the iniquity of the House of Israel" (Ezek 4:4–5).

The *Yaḥad* millenarians took the figure of 390 at face value. When recounting the history of their group at the opening of the Damascus Document [as preserved], they refer to the end of that period of 390 years as the beginning of the expected restitution of their own good fortunes. By means of a piece of midrash-type exegesis they construe the end of the period of doom to coincide with the onset of the new era of bliss: "At the appointed termination

24. See: S. Talmon, "Polemics and Apology in Biblical Historiography – 2 Kings 17:24–41", *The Creation of Sacred Literature, Composition and Redaction of the Biblical Text*, ed. R.E. Friedman (Berkeley/Los Angeles/London, 1981) 67–68; *id.*, "Exil und Rückkehr", *Geschichte der Juden – Von der biblischen Zeit bis zur Gegenwart*, ed. F.J. Bautz (München, 1983) 44ff.

of the epoch[25] of wrath, three hundred and ninety years after having delivered them into the hand of Nebuchadnezzar king of Babylon, he remembered them (cp. *ib.* VI:2–5) and caused the root he had planted to sprout[26] from Israel and Aaron,[27] to possess [again] his land and to wax fat in the goodness of its soil" (CD I:5–8).

A count of 390 years after the destruction of the Temple and the capture of Jerusalem in 586 brings us down to the beginning of the 2nd ctry. B.C.E. Most surprisingly, the date arrived at by a calculation based on millenarian arithmetics tallies with the date arrived at by scholarly arguments. Linguistic, palaeographic, archaeological and historical evidence led students of the Scrolls to resolve that the Community of the Covenanters emerged in the Hasmonaean Period, in the early 2nd ctry. B.C.E. This concurrence lends additional weight to the thesis that the *Yaḥad* millenarians indeed ascribed historical accuracy to Ezekiel's symbolic act.

The character of their 'Age to Come' is largely restorative. The new aeon unfolds for them in the geographical frame of the Land of Israel to which the *Yaḥad* returns victoriously. The Qumranians expected a new *'Landnahme'*, culminating in the capture of Jerusalem. Their 'New Jerusalem' is portrayed as a lofty and shining, infinitely improved, but nonetheless realistic version, not a spiritualized replica of the historical city. The 'New Age' will be experienced by the Covenanters as a structured ethnic-national entity, as the renewed 'People of Israel', not individually, as inspired members of a credal community. This notion again reflects that of biblical and early postbiblical Israel, at the same time diverging from Christian Messianism. However, in distinction from Pharisaic Judaism, the Covenanters circumscribe the fellowship of the 'redeemed' not alone in ethnic-national terms. They infuse into the designation 'People of Israel', by definition a term with an ascriptive connotation, the notion of elective association. They view themselves as the chosen remnant of biblical Israel whom alone, out of all his people, God had granted a new lease

25. The term קץ is used here in a *double entendre*: 'appointed time' and 'end'. The first connotation prevails in Qumran literature, reflecting a late biblical usage. See: "Eschatologie und Geschichte etc." (above n. 9), 27; "Waiting for the Messiah etc." (above n. 10); L. Ginzberg, An Unknown Jewish Sect (New York, 1976), tr. from the German ed. (New York, 1922) 29–30.
26. In the Bible plant imagery is frequently applied to the Davidic House (see *e.g.* 2 Sam 7:10 = 1 Chron 17:9; Isa 11:1, 11; Jer 23:5–6; 33:15; Ezek 17:19; Zech 3:8; 6:12). In CD I:5–8 it is also applied to the Aaronide priesthood (cp. Zech 4:12–14 *et al.*).
27. Possibly a proleptic reference to the 'Twin Messiahs' (see below).

on life, the right to rebuild the new temple and reconstitute Israel's sovereignty.[28]

A comparison of the *Yaḥad* concept of the 'Age to Come' with those of rabbinic Judaism and Christianity, puts in relief a distinct feature of the Qumranians' vision. The rabbinic view of the ideal future aeon is characterized by its markedly ethnic-national circumscription. Christian eschatology aims at the community of inspired individuals – irrespective of ethnic or national affiliation – bound together by the shared belief in the Messiah who had arisen.

Membership in the *Yaḥad*, the commune of the elect who await the 'Kingdom to Come' is defined, like in the rabbinic view, by the 'comprehensive' ascriptive-ethnic quality which inheres in their being the People of Israel. But at the same time their group, like the original Christian community, believed to exclusively possess a revealed interpretation of Israel's true heritage. This invested their fellowship with the elective-inspired specifity of a 'creed'.[29] Thus, the *Yaḥad* presents to the viewer a peculiar fusion of religious and societal values which, at the end of the Second Temple Period, severally characterized 'normative' Judaism and Christianity, respectively their distinct visions of a future aeon. A non-Israelite could never be admitted to the 'Commune of the Righteous'. But admittance was restricted to those Israelites only, who by joining the 'New Covenant' proved that they had been originally destined to enter the Commune of the Elect.

TWO ANOINTED

In the final count, also the *Yaḥad* appears to have harbored a predominantly 'diffuse' conception of the future ideal age, once again exhibiting a distinct similarity to biblical and rabbinic notions. Concomitantly, their vision encapsules a 'Messiah-orientation' which is decidely more pronounced than in biblical or early rabbinic Judaism. In this respect, the *Yaḥad* concept exhibits a strong similarity with Christian eschatology. However, this statement requires qualification. A decisive difference gives quite special contours to the messianic idea entertained by the Qumran community which emerges in the *Yaḥad* literature in a peculiar bifurcation. The Covenanters expected the advent of two messianic figures: One is a scion of the House of David, the other derives from and represents the priestly House of Aaron. While vestiges of the 'Twin-

28. See: "The Emergence etc.", in this vol. 181.
29. This type-distinction was proposed by M. Weber. Cp. "The Emergence etc." (above n. 4), in this volume 184–186.

Messiah' vision turn up also in some apocryphal writings,[30] this concept holds a quite special importance in the Qumran world of ideas.

The expectation of 'Two Anointed', two *mešîḥîm*, proves the Qumran vision of the future aeon to differ intrinsically from Christian eschatology which culminates in the one and only Messiah figure. The difference is of a decisive qualitative, not merely a quantitative nature. In this distinctive variant of the Messiah idea found at Qumran, we may discern the prevailing 'restorative' orientation which marks the biblical hope for an attainable ideal future, as well as the vision entertained by the 'normative' stream in Judaism of the Second Temple Period. The 'messianic duality', the expectance of an 'Anointed' descended from the royal stock of David together with a priestly 'Anointed' descended from the House of Aaron, appears to reflect a concept of religio-political communal structure, rooted in biblical literature of the early post-exilic period. At that time, the prophet Zechariah had proffered to the Returnees from the Babylonian exile a 'blue-print' for organizing the Province of Jahud as a state *in nuce* in the framework of the Persian Empire. He drew a clear demarcation line between the spheres of competence of the Davidic Prince Zerubbabel and the High Priest Joshua (Zech 3–4). Monarchy and priesthood are to complement, not to war with each other. Their mutual relations should be guided by a 'counsel of peace' (*ib.* 6:13). The resulting coordination of their actions would provide the basis for national unity, and guarantee peaceful communal life (*ib.* 7–8), concentrated on the royal metropolis Jerusalem on the one hand, and on the other hand, on the Temple in her midst, the High Priest's legitimate domain of influence (*ib.* 3:7). This concept had been intended to be realized by the community of the Returnees in the Province of Jahud. It was viewed by the *Yaḥad* as the prototype, the image of the *Urzeit* upon which the ideal future aeon would be modelled.

In those 'Days to Come', the Covenanters' commune no longer will lead the life of a disadvantaged minority, of non-tolerated *metoikoi*, not alone vis à vis other peoples and nations, but also within the Jewish 'normative' majority, as was their lot in actual history. The *Yaḥad* then will become the kingpin in a world freed from all tensions that had still afflicted the prototypical *Urzeit*. They perceive of the 'New Jerusalem' as a shining creation, healed from all religious blemishes and social evils which had marred the historical city also in the days of that other 'Return' in the days of Zerubbabel, Joshua the Highpriest, Ezra and Nehemiah.

30. The pertinent texts were assembled and discussed by A.S. van der Woude, *Die messianischen Vorstellungen der Gemeinde von Qumran* (Assen, 1957). See further Ginzberg, *op. cit.* (above n. 25) 227–233.

However, contrary to expectation, the advent of the ideal 'New Age' did not materialize at the 'authoritatively' established date. This failure must have thrown the founding members of the group into utter confusion. It could have nipped in the bud any further promulgation of their teaching, prevent the consolidation of the just created nucleus of a community, and cause its dissolution.[31] The resulting frustration and its inherent dangers, were overcome by extending the millenarian extrapolation of the above mentioned Ezekiel passage to cover also a time of desolation for Judah which was to last for 'forty years': "... ly again on your right side and bear the iniquity of the House of Judah forty days. I have appointed each day for one year" (*ib.* 4:6). The schematic 'forty years period of punishment and preparation', hallowed by tradition,[32] was possibly subdivided with a typological intent into two units of twenty years each. The first, that of 'punishment', is referred to in a piece of *pesher*-type exegesis. The retardation of the advent of the 'New Era' is explained to have resulted from the sinfulness of the group's members. It caused that "they were like the blind ... groping their way for twenty years" (CD I:9–10). The second phase, that of 'preparation', was probably seen to coincide with the life-time of the *mōrēh haṣedek*, the 'Righteous Teacher' whom God in his mercy had appointed to lead them out of their bewilderment (*ib.*). However, it must be conceded that this supposition cannot be substantiated by an explicit *pesher*.[33]

It may be presumed that the exegetical procedure outlined above, enabled the Covenanters to explain, or 'rationalize', their disappointment with Alexander Jannaeus. Initially, they seem to have accepted him as the 'Anointed of the House of David' whom they expected to arise and preside over the *New Israel* in 'peaceful concordance' with the 'Anointed of the House of Aaron' (Zech 3–4; 6:9–15). However, they soon realized that Jannaeus was not the man to fill the role of the fervently expected 'ideal king'. Even if one were to disregard his other misdoings, after usurping the high-priestly office in addition to occupying the Davidic throne, he would not anymore qualify for that sublime status. By combining both these functions in his person, Jannaeus upset the 'balanced duality' of Kingship and Priesthood, the very fundament of the 'political program' which the prophet Zechariah had advocated in the days of the 'Return from the Exile' and which the *Yaḥad* had incorporated into its vision of the 'Age to Come'.

31. See: "The Emergence etc.", in this vol. 198–208; "The New Covenanters etc." (above n. 10). 76–78.
32. See: "The Desert Motif etc." (above n. 21), 55–63.
33. See: "Waiting for the Messiah etc." (above n. 10).

When Jannaeus had lost credibility and could not be anymore viewed as the 'Anointed' of the ideal aeon, its expected realization needed to be deferred, *nolens volens*, beyond the date which the Covenanters had extrapolated from the Book of Ezekiel. The form in which the deferment was conceived again places the *Yaḥad* in an intermediate position between rabbinic Judaism and Christianity. With the Coming of Christ, Christianity actually had entered the 'messianic era', even though subsequent events proved that the 'experienced' eschaton was not final. In contrast, for reasons which cannot be elucidated here, 'normative Judaism' of the Second Temple Period did not expect its vision of the perfect aeon to be realized in an attainable historical future time. In this its view differs from the one which obtained in the biblical world of ideas.[34] The *Yaḥad* cannot be aligned unqualifiedly with either of these two contemporaneous religious trends. On the one hand, its members understood themselves to be the "last [or: latest] generation" (CD I:12), and expected to be imminently transported into the 'Messianic Age'. The certainty of 'knowing' the exact date of the impending onset of the glorious future, brings their stance close to the 'realized Messianism' which marks Christianity. On the other hand, the necessity of deferring the 'Messianic Age' to an uncharted future after it had failed to materialize in their own days, opened up a gaping chasm between the impure 'Now' and the impeccable 'Then'. In this respect, the *Yaḥad* concept displays affinities with the clear division between 'This World' and the 'World to Come', which prevailed in mainstream Judaism. Figuratively speaking, the Covenanters were caught standing on the threshold of their 'Kingdom to Come', but never gained admittance into it.

The unrealized millennial hope gave rise to a new vision of the 'Latter Days' for which they could not predict a fixed date of departure or did not anymore dare to do so. This uncertainty necessitated a redefinition of the belief that they had been selected to "prepare the way" (Isa 40:3) for the advent of that sublime event. The unfathomable gap which separated actual history from the 'ideal age' caused that now the severance of ties with their fellow Jews and the 'Retreat into the Desert' by themselves were judged insufficient means for achieving that end. New ways had to be found for bridging the gap, and for making sure that the Covenant members would continue to stand in readiness for the advent of the millennium. The erstwhile chiliastic anarchists had to be hammered into a well defined communal structure. This task was achieved by the מורה הצדק and his immediate successors. He fashioned the tools for establishing the required social and religious framework by creating the Code

34. See: Biblical Visions of the Future Ideal Age etc.", in this vol. 140–164.

of Laws which was to serve the *Yaḥad* as its institutional fundament. Also the depiction of the transition from actual history to the 'Age to Come' underwent drastic changes. The certitude that the passage from one to the other, being divinely decreed, would be achieved without impediment, had generated in the founding-members a basically 'quietist' stance. The sense of failure which took hold of them with the uneventful passing of the appointed date, appears to have brought about an extreme chiliastic-militant orientation. The retardation of the onset of the 'New Era', was now explained to have been caused not solely by their own sinfulness, but was also blamed on evil forces that blocked its realization. These forces must be vanquished so that the predetermined progress of history can smoothly run its course.

As a result of these transformations, the interim period which is expected to precede the 'New Age', became invested with apocalyptic motifs, molded upon patterns drawn from biblical prophecy, especially from Ezekiel's visions of the war against Gog, King of Magog and his multitude in the 'latter days' (Ez 38–39). Since the certainty about the datable onset of the 'Ideal Aeon' had been undermined, the conviction emerged that its realization will take the form of an undeterminable violent cosmic upheaval. For reasons which cannot be fully fathomed, the Covenanters did not avail themselves of references in the Book of Daniel to a world-period of 7×70=490 years (Dan 9:20–27) which could have served as a launching pad for 'emended' millenarian calculations. Unlike the prophet Ezekiel's symbolic acts, these utterances were presumably not considered to have been made under divine inspiration, and therefore were not considered to be imbued with the divine authority which is a *sine qua non* for basing millenarian calculations on a given text.[35]

While the onset of the 'New Age' could not anymore be figured out, the prerequisite pegs for its calculation not being available, the duration of the final war which is to precede it could yet be established. For this purpose, one could rely on undisguised, plainly recognizable biblical motifs, without having to take

35. The status of the Book of Daniel at Qumran may have been somewhat different from that of the books included in the collection which later became the Biblical Canon. Two fragments of Daniel found in the first Qumran Cave (1QDan^{a,b}) were written in a manner which deviates from the way in which Qumran biblical manuscripts usually are penned (*cp.* 4QPsDan^{a,b,c}). A fragment of Daniel which hails from Cave 6 (p6QDan) is the only piece of biblical literature written on papyrus. In addition, the *Prayer of Nabonid* (4QPrNab) shows that at Qumran Daniel-material was yet known in a pre-Canon form. All this prompts the surmise that the Book of Daniel was considered by the Qumranians to be 'worthy of reading' (m. *Yoma* 1:6) but possibly was not included in the definite collection of 'sanctified writings'. Thus, D. Barthélemy: "Certain indices permetraient de penser que Daniel n'était peut-être pas considéré à Qumrân comme un livre canonique". *DJD* I (Oxford, 1955) 150.

recourse to the extrapolation of inspired scriptural texts. The 'Final War' which paved the transition from the negative pole of 'Now' to the positive of 'Then', assumed the character of a 'rite de passage', approximating in content and meaning the time of Israel's 'Wanderings in the Desert', between the Exodus from Egypt and the attainment of the 'Promised Land'.[36] Like that former interim phase in history, the 'Final War' is to last 40 years. After its termination, the victorious millenarian messianists will regain the Holy City of Jerusalem. They will establish in her the Temple of Israel's God, over which the 'Anointed of Aaron' will preside, sharing the leadership of the *New Israel* with the 'Anointed to David'. The portrayal of the Messianic Age mirrors the prototypical *Urzeit*, the days of the Return from the Babylonian Exile.

Viewed against the background of the above, predominantly restorative types of messianic expectation, anchored in different strata of Hebrew biblical literature and concepts, Christian Messianism must be considered an entirely new breakthrough. The followers of Jesus Christ piously believed to have entered the realized 'Kingdom of Heaven' of the 'Messianic Age'. The eschaton had become actual history for them. Herein becomes visible the decisive difference between Christology and the crystallizations of messianic expectation in the late Second Temple Period which did not achieve the stage of realization: that of the Samaritans, the Qumran Covenanters, and rabbinic Judaism.

Not less important is one additional factor. When the pious believers in Jesus realized that they had not as yet attained the redemptive age in finality, its realization too was translated to a distant future. But in distinction from the other three types of messianic expectation, Christianity conceived its deferred *Endzeit* in the image of a prototypical *Urzeit* which lay beyond the horizon of the biblical age and of Hebrew biblical literature. It is the 'eschaton gained and lost' in the lifetime of Jesus, which became the *Urzeit* upon which the portrayal of the future eschaton was modelled, culminating in the renewed advent of Jesus ὁ χριστός, the Messiah. The Golgatha event is invested with the values which 'Normative Judaism' perceived in the glorious days of the kingdom of David and Solomon, the Qumran Covenanters in the era of the Return from the Babylonian Exile, and the Samaritans in the age of Moses. The parting of ways between Christianity and all other types of messianic expectation which were anchored in the Hebrew Bible, became total and final.

36. See: "The Desert Ideal etc." (above n. 21).

LIST OF ABBREVIATIONS

AAAH Acta Academicae Aboensis Humaniora

AES Archives Européenne de Sociologie

AfO Archiv für Orientforschung

AJS American Journal of Sociology

ANEP The Ancient Near East in Pictures Relating to the Old Testament, ed. J.B. Pritchard

ANET Ancient Near Eastern Texts Relating to the Old Testament, ed. J.B. Pritchard

AO Der Alte Orient

ARW Archiv für Religonswissenschaft

BA Biblical Archaeologist

BAR Biblical Archaeologist Reader

BASOR Bulletin of the American Schools of Oriental Research

BEThL Bibliotheca Ephemeridum Theologicarum Lovaniensium

Bibl Biblica

Bibl Or Bibliotheca Orientalis

BIES Bulletin of the Israel Exploration Society

BJPES Bulletin of the Jewish Palestine Exploration Society

BZ Biblische Zeitschrift

BZAW Beihefte zur Zeitschrift für die Alttestamentliche Wissenschaft

CBQ Catholic Biblical Quarterly

CSSH Comparative Studies in Society and History

EcR Ecumenical Review

HiJ The Hibbert Journal

HThR Harvard Theological Review

HUCA Hebrew Union College Annual

IEJ Israel Exploration Journal

Iraq Quarterly of the British School of Archaeology in Iraq

JAOS Journal of the American Oriental Society

JBL Journal of Biblical Literature

JES Journal of Ecumenical Studies

JJS Journal of Jewish Studies

JNES Journal of Near Eastern Studies

JQR Jewish Quarterly Review

JSS Journal of Semitic Studies

JThS/NS	Journal of Theological Studies
JWH	Journal of World History
Judaism	A Quarterly Journal
Kedem	Studies in Jewish Archaeology
Leshonenu	A Journal for the Study of the Hebrew Language and Cognate Subjects
NT	Novum Testamentum
OA	Oriens Antiquus
OLZ	Orientalistische Literaturzeitung
PAAJR	Proceedings of the American Academy for Jewish Research
PJB	Palästinajahrbuch
PEFQ	Palestine Exploration Fund Quarterly Statement
PSBA	Proceedings of the Society of Biblical Archaeology
RB	Revue Biblique
REJ	Revue des Études Juive
RhPhR	Revue d'Histoire et de Philosophie Religieuses
RHR	Revue de l'Histoire des Religions
RQ	Revue de Qumrân
SBWA	Sitzungsberichte der Deutschen Akademie der Wissenschaften zu Berlin
Sem	Semitics
Sinai	A Monthly for Torah, Science and Literature
SR	Social Research
StBTh	Studies in Biblical Theology
Syria	Revue d'Art Oriental et d'Archéologie
Tarbiz	A Quarterly for Jewish Studies
Textus	Annual of the Hebrew University Bible Project
ThLZ	Theologische Literaturzeitung
ThZ	Theologische Zeitschrift
UF	Ugaritforschung
VT	Vetus Testamentum
VTS	Supplements to Vetus Testamentum
ZA	Zeitschrift für Assyriologie
ZAW	Zeitschrift für die Alttestamentliche Wissenschaft
ZDMG	Zeitschrift der Deutschen Morgenländischen Gesellschaft
ZKTh	Zeitschrift für Katholische Theologie
ZThK	Zeitschrift für Theologie und Kirche

INDEXES

SOURCES

HEBREW BIBLE

2 Samuel

1 Kings

Jeremiah

Ezekiel

QUMRAN MANUSCRIPTS

RABBINIC LITERATURE

MIDRASH

AUTHORS

ACKNOWLEDGEMENTS

I wish to thank the original publishers and editors of these studies for their kind permission to reprint them in this volume:

Kingship and the Concept of State in Biblical Israel, *The World History of the Jewish People, The Age of the Monarchies: Culture and Society*, ed. A. Malamat (Jerusalem: Massada Press Ltd., 1978) 3–26.

'In Those Days There was no מלך in Israel' – Judges 18–21, translated from the Hebrew original, *Proceedings of the Fifth World Congress of Jewish Studies*, Jerusalem 3–11 August 1969 (Jerusalem: World Union of Jewish Studies, 1972) 135–144.

'The Rule of the King' – 1 Samuel 8:4–22, translated from the Hebrew original, *Publications of the Israel Society of Bible Research*, II – *A. Biram Jubilee Volume* (Jerusalem: Kiryath Sefer, 1956) 45–56.

The Judean *ʿam ha'areṣ* in Historical Perspective, *Papers of the Fourth World Congress of Jewish Studies*, Jerusalem 25.7–1.8.1965 (Jerusalem: World Union of Jewish Studies, 1967) 71–76.

The New Hebrew Letter from the Seventh Century B.C.E. in Historical Perspective, *Bulletin of the American Schools of Oriental Research* 177 (1965) 29–39.

The Gezer Calendar and the Seasonal Cycle of Ancient Canaan, *Journal of the American Oriental Society* 83 (1963) 177–187.

Jeroboam's Cult and Calendar Reform, published as: Divergences in Calendar Reckoning in Ephraim and Judah, *Vetus Testamentum* 8 (1958) 48–74.

The Emergence of Jewish Sectarianism in the Early Second Temple Period, a shortened version of the German original: Jüdische Sektenbildung in der Frühzeit der Periode des Zweiten Tempels. Ein Nachtrag zu Max Webers Studie über das antike Judentum, in: *Max Webers Sicht des antiken Christentums. Interpretation und Kritik*, ed. W. Schluchter (Frankfurt a/M: Suhrkamp, 1985) 233–280. This English version was prepared for and will be published in the forthcoming F.M. Cross *Festschrift*.

Types of Messianic Expectation at the Turn of the Era, translated from the German original, *Probleme Biblischer Theologie. G. v. Rad zum 70. Geburtstag*, ed. H.W. Wolff (München: Kaiser, 1971) 511–588.